Simon Kerl

An Elementary Grammar of the English Language

Twenty-First Edition

Simon Kerl

An Elementary Grammar of the English Language
Twenty-First Edition

ISBN/EAN: 9783337086046

Printed in Europe, USA, Canada, Australia, Japan

Cover: Foto ©Paul-Georg Meister /pixelio.de

More available books at **www.hansebooks.com**

AN

ELEMENTARY GRAMMAR

OF THE

ENGLISH LANGUAGE.

BY SIMON KERL, A.M.

TWENTY-FIRST EDITION.

NEW YORK:
IVISON, PHINNEY, BLAKEMAN & CO.,
CHICAGO: S. C. GRIGGS & CO.

1868.

KERL'S
SERIES OF ENGLISH GRAMMARS.

Kerl's Elementary English Grammar.—In the rapidity of its sales, this little treatise, according to its age, has surpassed every similar book ever published in this country. It contains, in a very compact and systematic form, about as much grammar as the majority of children have time to learn in our common public schools. It is, at the same time, so nearly identical with the first part of the large Grammar, as to enable the pupil to begin that book at Part Second, or even on p. 122. Pages, 164; well printed and bound.

Kerl's Comprehensive English Grammar.—This book is designed to be a thorough Practical Grammar, for the use of Common Schools. Nearly all that it contains beyond what the generality of Grammars have, will be new and useful. To its sections on VERBS, PREPOSITIONS, CONJUNCTIONS, PARSING, ANALYSIS, VERSIFICATION, PUNCTUATION, CAPITAL LETTERS, RHETORICAL FIGURES, and FALSE SYNTAX, particular attention is directed; and also to the arrangement of matter and to the copious ILLUSTRATIONS and EXERCISES. 375 pp., 12mo.

Kerl's Common-School Grammar.—This book is of an intermediate grade between the two foregoing ones; and it contains, besides, the most important historical elements of the English language. It is, however, so elementary, and yet so comprehensive, that it does not require either of the other books. Great care has been taken to make it, in matter, method, arrangement, and typography, as good as it can be made. About 300 pages. *Nearly ready.*

Kerl's Treatise on the English Language.—This book is designed for High-Schools, Colleges, and Private Students. Large 8vo. *In preparation.*

Entered according to Act of Congress, in the year 1862,
By SIMON KERL,
In the Clerk's Office of the District Court for the District of Columbia.

Entered according to Act of Congress, in the year 1864,
By SIMON KERL,
In the Clerk's Office of the District Court for the Southern District of New York.

Electroyped by SMITH & McDOUGAL, 82 & 84 Beekman-street.

PREFACE.

This little book is designed for beginners, for Public Schools, and as an introduction to the Comprehensive Grammar.

It is the result of much labor and care, and of considerable experience in teaching. In proportion to its size, it contains more grammar, with all the necessary illustrations and exercises, than any similar book with which the author is acquainted. It affords the pupil ample facilities for mastering all the parts of speech, for analyzing plain sentences, and for correcting the common errors of language.

The arrangement of matter is unusually simple, progressive, and logical. According to the present system of teaching the English language, the main object of an English grammar should be, to show the construction of the language, and to correct the popular errors, which, from ignorance or carelessness, naturally grow out of this construction. Hence I have first presented the etymological properties, attended below by a set of exercises running parallel with the text; then the syntactical properties, with exercises; then the etymological and syntactical properties combined, first, in the whole circuit of right construction, called Parsing, and, secondly, in the whole circuit of misconstruction, called False Syntax; then the construction of language on that grander scale which is called Analysis; and, lastly, under the head of Prosody, whatever is needed, as finish and ornament, to complete the subject.

I have endeavored to make the study of grammar as interesting and practical as it can possibly be made; to simplify and abridge definitions and classifications; to simplify Parsing and Analysis, by removing all superfluous machinery, and making them more of a self-evident and common-sense affair; to follow everywhere the natural order of things, except where the pupil's limited ability requires variation; and to introduce difficult subjects by familiar and striking explanations, without requiring the pupil to learn a series of questions and answers from which he can but guess the principles.

The catechetic system has been adopted to some extent, because it seems to be the best for beginners; but care has been taken not to abuse it. The arrangement of *question, answer*, and *illustrations*, is simple and direct. The labor of the pupil, too, can be thus often lightened, by throwing the less important matter into the question, and burdening his mind with not more than the chief idea. Where definitions seem rather long, it will generally be found that they are enumerative, or consist of contrasted parts, and are therefore more easily learned.

We should show to children not merely the essence in an apothecary's bottle, but take them to the bush on which the roses grow. The examples to illustrate the text are therefore numerous and prominent, and the parts referred to are made obvious by means of Italics and small capitals. This mode of presenting the subject is not unlike the approved method of teaching by "object lessons."

Since difficult words could not always be well avoided, most of them have been explained on the lower margins of the pages. To understand fully what we are to learn, is the first great requisite in studying; pupils can not, therefore, acquire too soon the habit of referring to a good dictionary for the meaning of every word which they do not understand.

Sometimes words are explained a little before the page to which they belong, and sometimes the exercises are a little beyond the page to which they belong; but all the related parts have been arranged as nearly together as typography would allow.

This little book is made so nearly identical with Part First of the Comprehensive Grammar, that, when the pupil has learned the Elementary Grammar, he may begin the Comprehensive at Part Second, and use Part First as a review of the smaller treatise.

SYNOPSIS.

1. Introductory View, or an *Outline.*—Letters, syllables, words, subjects, predicates, phrases, propositions, clauses, sentences.

2. Nouns and Pronouns.—CLASSES: *nouns*, proper and common; *pronouns*,—personal, relative, and interrogative. PROPERTIES: *genders*,—masculine, feminine, common, and neuter; *persons*,—first, second, and third; *numbers*,—singular and plural; *cases*,—nominative, possessive, and objective. Declension. Exercises.

3. Articles.—Kinds; definite and indefinite. How *a* and *an* should be used. Exercises.

4. Adjectives.—CLASSES: descriptive, and definitive with sub-classes. *Degrees of comparison;* positive, comparative, and superlative. List of adjectives that are not regularly compared. Exercises.

5. Verbs.—CLASSES: verbs finite, participles, and infinitives; regular verbs, irregular verbs, list of irregular verbs; transitive and intransitive. PROPERTIES: *voices*,—active and passive; *moods*,—indicative, subjunctive, potential, imperative, infinitive; *tenses*,—present, past, future, perfect, pluperfect, future-perfect, with *forms*—common, emphatic, progressive, and passive; *persons* and *numbers*. Participles and infinitives. Auxiliary verbs. Formation of the tenses. Conjugation. Exercises.

6. Adverbs.—Their chief characteristics. Large list, carefully classified. Exercises.

7. Prepositions.—Their chief characteristics. Adjuncts. List of prepositions. Exercises.

8. Conjunctions.—CLASSES; coördinate, subordinate, corresponding. List of conjunctions, classified according to their meanings. Exercises.

9. Interjections.—List, classified according to the emotions.

10. Rules of Syntax.—The relations of words to one another, in the structure of sentences. Exercises under each Rule.

11. Parsing.—Formulas, models, and examples.

12. False Syntax.—Examples to be corrected, under the Rules and other principles of grammar.

13. Analysis of Sentences.—Principles, with exercises. Formulas. Sentences analyzed. Thought and its expression. The six elements. Exercises. Gray's Elegy.

14. Prosody.—Punctuation, figures, and versification.

ELEMENTARY GRAMMAR.

1. INTRODUCTORY VIEW.

What is language?
Language is the medium by which we express our thoughts.

Of what does language consist?
Of a great variety of sounds, which are used as the signs of our ideas, and are called *words*.

To what may all these sounds be reduced?
To a small number of simple sounds, which are made intelligible to the *eye*, as well as to the *ear*, by means of certain marks called *letters*.
Language thus becomes both *spoken* and *written*.

What is a letter?
A **letter** is a character that denotes one or more of the elementary sounds of language.

EXAMPLES: A, b, c; age, at, art, all; bubble; cent, cart.

☞ Always read the examples carefully, reflecting upon each, so that you may learn clearly and fully what is meant by the definition.

Grammar is the science which teaches us to speak and write correctly. **English Grammar** teaches how to speak and write the English language correctly.

Grammar may be divided into five parts; *Pronuncia'tion, Orthog'raphy, Etymol'ogy, Syn'tax,* and *Pros'ody*. (Spelling, pronunciation, and derivation, should be learned chiefly from spelling-books.)

Words Explained.—*Grammar* is derived from the Greek word *gramma*, a *letter*, and thence *writing;* because the need of a knowledge of language is greatest, or most felt, when we undertake to write it, and hence language became an object of study chiefly with a view to writing it. A *sci'ence* is a branch of knowledge put together in some proper order. *El-e-ment'-a-ry*, simple, what we begin with; containing what is most important. *Introduc'tory*, leading in. *Lan'guage*, from the Latin *lingua*, tongue; because the tongue is the chief organ of speech. *Me'-di-um;* that through which a thing passes, or by which it is conveyed. *Ide'ā;* the picture or notion of a thing, in the mind. *Intel'ligible*, such that it can be understood. *Char'acter*, a mark or sign. *Exam'ple*, what shows or proves, a pattern. *Reflecting*, thinking back upon. *Defini'tion;* a short description of a thing, to distinguish it from different things, by telling what it is.

How many elementary sounds has our language, and how many letters to represent them?

About *forty* elementary sounds, and *twenty-six* letters to represent them.

Into what two classes are the letters divided?

Into *vowels* and *consonants*.

What is a *vowel?* and what is a *consonant?*

A *vowel* is a letter that denotes pure sound only; a *consonant* is a letter that generally denotes a contact of some of the organs of speech.

Which are the vowels?

A, e, i, o, u, and sometimes *w* and *y*.

W or *y* is a consonant, only when it is followed by a vowel sound in the same syllable; as in *water, young, away, Bunyan*.

What is a *syllable?*

A **syllable** is a letter, or two or more combined, pronounced as one unbroken sound.

Ex.—A, I, on, no, not, stretched, barb'dst, a-e-ri-al, pro-fu-sion.

What is a *word?*

A **word** is a syllable, or two or more combined, used as the sign of some idea.

Ex.—Man, tree, sky, pink, beauty, strikes, well, fair, alas, because.

How are words classified according to their syllables?

Into *monosyllables, dissyllables, trisyllables,* and *polysyllables*.

Exercises.

Tell which of the following letters are vowels, and which are consonants:—

A, b, c, d, e, f, g, h, i, j, k, l, m, n, o, p, q, r, s, t, u, v, w, x, y, z; bar, bed, kind, fond, turn, Baltimore.

Words Explained.—*Rep-re-sent'*, to stand in the place of, to show. *Class;* things put together because alike, or because alike in certain respects. *Con'so-nant*, sounding with, sounded with a vowel; a consonant can be sounded only with a vowel. *Organs of speech;* the glottis, palate, tongue, teeth, and lips. *Combined'*, put together. *Con'tact*, a touching, junction. *Clas'sified*, put into classes. *Monos*, alone, one; *dis*, double; *tri*, three; *polys*, many.

Pronunciation treats of sounds; *Orthography*, of letters; *Etymology*, of words; *Syntax*, of sentences; and *Prosody*, of the finish and ornaments of sentences.

Define these classes.

A *monosyllable* is a word of one syllable; a *dissyllable*, of two; a *trisyllable*, of three; and a *polysyllable*, of four or more.

Ex.—I, song; baker; ornament; customary, incomprehensibility.

How are words classified according to their formation?

Into *primitive, derivative,* and *compound.*

Define these classes.

A *primitive* word is not formed from another word; a *derivative* word is formed from another word; and a *compound* word is composed of two or more other words.

Ex.—*Primitive:* Breeze, build. *Derivative:* Breezy, builder, rebuild. *Compound:* Sea-breeze, newspaper.

How are words divided according to their meaning?

Into nine classes, called PARTS OF SPEECH.

Name them.

Nouns, Pronouns, Articles, Ad'jectives, Verbs, Adverbs, Prépositions, Conjunctions, and *Interjections.*

FAMILIAR EXPLANATION.—I might present to your mind, by words alone, all that I have ever seen or experienced. To do this, I should have to use *nouns* and *pronouns*, to denote objects; *articles*, to aid the nouns; *adjectives*, to express the

---

Exercises.

Tell which are monosyllables, dissyllables, trisyllables, polysyllables, and why:—

Pink, lily, daffodil, ordinary, gold, silver, golden, silvery, book, grammar, grammatical, grammatically, arithmetic, behavior, punishment, home, mother, relative, relatives, unassisted.

Whether primitive, derivative, or compound, and why:—

Play, playing, play-day, snow, snowy, ball, balls, snowball, snowballs, noble, nobly, noble-minded, plant, transplant, planter, plantation, tea-plant, water-melon, he, hero, heroic, nothing, nevertheless.

Words Explained.—*Prim'-i-tive*, first, simple. *De-riv'-a-tive*, drawn from. *Com'pound*, made up of others. *Denote'*, to stand as the sign of. *Ob'ject*, any thing that can be thought of as being something. *Express'*, make known. *Exercise*, a drilling to give us a better or practical knowledge of something.

Pronunciation treats of the sounds of letters and syllables, and of accent. The word is derived from the Latin words *pro*, forth, and *nuncius*, a messenger; uttering forth aloud.

Orthography treats of the forms of letters, and of spelling. From the Greek *orthos*, correct, and *graphè*, writing; correct writing or spelling.

qualities, conditions, or circumstances of objects; *verbs*, to express their actions, or states of existence; *adverbs*, to describe their actions, or to show the nature or degree of their qualities; *prepositions*, to express their positions or relations to one another; *conjunctions*, to continue the discourse, or to connect its parts; and *interjections*, to give vent to any feeling or emotion springing up suddenly within me.

Ex.—*Nouns:* In *spring*, the *sun* shines pleasantly upon the *earth*, *leaves* and *flowers* come forth, and *birds* sing in the *woods*.

Pronouns: Roses encircle *my* window, and the roses adorn the window. *they* adorn *it*.

Articles: The church stands on *a* hill.

Adjectives: Ripe strawberries are *good*. *That* man owns *two* farms.

Verbs: Rivers *flow*, stars *shine*, men *work*, and boys *study* and *play*.

Adverbs: Below us, a *most* beautiful river flowed *very smoothly*.

Prepositions: There are cedars *on* the hill *beyond* the river.

Conjunctions: John *and* James are happy, *because* they are good.

Interjection: All seek for happiness; but, *alas!* how few obtain it.

SUGGESTION TO THE TEACHER.—Take a walk with your class, during some leisure interval, and teach them the parts of speech, from the surrounding scenery.

Of what, at least, must every thought or saying consist?

Of a SUBJECT and a PRED'ICATE.

What is meant by the *subject?*

The **subject** denotes that of which something is affirmed.

Ex.—*The cannons* were fired. *The leaves and flowers in the garden* have been killed by the frost.

What is meant by the *predicate?*

The **predicate** denotes what is affirmed.

Ex.—The cannons *were fired.* The leaves and flowers in the garden *have been killed by the frost.*

Exercises.

Tell which is the subject, and which is the predicate, and why:—

Birds sing. Flowers bloom. Cats catch mice. The dew refreshes the flowers. The stars gem the sky. The Indians' tents

Words Explained.—Subject, from *subjectus*, thrown under, because viewed as being the foundation on which the proposition or sentence is based. *Pred'icate*, from *prædico*, I speak or say. To *affirm*, in grammar, means to assert positively or negatively, to ask, or to command.

Etymology treats of the true roots and meanings of words, and of the true or right forms of words to be put into sentences according to Syntax. From the Greek *etymos*, true, and *logos*, a word or discourse; the right words or forms.

How are subjects and predicates classified?
Into *simple* and *compound*.

Define *simple* subjects and *compound* subjects.

A *simple* subject has but one nominative to which the predicate refers; a *compound* subject has more than one.

Ex.—*Simple:* "The boy learns;" "The boy who is studious, learns."
Compound: "The boy and his sister learn;" "The boys and girls who are studious, learn."

Define *simple* predicates and *compound* predicates.

A *simple* predicate has but one finite verb referring to the subject; a *compound* predicate has more than one.

Ex.—*Simple:* "Boys study;" "Boys study the lessons which are given to them." *Compound:* "Boys study, recite, and play;" "Boys study and recite the lessons which are given to them."

What is a *phrase?*

A **phrase** is two or more words rightly put together, but not making a proposition.

Ex.—In the next place. Riding on horseback. To gather roses while they bloom.

Exercises.

stood along the river. John caught a fish. The fish was caught by John. William studies his lesson. A guilty conscience needs no accuser. The grass is growing. The bird has been singing. In a few years, these tribes will have disappeared.

The subject and the predicate, and why; whether simple or compound, and why:—

The stars twinkle. The sun and moon shine. The sun rises and sets. Emma was gathering roses. Trees and flowers grow, flourish, and decay. The troubled ocean roars. Honeysuckles and roses overspread our portico. Laura brought a fresh rose, and gave it to me. A dark cloud hides the sun. The sun is hidden by a dark cloud. You and he may go and recite. The soldiers' horses were in the pasture. The cannons which the soldiers brought, were captured in the battle. Do well, but boast not. (Supply *thou*.)

Words Explained.—*Nom'inative*, naming, chief word in meaning. *Refers*, hangs to in sense. *Fi'nite*, not free, drawn to some particular thing; a *finite* verb has a particular form (called its *person and number*), which confines it to a particular kind of subject. *Phrase*, from a Greek word that signifies to *speak* or *say*.

Syntax treats of the relations and arrangement of words in the formation of sentences. From the Greek *syn*, together, and *taxis*, a placing; placing together.

What is a *proposition?*

A proposition is a subject combined with its predicate.

Ex.—Stars shine. And if | my hopes must perish.

A *proposition* is an expression viewed as having a subject and a predicate; a *clause* is a proposition viewed as making but a part of a sentence.

What is a *clause?*

A clause is any one of two or more propositions which together make a sentence.

Ex.—The morning was pure and sunny, the fields were white with daisies, the hawthorn was covered with its fragrant blossoms, the bee hummed about every bank, and the swallow played high in air about the village steeple.—*Irving.* This sentence has five clauses, separated by the comma.

What is a *sentence?*

A sentence is a thought expressed by words, and comprised between two full pauses.

Ex.—Every man is the architect of his own fortune. Is life so dear, or peace so sweet, as to be purchased at the price of chains and slavery?

A sentence is *simple*, when it consists of but one simple proposition; it is *compound* or *complex*, when it can be resolved into two or more propositions.

Exercises.

Whether a phrase or a sentence, and why :—

Far away. The dark storm approaches. John's slate. Many small pieces. John's slate is broken into many small pieces. The rising sun. The sun is rising. A large red apple. Give me a large red apple. To write a letter. I wish to write a letter.

Whether a simple sentence or a compound, and why; and if compound, mention the clauses :—

Hope gilds the future. True praise takes root and spreads. The rain is pouring down heavily, and the river is rapidly rising. The sun illuminates the distant hills. Billows are murmuring on the hollow shore. Gold can not purchase life, nor can diamonds bring back the moments we have lost. God has robed the world with beauty. From flower and shrub arose a sweet perfume. Prosperity produces wealth; and wealth, corruption.

Words Explained.—*Proposition*, from the Latin *pro*, before, and *positio*, placing; something placed before a person's mind to be thought upon. *Clause*, something that fills up or closes the sense. *Sentence* is derived from the Latin word *senten'tia*, a thought or an opinion. *Com'plex*, knit together, tangled; consisting of parts closely connected.

Prosody treats of punctuation, figures, and versification. From the Greek *pros*, to, and *odè*, tone added; and thence, whatever is added to unadorned language to make it clearer or more expressive.

2. NOUNS AND PRONOUNS.

What is a *noun?*
A **noun** is a name.

Ex.—God, Mary, man, George Washington, sky, sun, city, St. Louis, street, flower, soul, feeling, sense, motion, behavior.

Names are given to persons, to spiritual beings, to brute animals, and to things. The word *objects* may be used as a general term for all these classes.

There are two kinds of nouns; *proper* and *common.*

What is a *proper* noun?

A **proper** noun is the name given to a particular object, to distinguish it from other objects of the same kind.

Ex.—George, Susan, William Shakespeare, New York, Mississippi, Monday, January; the *Robert Fulton;* the *Intelligencer;* the *Azores.*

What is a *common* noun?

A **common** noun is a name that can be applied to every object of the same kind.

Ex.—Boy, tree, house, city, river, horse, chair, ink, bird, blackbird.

All the objects in the world may be divided into a limited number of classes; as, rivers, valleys, hills, cities, leaves, flowers. A few of these classes—namely,

---

Exercises.

The nouns, and why:—

A house of marble. There are lions and ostriches in Africa. John and Joseph drove the horses to the pasture. There are roses, pinks, lilies, and tulips in our garden. The groves were God's first temples. Love and kindness go together. Col. Thomas H. Benton died in the year 1858. There was much Indian fighting in the settling of this country. I like apples. I like to skate. A home on the rolling deep. Learn the *how* and the *why.* You is a pronoun. Why he did not go, is obvious. (What is obvious?) I know that you are wrong. (I know what?)

  The pear and quince lay squandered on the grass;
  The mould was purple with unheeded showers
 Of bloomy plums;—a wilderness it was
  Of fruits, and weeds, and flowers!—*Hood.*

Words Explained.—*Spir'itual beings,* such as God and angels. *Brute animals,* all the animals of the earth except man. *General term,* a word that denotes different things. *Prop'er noun,* a name that belongs to a person or thing just as private property belongs to its owner. *Common,* belonging to every one, found everywhere. *Applied,* given to. *Distinguish,* to set off so that we may know from others. *Limited,* within reach or command.

persons, places, months, days, ships, boats, horses, oxen, rivers, mountains, and some others—are of so much importance to us in our daily affairs, that we have an extra name for each object of the class; as, *Thomas, Smith, Chicago, Missouri*. The names of the former kind are *common* nouns; those of the latter, *proper* nouns. The common noun rather tells *what* the object is; and the proper noun, *who* or *which* it is. A proper noun begins with a capital letter.

What is a *collective* noun?

A **collective** noun is a common noun that always denotes, in the singular form, more than one object of the same kind.

Ex.—Family, army, swarm, multitude, congregation, class.

Sub'stantive is often used as a general term to denote either a noun or a pronoun, or whatever is used in the sense of a noun.

What is a *pronoun?*

A **pronoun** is a word that supplies the place of a noun.

Ex.—"William promised Mary that William would lend Mary William's grammar, that Mary might study the grammar," is expressed more agreeably by saying, "William promised Mary that *he* would lend *her his* grammar, that *she* might study *it*." Pronouns enable us to avoid disagreeable repetitions of nouns.

What is the *antecedent* of a pronoun?

The *antecedent* of a pronoun is the word or expression which it represents.

William, Mary, and *grammar,* above, are the antecedents of *he, she,* and *it*.

Exercises.

The nouns, and why; whether proper or common, and why:—

Girl, Susan, boy, George, country, day, Europe, Saturday, month, September, holiday, Christmas, bird, blackbird, parrot, Polly, river, Mississippi, mountains, Andes, island, Cuba, chain, Jane, Louis, Louisa, Louisiana, state, city, New York, year, 1860, soil, mind, hope, army; Mrs. Amelia Welby; the prophet Jonah; Cape Lookout. Ferdinand and Isabella, the king and queen of Spain, enabled Columbus, a Genoese, to discover America. The clamor of most politicians is but an effort to get the *ins* out and the *outs* in.

Words Explained.—*Collec'tive,* gathering together or into one. *Sub'stantive,* from *sub,* under, and *stans,* standing; standing under, upholding qualities: this word is applied to nouns and pronouns, because objects, denoted by them, have a sort of independent existence; while qualities and actions are in a manner dependent on objects. *Pro* means *for,* or *in stead of;* hence *pronoun* means *for a noun. Antece'dent,* from *ante,* before, and *cedens,* going; going before: the *antecedent* of a pronoun generally precedes it.

There are three chief classes of pronouns; *personal*, *relative*, and *interrog'ative*.

What is a *personal* pronoun ?

A **personal** pronoun is one of that class of pronouns which are used to distinguish the three grammatical persons.

Ex.—*I* told *you he* was not at home. *We* told *him* who *you* are.

Persons, in grammar, are properties of words to distinguish the speaker, what is spoken to, and what is spoken of, from one another.

Which are the chief or leading personal pronouns ?

I, thou or *you, he, she,* and *it.*

What is a *relative* pronoun ?

A **relative** pronoun is one whose clause generally *relates* to and describes a preceding word, and is always a dependent part of the sentence.

Ex.—"There is the man *whom* you saw;" "From the side of a mountain gushed forth a little rivulet, *which* lay, like a silver thread, across the meadow;" "I do not know *who* took your hat;" "No one knows *what* ails the child." Observe that the Italic words with what follows each, can make sense only in connection with the other words, and hence the relative clauses are said to be *dependent.*

Which are the chief or leading relative pronouns ?

Who, which, what, that, and *as.*

Relative pronouns may be divided into *common* and *responsive.* "Who came?" "I do not know *who* came." (Responsive relative.) "I do not know the man *who* came." (Common relative.) Observe that the second sentence differs, in meaning, from the third. *Who came*, of the second sentence, is the preceding question made responsive; but since the clause is *dependent*, and *not* interrogative, its pronoun may be classed with relatives rather than with interrogatives.

Exercises.

Mention the pronouns and their antecedents; also put nouns for the pronouns:—

The tree has shed its leaves. Liberty has God on her side. Let every man take care of himself. John, you, and I, must learn our lessons. John and James know their lessons. Neither John nor James knows his lesson. Henry, you must study. And there her brood the partridge led.

Words Explained.*—Rel'ative*, referring. *Dependent*, hanging to something else for support—in grammar, for complete sense. *Respon'sive*, answering. *Grammatical*, belonging to grammar. or right according to grammar.

What is an *interrogative* pronoun?

An interrogative pronoun is one used to ask a question.

Ex.—*Who* took my hat? *Which* is yours? *What* ails the child?

Which are the chief or leading interrogative pronouns?

Who, which, and *what.*

What other words are frequently used as pronouns?

One, ones, oneself, none; other, others; that, those; each other, one another.

Ex.—" Take this horse, and leave the other *one ;*" *i. e.*, other *horse.* " The course of life is short; *that* [*the course*] of glory, eternal." " They deemed *each other* oracles of law."—*Pope.*

What is a *compound* pronoun?

A **compound** pronoun is a simple pronoun with *self, selves, ever, so,* or *soever* annexed to it; or it is a pronoun consisting of two words.

Ex.—My, *myself;* them, *themselves;* who, *whoever;* each *other.*

What properties have nouns and pronouns?

Genders, persons, numbers, and **cases.**

Just as every apple, for instance, must have size, color, flavor, etc.

Exercises.

Put nouns for the pronouns :—

John knows his lesson. Mary has lost her bonnet. He met her. I saw him and you. He showed them the lesson, that they might learn it. The girl went with her father, and the boy went with his mother, and they were good children. Who knows who he is? (*What person * * * that man, etc.*) Bad boys spoil good ones. Take what you like.

The pronouns, and why; what kind, and why :—

He saw me. We love them. She deceived herself. Know thyself. When a dandy has squandered his estate, he is not apt to regain it. The lady who had been sick, received the peaches which were ripe. This is the same marble that you gave me, and it is the best one that I have. Who came? Who is he? Which is he? What is he? We bought only such mules as we needed. (—*those mules which*—) Love what is worthy of love. (—*the thing which*—) This apple is neither yours nor mine, but hers. (—*your*

Words Explained.—*Interrog'ative,* asking. *Annexed',* joined to the end. *Def'-i-nite,* particular, exact. *Prop'erty,* what belongs to a thing, or is a part of its nature.

NOUNS AND PRONOUNS. 11

a. The pupil should constantly bear in mind, that language is made to suit the world, and not the world to suit language. The properties of words arise generally from the nature or relations of objects. We can readily observe that the objects around us are either males, females, or neither; and to enable us to be sufficiently definite in these respects, words have what grammarians call *genders*. What, then, is *gender?*

Gender is the meaning of a word in regard to sex. There are four genders; the *mas'culine*, the *fem'inine*, the *common*, and the *neuter*.

What does the *masculine* gender denote?

The **masculine** gender denotes males.

Ex.—Man, Charles, brother, horse, ox, drake, instructor, he, his, him.

What does the *feminine* gender denote?

The **feminine** gender denotes females.

Ex.—Woman, Susan, niece, cow, duck, instructress, she, her.

What does the *common* gender denote?

The **common** gender denotes either males or females, or both.

Ex.—Parent, child, cousin, people, animal, I, we, thou, your, who.

Sometimes the sex may be ascertained more definitely from some other word in the sentence, and then the words should be parsed accordingly; as, "The child and *his* mother were in good health." Here *child* is masculine, as shown by *his*.

Exercises.

apple nor my apple, but her apple.) By others' faults, wise men correct their own. (*By other men's faults, etc.*) None are completely happy. (*No persons are, etc.*) He loves no other land so much as that of his adoption. (—*as the land*—) Whatever comes from the heart, goes to the heart. Do you know who he is? Teach me what truth is.

The **personal pronouns:** *I, my, mine, myself, me ; we, our, ours, (ourself,) ourselves, us ;—thou, thy, thine, thyself, thee ; you, ye, your, yours, yourself, yourselves ;—he, his, him, himself ; she, her, hers, herself ; it, its, itself ; they, their, theirs, them,* and *themselves.*

The **relative pronouns:** *Who, whoever, whosoever ; whose, whosever, whosesoever ; whom, whomever, whomsoever ; which, whichever, whichsoever ; what, whatever, whatsoever ; that ;* and *as.*

Whoso and *whatso* are sometimes found as shortened forms of *whosoever* and *whatsoever.*

Words Explained.—*Grammarians*, persons that make grammar their business, or understand it well. *Gender* is a property of words, but *sex* is a property of objects ; hence there can be but two sexes, yet there may be four genders. *Common*, as applied to gender, means applicable to either sex ; *neuter*, to neither sex. *Applicable*, may be given to.

What does the *neuter* gender denote?

The **neuter** gender denotes neither males nor females.

Ex.—Book, rock, rose, wisdom, cloud, happiness, it, what, flocks.

A collective noun that denotes a group of persons or other beings as one thing, is *neuter;* as, "The *army* was checked in *its* desolating career."

How is a word naturally neuter, sometimes regarded by *personification?*

As *masculine,* if the object is noted for size, power, or domineering qualities; as *feminine,* if the object is noted for beauty, amiability, productiveness, or submissive qualities.

Ex.—Now *War* aloft *his* bloody standard bears. The *sun* seemed shorn of *his* beams. The *ship,* with *her* snowy sails and flaunting banner.

In what three different ways do we commonly distinguish the sexes?

By the use of different words, by difference of ending, or by prefixing a distinguishing word.

Ex.—Boy, *girl;* actor, *actress;* he-bear, she-bear.

What are the most common endings that denote females.

Ess, ix, ine, and *a.*

Ex.—Lion, *lioness;* administrator, *administratrix;* hero, *heroine;* Cornelius, *Cornelia.*

Exercises.

The gender, and why :—

Brother, seamstress, Julius, Julia, parent, father, mother, son, daughter, child, duck, gander, robin, snow, book, mouse, he, him, hymn, she, hers, it, they, we, I, eye, you, it, its, himself, herself, themselves, nations, party, clergy, game, person, corpse, spirit, who, which, what; lady's hand; lady's-slipper. Hope enchanting smiled, and waved her golden hair. *John* is a noun, and *she* is a pronoun.

Give the feminine to each masculine term, then the masculine to each feminine term:—

Boy, *girl;* brother, *sister;* beau, *belle;* bridegroom, *bride;* buck, *doe;* hart, *roe;* stag, *hind;* bull, *cow;* bullock or steer, *heifer;* drake, *duck;* father, *mother;* friar or monk, *nun;* gander, *goose;* gentleman, *lady* (formerly, *gentlewoman*); lord, *lady;* landlord, *landlady;* horse, *mare;* husband, *wife;* king, *queen;* lad, *lass;* male, *female;* man, *woman;* master, *mistress;* master, *miss;* nephew,

Words Explained.—*Personification* is a lively mode of speaking, in which objects that are not persons, are spoken of as if they were persons, or as males or females; as, "All *Switzerland* is in the field; *she* will not fly, *she* can not yield." *Domineer'ing,* ruling, tyrannical. *Submissive,* yielding, obedient.

NOUNS AND PRONOUNS.

b. In speaking, we may refer either to ourselves, to something spoken to, or to something spoken of, and there are no other ways of speaking; hence words have what grammarians call *persons*. What, then, is *person?*

Person, in grammar, is that property of words which shows whether the speaker is meant, what is spoken to, or what is spoken of.

There are three persons; the *first*, the *second*, and the *third*.

What does the *first* person denote?

The **first** person denotes the speaker.

Ex.—*I* Andrew Jackson, President of the United States. *I* Paul have written it. *We*, the *people* of these colonies.

What does the *second* person denote?

The **second** person represents an object as spoken to.

Ex.—*Thomas*, come to me. *Gentlemen* of the jury. O *Happiness!* our being's end and aim. *Thou, thou*, art the man.

What does the *third* person denote?

The **third** person represents an object as spoken of.

Ex.—The *stars* shone out brilliantly from *their* blue *depths*. *He* knew *it* was *what she* wanted *him* to buy. I am a *friend* to you.

Exercises.

niece; ram or buck, *ewe;* sir, *madam;* uncle, *aunt;* wizard, *witch;* youth, *damsel* or *maiden;* bachelor, *maid;* Charles, *Caroline*.

Abbot, *abbess;* actor, *actress;* ar'biter, *ar'bitress;* bar'on, *bar'oness;* benefac'tor, *benefac'tress;* count or earl, *countess;* duke, *duch'ess;* emperor, *empress;* enchant'er, *enchant'ress;* gov'ernor, *gov'erness;* heir, *heiress;* hōst, *hōstess;* hunter, *huntress;* instructor, *instructress;* Jew, *Jewess;* lion, *lioness;* marquis, *mar'chioness;* negro, *negress;* patron, *patroness;* peer, *peeress;* poet, *poetess;* priest, *priestess;* prince, *princess;* prior, *pri'oress;* prophet, *prophetess;* protector, *protectress;* shep'herd, *shep'herdess;* sor'cerer, *sor'ceress;* tiger, *tigress;* tutor, *tutoress;* vis'count, *vis'countess;* widower, *widow;* administra'tor, *administra'trix;* exec'utor, *exec'utrix;* testa'tor, *testa'trix;* he'ro, *hĕr'oïne;* Joseph, *Jo'sephine;* don, *donna;* sign'or, *signo'ra;* sultan, *sulta'na* or *sul'taness;* tzar, *tzari'na;* Augustus, *Augusta*.

Words Explained.—*Person*, from the Latin *perso'na*, a mask; borrowed from stage-playing, in which different masks, or styles of dress, enable the same person to represent different persons or characters.

NOUNS AND PRONOUNS.

c. There are more than one of almost every kind of objects; and in speaking we are continually referring either to one object or to more, of the different kinds with which we have to do; hence words have what grammarians call *numbers*. What, then, is *number?*

Number, in grammar, is that property of words which shows whether one object is meant, or more than one.

There are two numbers; the *singular* and the *plural.*

What does the *singular* number denote?

The **singular** number denotes but one.

Ex.—Desk, leaf, boy, Arthur, swarm, I, thou, yourself, he, she, itself.

What does the *plural* number denote?

The **plural** number denotes more than one.

Ex.—Desks, leaves, boys, swarms, we, our, ye, they, them, themselves.

How is the plural number of nouns generally formed?

By adding *s* to the singular.

Ex.—Glove, *gloves;* chair, *chairs;* chimney, *chimneys;* nation, *nations.*

Exercises.

He-goat, *she-goat;* buck-rabbit, *doe-rabbit;* cock-sparrow, *hen-sparrow;* man-servant, *maid-servant;* male descendants, *female descendants;* Mr. Reynolds, *Mrs. Reynolds, Miss Reynolds.*

The person, and why:—

I, you, he, we, my, myself, us, thee, yourselves, mine, thine, thyself, himself, themselves, it, she, hers, others; a drooping willow; my dictionary; your grammar. I am the captain, sir. We passengers have poor fare. Then said I to him, "Well, my little friend, how fare the schoolboys?"

> My mother! when I learned that thou wast dead,
> Say, wast thou conscious of the tears I shed?
> Hovered thy spirit o'er thy sorrowing son,
> Wretch even then, life's journey just begun?
> I heard the bell tolled on thy funeral day,
> I saw the hearse that bore thee slow away,
> And, turning from my nursery window, drew
> A long, long sigh, and wept a last adieu!—*Cowper.*

Change into the other persons:—

John writes. The girls study. Henry, you may play. I William Ringbolt hold myself responsible. Shall Hannibal compare himself with this half-year captain?

The number, and why:—

Book, books, rose, roses, partridge, partridges, geese. family, families, scissors, ashes, letters, love, swarm, hay, honey, molasses, I, we,

NOUNS AND PRONOUNS. 15

To what nouns must *es* be added, to make them plural?

To nouns ending with *s*, *x*, *z*, *sh*, or soft *ch*; and also to nouns ending with *i*, *o*, *u*, or *y*, preceded each by a consonant.

Ex.—Glass, *glasses;* fox, *foxes;* to'paz, *to'pazes;* bush, *bushes;* church, *churches;* al'kali, *al'kalies;* negro, *negroes;* gnu, *gnues;* story, *stories.* (*Y* is changed to *i.* See page 153.)

Proper nouns, foreign nouns, and unusual nouns, to prevent the liability of mistaking them, are changed as little as possible, and hence often assume *s* only; as, Leary, the *Learys;* Peri, *Peris;* canto, *cantos;* "several *tos*" [or *to's*].

Owing to their *foreign* tinge, we still find, in good use, *cantos, duodecimos, frescos, grottos, halos, juntos, mementos, octavos, pianos, porticos, quartos, salvos, solos, tyros, zeros,* in stead of *cantoes* from *canto, grottoes* from *grotto,* etc., which are also coming into use.

How is the plural of compound words generally expressed?

By making plural that part of the word which is described by the rest.

Ex.—Mouse-trap, *mouse-traps;* spoonful, *spoonfuls;* brother-in-law, *brothers-in-law;* commander-in-chief, *commanders-in-chief.*

When the title *Mr., Miss,* or *Dr.,* is used with a name, how is the whole term made plural?

By making plural the title only.

Mr. Harper, *Messrs. Harper;* Miss Brown, the *Misses Brown;* Dr. Lee, *Drs. Lee.*

When the title is *Mrs.*, or when the word *two, three,* etc., stands before the title, the latter noun is made plural. "The Mrs. Barlows."—IRVING. "The two Miss *Scotts* had been gathering flowers."—*Irving.*

Exercises.

you, thou, him, themselves, they, his, several, one, ones, none, one another, our, ours, my, a, an, each man, either man, every man, neither road, two, a two, two twos, a twin, twins, a pair, two pair.

Spell the plurals of the singulars, then the singulars of the plurals:—

Man, *men;* woman, *women;* child, *children;* ox, *oxen;* foot, *feet;* goose, *geese;* tooth, *teeth;* mouse, *mice;* louse, *lice;* cow, *cows* or *kine;* this, *these;* that, *those;* I, *we;* thou, *ye;* he, *they.*

Brother, *brothers* (of the same family), *brethren* (of the same society); die, *dies* (stamps for coining), *dice* (small cubes for gaming); fish, *fishes* (individuals), *fish* (quantity, or the species); genius, *geniuses* (men of genius), *genii* (spirits); in'dex, *in'dexes* (tables of reference), *in'dices* (algebraic signs); penny, *pennies* (pieces of money), *pence* (how much in value); staff, *staves* (sticks—better, *staffs*), *staffs,* officers; flagstaff, *flagstaffs;* distaff, *distaffs.*

Beef, *beeves;* calf, *calves;* elf, *elves;* half, *halves;* knife, *knives;* leaf, *leaves;* life, *lives;* loaf, *loaves;* self, *selves;* sheaf, *sheaves;* shelf, *shelves;* thief, *thieves;* wife, *wives;* wolf, *wolves;* wharf, *wharfs* or *wharves.* Other words ending with *f* or *fe,* assume merely *s*: Fife, *fifes;* skiff, *skiffs.*

How are words adopted from the Latin or Greek language, made plural?
The ending *us* is generally changed into *i*; *um* or *on*, to *ä*; *is*, to *ēs*; *a*, to *œ*; and *x* or *ex*, to *cēs* or *icēs*.

Ex.—Stimulus, *stimuli*; arca'num, *arca'na*; crisis, *crises*; vor'tex, *vor'tices*.

Some nouns do not change their form, to express either number; as, *Deer, sheep, swine, vermin, grouse, head* (cattle), *sail* (ships), *pair, dozen, series, species, appara'tus, corps, means, news* (generally singular), *alms, wages* (generally plural), *odds, amends, ethics, mathematics,* etc.

Some nouns, denoting generally objects that consist of two or many parts, are nearly always used in the plural number only; as, *Tongs, scissors, snuffers, ashes, stairs, dregs, pincers, lungs, trousers, drawers, hose, bowels, annals, ar'chives, ides, chops, clothes, thanks, riches, goods, bitters, victuals, oats, vetches, aborig'inēs, mamma'lia,* etc.

How do you determine the number of a collective noun that is singular in form?

A collective noun is *singular*, when we regard the entire collection as one thing; *plural*, when we refer to the individuals composing the collection.

Ex.—The *committee* was large. The *committee* were not unanimous.

Exercises.

Atlas, *atlases*; halo, *haloes*; folio, *folios*; torch, *torches*; monarch, *monarchs*; story, *stories*; money, *moneys*; German, *Germans*; Mussulman, *Mussulmans*; larva, *larvæ*; lam'ina, *lam'inæ*; minu'tia, *minu'tiæ*; alum'na, *alum'næ*; alum'nus, *alum'ni*; ma'gus, *ma'gi*; ra'dius, *ra'dii*; fo'cus, *fo'ci*; nu'cleus, *nu'clei*; arca'num, *arca'nā*; da'tum, *da'ta*; memoran'dum, *memoran'da* or *memoran'dums*; stratum, *strata*; phenom'enon, *phenom'ena*; sta'men, *stam'ina*; ge'nus, *gen'era*; axis, *axēs*; crisis, *crisēs*; o'asis, *o'asēs*; the'sis, *the'ses*; pha'sis, *pha'ses*; ellip'sis, *ellip'ses*; em'phasis, *em'phases*; hypoth'esis, *hypoth'eses*; paren'thesis, *paren'theses*; synop'sis, *synop'ses*; syn'thesis, *syn'theses*; appen'dix, *appen'dices*; beau, *beaux*; monsieur, *messieurs*; cherub, *cherubs* or *cher'ubim*; seraph, *seraphs* or *ser'aphim*; bandit, *bandits* or *bandit'ti*; brother-in-law, *brothers-in-law*; sister-in-law, *sisters-in-law*; court-martial, *courts-martial*; aid-de-camp, *aids-de-camp*; billet-doux, *billets-doux*; cupful, *cupfuls*; spoonful, *spoonfuls*; man-servant, *men-servants*; ignis fatuus, *ignēs fatui*; Miss Warner, the *Misses Warner*; Mr. Hunter, the *Messrs. Hunter*; Dr. Hunter, *Drs. Hunter*.

Words Explained.—*Singular*, single, odd. *Plural*, from the Latin *plus*, more; more than one. *Mr.* is abbreviated from *Mister*; *Messrs.*, from the French *Messieurs*. *Case* ordinarily means *state* or *condition*. *Relation*, how one thing is to another. *Sense*, meaning. *Con'strued*, arranged according to the sense. *Independently*, having nothing to do with others. *Ab'solutely*, absolved, freed from something. *Address*, speak to. *Exclaim*, cry out. *Participles* and *infinitives*, forms of the verb. *Verb*, a word expressing action or state.

d. If I say, "*Your brother's friend* sent *James* to *me*;
Your friend's brother sent *me* to *James*;
My brother's friend sent *James* to *you*;
James sent *your brother's friend* to *me*;
I sent *your friend's brother* to *James*;
You sent *James* to *my friend's brother*;" you can easily see that all these sentences differ much from one another in meaning. The difference of meaning arises from the different relations of the words to one another, and these different relations are called *cases*. That objects exist or act, that objects are owned, or make parts of other objects, and that objects are acted upon, are the three chief conditions of things, on which *cases* are based. What, then, is *case?*

Case is the sense or form in which nouns and pronouns are construed with other words, to express thought.

There are three cases; the *nominative*, the *possessive*, and the *objective*.

What does the *nominative* case denote?

The **nominative** case denotes the condition of a noun or pronoun that is used as the subject of a predicate.

Ex.—*John* struck James. (Who struck James?) The *rose* is beautiful. (What is beautiful?) *Fishes* swim in the sea, and *birds* fly in the air. Mary's *bunch* of flowers is fading.

A noun or pronoun is also in the *nominative case*, when it is used *independently* or *absolutely*.

Ex.—*Independently:* "*John*, come to me;" "Alas, poor *Yorick!*" "The Pilgrim *Fathers*,—where are they?" "Merchants' *Bank*." *Absolutely:* The *tree* having fallen, we returned;" "*Bonaparte* being banished, peace was restored;" "To become a *scholar*, requires exertion."

Independently; used in addressing persons or other objects, in exclaiming, or in simply directing attention to an object. **Absolutely;** used before a participle, or after a participle or an infinitive, without being governed by it or controlled by any other word.

Exercises.

Spell the plural of the following words:—
Sofa, larva, house, mouse, feather-bed, booth, tooth, ox, box, root, foot, turf, wolf, genus, genius, isthmus, trio, cargo, valley, sally, alley, ally, rabbi, crutch, stomach, trellis, ellipsis, Mr. Jones, Mrs. Jones.

Words Explained.—*Possessive*, owning. *Apos'trophe*, turning or cutting off, something that shows omission: *kingis crowne* has become *king's crown*.

What does the *possessive* case denote?

The possessive case denotes possession.

Ex.—*John's* horse. *My* slate. The *children's* books. *Boys'* sports. Possession may be past, or future and merely intended, as well as present and actual; as, "*Webster's* Dictionary;" "*Men's* boots for sale here." The former example implies *origin*; the latter, *fitness*.

What is the regular sign of the possessive case?

An apostrophe, or comma above the line, followed by the letter s.

Ex.—*Mary's* slate. *Burns's* poems. *Men's* affairs.

Is the possessive *s* always expressed?

It is omitted from plural nouns ending with s, and sometimes also from singular nouns ending with s, or an s-sound.

Ex.—The *soldiers'* camp. For *conscience'* sake.

A singular noun ending with an *s*-sound, should generally have the apostrophe and *s*; as, "Dennis's Works."—*Pope*. "Louis's reign."—*Macaulay*. "Charles's affairs."—*Prescott*. It is often better to use *of*, or to make the possessive word an adjective; as, "The death of Socrates;" "Lucas Place."

"For conscience' sake," "For goodness' sake," etc., are rather idiomatic exceptions to the rule, than fair illustrations of a general principle.

What does the *objective* case denote?

The objective case denotes the condition of a noun or pronoun that is used as the object of a verb or preposition.

Ex.—This stream turns a *mill*. (Turns what?) The water flows over the *dam*. (Over what?) I saw *her* with *him?* (Saw whom? with whom?)

The object of a transitive verb or of a preposition, is the noun or pronoun required after it to make sense; as, "I rolled a *stone* down the *hill*." Here *stone* is the object of the verb *rolled*, and *hill* is the object of the preposition *down*.

Exercises.

The noun or pronoun, and why; then the case, and why:—

John found Mary's book. Lucy's lamb nips the grass. Fair blooms the lily. He wrote his name in his book. John shot some squirrels in your father's field. Sweet fountain, once again I visit thee. The Greeks were more ingenious than the Romans [were]. The plough, the sword, the pen, and the needle,—how

Words Explained.—*Idiomat'ic*, peculiar, formed by custom without regard to rules. *Principle*, a rule or law, a truth that applies to many particulars. *Objec'tive*, denoting an object; and *object*, something thrown in the way, something aimed at or affected. *Prĕp-o-sĭ'-tion*, from *pre*, before, and *positio*, placing; a word placed before others to show position or relation. *Repetition*, telling again. *Explanation*, telling what a thing is.

When must a noun or pronoun agree in case with another noun or pronoun?
When it is but a repetition of the other, or when it denotes, by way of explanation, the same thing.

Ex.—I, *I*, am the man. Friends, false *friends*, have ruined me. Smith is a *barber*. Smith the *barber* is my *neighbor*.

How can the different cases of nouns be distinguished?
By their meanings: or, the *nominative* may be found by asking a question with *who* or *what* before the verb; the *objective*, with *whom* or *what* after the verb; and the *possessive* is known by the apostrophe.

Ex.—" Mary plucked flowers for John's sister." Who plucked?—plucked what?—for whom?

e. Having now shown you what properties nouns and pronouns have, I shall next show you, briefly and regularly, how the different nouns and pronouns are written to express these properties. This process is called *declension*.

What, then, is it, to *decline* a noun or pronoun?
To **decline** a noun or pronoun, is to show, in some regular way, what forms it has to express its grammatical properties.

Observe that nouns sometimes remain unchanged, and that pronouns are sometimes wholly changed, to express their properties.

Exercises.

mighty! To retreat was to lose all. (What was what?) I know that you can learn. (I know what?) Why he went, is plain. (What is plain?) Promising and performing are two different things.

On that day of desolation,
Lady, I was captive made;
Bleeding for my Christian nation,
By the walls of high Belgrade.—*Campbell.*

Spell the possessive singular; then the possessive plural, if the word can have it:—

Sister, (thus: S-i-s-sis—t-e-r-apostrophe-s-ter's—Sister's,) John, day, Sparks, prince, horse, St. James, John Henry Thomson, he, one, who, other, she, it, court-martial, brother-in-law, bookkeeper; the duke of Northumberland; Allen and Baker; Morris the bookseller; Morris, the bookseller.

Words Explained.—*Decline'*, to change from one state or form into another. *Supersede'* ; to take the place of, because preferred. *Style*, mode of writing or speaking. *Authority* ; right to govern from greater merit, or through power derived from others. *Emphat'ic*, expressing an idea with greater force. *Reflex'ive*, turning back upon itself, that the act or relation reverts to the subject.

DECLENSION OF NOUNS AND PRONOUNS.

Nouns.

_____ SINGULAR _____			_____ PLURAL _____		
Nominative.	*Possessive.*	*Objective.*	*Nominative.*	*Possessive.*	*Objective*
Boy,	boy's,	boy;	boys,	boys',	boys.
Man,	man's,	man;	men,	men's,	men.
Lady,	lady's,	lady;	ladies,	ladies',	ladies.
Fox,	fox's,	fox;	foxes,	foxes',	foxes.
John,	John's,	John.			

Pronouns.

	_____ SINGULAR _____			_____ PLURAL _____		
	Nom.	*Poss.*	*Obj.*	*Nom.*	*Poss.*	*Obj.*
1st Pers.	I,	my *or* mine,	me;	we,	our *or* ours,	us.
2d Pers.	Thou,	thy *or* thine,	thee;	ye,	} your *or* yours, you	
	You,	your *or* yours,	you;	you,		
3d Pers. { *Mas.*	He,	his,	him;	} they, their *or* theirs, them.		
{ *Fem.*	She,	her *or* hers,	her;			
{ *Neut.*	It,	its,	it;			

	Nom. or *Obj.*			*Nom.* or *Obj.*		
1.	Myself (*or* ourself);			ourselves.		
2.	Thyself *or* yourself;			yourselves.		
3.	Himself, herself, itself;			themselves.		

	Nom.	*Poss.*	*Obj.*	*Nom.*	*Poss.*	*Obj.*
	One,	one's,	one;	ones,	ones',	ones.
	Other,	other's,	other;	others,	others',	others.

Sing. or *Plur.* {	Who,	whose,	whom.	(—ever *or* soever.)	
	Which,	whose,	which.	"	
	That,	whose,	that.	——	
	What,	———	what.	"	
	As,	———	as.		
	None,	———	none.		

Decline *John, man, boy, lady, fox, farmer, Benjamin, city.*

Decline *I, thou, you, he, she, it, myself, thyself, yourself, himself, herself, itself, one, other, who, whoever, whosoever, which, whichever, what, that, as, none.*

Thou is now superseded, in common usage, by *you.* Thou is still preferred in addressing the Deity, and often in Scriptural or poetic style.

We may include, with the speaker, the person addressed, and the person spoken of. *You* may include, with the person addressed, the person spoken of. *You, he,* and *I—we; thou* or *you* and *he—you.*

Editors, in speaking of themselves editorially, generally prefer *we* to *I.* This use of the plural pronoun denotes greater modesty or authority; for it implies that the speaker is not alone in his opinion.

Ours, *yours, hers,* etc., are each equivalent to the simple possessive pronoun and a noun; as, "This is my hat, and that is *yours,*" i. e., *your hat.*

It sometimes denotes merely the state or condition of things; as, "*It* snows;" "*It* was moonlight on the Persian sea;" "*It* is too dark here to read." Sometimes it introduces a sentence, and is explained by a following word, phrase, or clause; as, "*It* is *he*;" "*It* is *she*;" "*It* was *they*;" "*It* is mean *to take advantage of another's distress*;" "*It* is perfectly plain *that a straight line must be the shortest distance between two points.*" (What is plain?)

It is sometimes applied to creatures whose sex is not obvious or not important; as, "We found a young *fawn,* and caught *it.*" The sex, most grammarians say, is disregarded in such instances, and the words are neuter. But, since the nouns must, in such cases, be nearly always of the common gender, and since we can say, "*It* is *he,*" "*It* is *she,*" it may be as well to say *it* is of the common gender. ("The *tiger* broke *its* chain," seems less proper to me than, "The *tiger* broke *his* chain.")

The **compound** personal pronouns of the first and the second person are composed of the simple possessive pronouns and *self* or *selves;* those of the third person, of the objective pronouns and *self* or *selves.* These pronouns are used only in the nominative and the objective case, and they are either emphatic or reflexive in sense; as, "He *himself* waited on his guest;" "She deceived *herself.*" To express possession emphatically, *own* is used with the simple possessive pronoun; as, "This is *my own* affair."

None (*no-one*) may be used either as singular or plural. *Each other* properly relates to two only; *one another,* to more.

Exercises.

What is the objective corresponding to—
I?—thou?—we?—ye?—he?—she?—it?—they?—you?—who?
What is the nominative corresponding to—
Me? — us? — thee? — him? — whom?—her?—hers?—them?—themselves?—herself?—it?—which?
Form the compound pronoun:—
My, our, thy, your, him, her, it, one, them, who, which, what.

Of what gender, person, number, and case is each of the following pronouns?—

Him, his, its, he, them, it, I, you, thy, their, she, thou, me, your, us, they, my, mine, thine, yours, it, hers, others, theirs, we, thee, our, ours, ye, myself, ourself, themselves, ourselves, thyself, yourselves, yourself, himself, itself, herself, one, none, one's, ones', other, others', who, what, which, whatever.

3. ARTICLES.

If I say, "Give me a book," you understand that any book will answer my purpose; but if I say, "Give me *the* book," you understand that I want some particular book. If I say, "Missouri is north of Arkansas," I mean States; but if I say, "*The* Missouri is north of *the* Arkansas," I mean rivers. These little words, *a* and *the*, which often have so important an effect on the sense of nouns, are called *articles*. What, then, is an *article?*

An **article** is a word placed before a noun, to show how the noun is applied.

Ex.—*Man* is made for society; but *a man* naturally prefers *the man* whose temper and inclinations best suit his own.

How many articles are there, and what are they?

Two: **the**, the *definite* article; and **a** or **an**, the *indefinite* article.

What does the *definite* article show?

The **definite** article shows that some particular object or group is meant.

Ex.—*The* horse, *the* horses, *the* stage, *the* Connecticut; *the* green meadows; *the* iron-bound bucket; *the* brave Pulaski.

What does the *indefinite* article show?

The **indefinite** article shows that no particular one of the kind is meant.

Ex.—*A* bird, *a* mouse, *an* apple, *a* cherry, *a* carriage; *an* idle boy.

How do *a* and *an* differ?

In application only; in meaning, they are the same.

Where is *an* used?

Before words beginning with a vowel sound.

Ex.—*An* article, *an* enemy, *an* inch, *an* urn, *an* hour, *an* honor.

Exercises.

The article, and why; whether definite or indefinite, and why; and to what it belongs:—

The roses in the garden. The rose is a beautiful flower. A fish from the river. A daughter of a duke. The daughter of the duke. A daughter of the duke. An eagle's nest.

Words Explained.—*Article*, joint; because, in the Greek language, from which the word is taken, it sometimes encloses a noun on each side, as two joints enclose a limb, or as *that* encloses *man* in the expression, "*that* MAN *that* I saw." *Understand*, see with the mind. *Definite*, setting bounds to. *Indefinite*, not definite. *Application*, a putting to something else.

Where is *a* used?

Before words beginning with a consonant sound.

Ex.—*A* banquet, *a* cucumber, *a* dunce, *a* fox, *a* horse, *a* jug, *a* king, *a* lion, *a* youth, *a* university, *a* eulogy; *a* one-horse carriage.

4. ADJECTIVES.

The nouns and pronouns, as you remember, denote objects. But our regard for objects depends not a little on their qualities and circumstances; and hence there is a large class of words to express these, for all the various purposes of life. The word *apple*, for instance, denotes something that may be *red, large, ripe, mellow, juicy.* And when I say, "*that* apple, *this* apple, *every* apple, *four* apples, the *fourth* apple," the slanting words show, without expressing quality, more precisely what I mean. These qualifying and designating—these descriptive and definitive words, which generally *add* an idea to that of the noun, are therefore called *adjectives*. What, then, is an *adjective?*

An adjective is a word used to qualify or limit the meaning of a noun or pronoun.

Ex.—Green, good, lazy, tall, wise, religious. A *bay* horse; a *sharp* knife; a *sharper* knife; a *bright* day; *golden* clouds; a *gold* watch; *Missouri* apples; a *rustling* aspen; *that* sun-tipped elm; a boy *nine* years *old*, who is *sick*.

Adjectives may be divided into two classes; *descriptive* and *definitive*. Instead of these words, *qualifying* and *specifying* may also be used.

What is a *descriptive* adjective?

A descriptive adjective describes or qualifies.

Ex.—A *rapid* river; the *blue* sky; a *modest* woman. She is *beautiful, amiable,* and *intelligent.* The *rippling* brook; *waving* woods; a *broken* pitcher. The last three adjectives, and others like them, are called *participial* adjectives.

Exercises.

Place the proper indefinite article before each of the following words or phrases:—

Razor, house, knife, humming-bird, chicken, ounce, insult, unit, ox, ball, hundred, African; interesting story; humble cottage; useful instrument; honest man; honorable deed.

Words Explained.—*Ad'jective*, from the Latin *ad*, to, and *jectus*, thrown; thrown or joined to something else, adding an idea to. *Quality*, the nature of a thing for a long time. *Condition*, the nature of a thing for a short time. *Cir'cumstances*, surroundings, what accompanies the main thing; thus, when an act is done, the time, place, manner, means, etc., are its circumstances. *Des'ignating*, pointing out. *Descriptive*, telling what something is. *Defin'itive*, showing which or how many. *Limits*, sets bounds to the meaning. *Modifies*, affects or varies the meaning. *Principal*, chief.

ADJECTIVES.

What is a *definitive* adjective?

A **definitive** adjective merely limits or modifies.

Ex.—*Four* peaches; *all* peaches; *some* peaches; *this* peach.

Which are the principal definitive adjectives?

All, any, both, certain, each, every, either, else, few, many, many a, much, neither, no, one, other, own, same, some, such, that, this, very, what, which, and *yon* or *yonder.*

Also, *one, two, three,* etc.; *first, second, third,* etc.

Nearly all the adjectives of the first class are usually called *pronominal* adjectives, some of them being occasionally used as pronouns; and those of the second class are called *numeral* adjectives. Since we may refer to objects *definitely, indefinitely,* or *distributively,* the pronominal adjectives are accordingly, some of them, *definite* or *demonstrative,* as *this, that, yonder;* some, *indefinite,* as *any, some, other;* and some, *distributive,* as *each, every, either, neither, many a.* And since we may either *count* or *number,* some of the numeral adjectives are called *cardinal,* as *one, two, three;* and the others, *ordinal,* as *first, second, third.*

Either and *neither* properly relate to one of two; *any, any one,* or *none,* should be applied to more. *This* refers to the nearer of two; *that,* to the more distant.

Since the same quality may exist in different objects, and in the same degree or in different degrees,—as, "*red* cheeks, *red* roses, *red* hair, *redder* cheeks, the *reddest* roses,"—adjectives have what grammarians call the *degrees of comparison.* What, then, is meant, in grammar, by *comparison?*

Comparison, in grammar, denotes the forms in which adjectives and adverbs are expressed, to show the quality and its degrees.

There are three degrees of comparison; the *positive,* the *comparative,* and the *superlative.*

Exercises.

The adjective, and why; whether descriptive or definitive, and why; and to what it belongs:—

The blue sky. The sky is blue. An aspiring man. A modest and beautiful woman, with eyes bright, blue, and affectionate. The night grew darker and darker. That field has been in cultivation four years. The first car is not full, having but one man in it. The landscape was fresh with dew and bright with morning light. The rosy-fingered Morn. The star-powdered galaxy. The apples

Words Explained.—*Pronom'inal,* resembling a pronoun. *Distrib'utively,* taken one by one. *Demon'strative,* pointing out exactly what is meant. *Numeral,* expressing number. *Car'dinal,* chief, the most important or common. *Or'dinal,* expressing order. *Degree,* a step or grade.

How does the *positive* degree describe an object?
The **positive** degree ascribes to an object the quality simply, or an equal degree of it.

Ex.—High, rocky, polite, black, prudent; as *white* as snow.

How does the *comparative* degree describe an object?
The **comparative** degree ascribes to an object the quality in a higher or a lower degree.

Ex.—Higher, rockier, politer, better, more prudent, less prudent.

How does the *superlative* degree describe an object?
The **superlative** degree ascribes to an object the quality in the highest or the lowest degree.

Ex.—Highest, rockiest, politest, best, most prudent, least prudent.

How are adjectives of one syllable compared, to express *increase* of the quality?
By adding *er* or *est* to the word in the positive degree.

Ex.—Pos. *great*, comp. *greater*, superl. *greatest*; wise, *wiser*, *wisest*. See p. 153.

What adjectives of two syllables are compared by annexing *er* and *est?*
Adjectives of two syllables ending in *y* or *le*, or accented on the second syllable.

Ex.—Pos. *lovely*, comp. *lovelier*, superl. *loveliest*; able, *abler*, *ablest*; serene, *serener*, *serenest*.

How do we compare other adjectives of two syllables, all adjectives of more syllables, and sometimes adjectives of any length?
Other adjectives of two syllables, all adjectives of more syllables, and sometimes adjectives of one syllable, are compared by placing *more* and *most* before the positive.

Ex.—Pos. *beautiful*, comp. *more beautiful*, superl. *most beautiful;* active, *more active*, *most active;* unlucky, *more unlucky*, *most unlucky*. The *more nice* and *elegant* parts.—*Johnson.* By far the *most rich* and *copious*.—*Pope.*

A foot *more light*, a step *more true*,
Ne'er from the heath-flower dashed the dew.—*Scott.*

Exercises.

boiled soft. Now fairer blooms the drooping rose. His hammock swung loose at the sport of the wind. He is asleep. This is a broad, deep, clear, swift, and winding river.

Words Explained.—*Pos′itive*, laid down, certain, referring to nothing else. *Compar′ative*, reckoned by comparison. *Super′lative*, from the Latin *super*, over, beyond, and *latus*, carried; beyond all others. *Irregular*, not according to rule, differing from most of its kind. *Propri′ety*, good sense as to fitness.

ADJECTIVES.

Some words are expressed in the superlative degree, by annexing *most* to them; as, *Inmost, innermost, utmost* (*out*most), *uppermost, nethermost.*

A high degree of the quality, without implying direct comparison, is expressed by *very, exceedingly, a most,* etc.; as, *Very respectful, exceedingly polite, a most ridiculous* affair.

Some adjectives are not compared according to the foregoing rules, and are therefore said to be *irregular.* The following is a list:—

Positive.	Compar.	Superl.	Positive.	Compar.	Superl.
Good,	better,	best.	Hind,	hinder,	hindmost.
Bad, ill, *or* evil,	worse,	worst.	Far,	farther,	farthest.
Much *or* many,	more,	most.	(Forth)	further,	furthest.
Little,	less,	least.	Near,	nearer,	nearest, *or* next.
Fore,	former,	foremost, *or* first.	Late,	later, latter,	latest, *or* last.
			Old,	older, elder,	oldest, *or* eldest.

Elder and *eldest* are applied to persons only; *older* and *oldest,* to persons or things. *Later* and *latest* refer to time; *latter* and *last,* generally to order in place.

How are adjectives compared when we wish to express *decrease* of the quality?

By *less* and *least.*

Ex.—Wise, *less wise, least wise;* arrogant, *less arrogant, least arrogant.*

A little of the quality may be expressed by annexing *ish* to the positive, or by placing before it, *rather, somewhat,* etc.; as, Black, *blackish;* salt, *saltish; disagreeable, somewhat disagreeable;* young, *rather young.*

Can all adjectives be compared?

Some can not be compared with propriety.

Ex.—Eternal, straight, equal, perpendicular, two-edged, speechless, four.

Exercises.

Compare, of the following adjectives, those which can be compared:—

Wise, studious, near, good, evil, melodious, high, tuneful, saucy, eloquent, expressive, lovely, nimble, late, many, much, few, little, old, glowing, accomplished, expert, half-finished, full, counterfeit, graceful, meagre, worthless, bottomless, fundamental, ornamental, vernal, green, sluggish, sunburnt, free, first.

Mention and spell the three degrees of comparison:—

Strong, weak, light, gay, rough, nice, coarse, fierce, white, ripe, thin, slim, dim, fit, hot, fat, glad, big, droll, dry, sprightly, manly, gentle, feeble, noble, idle, discreet, remote, sublime, profound.

Compare by using LESS *and* LEAST:—

Broad, convenient, confident, oily, troublesome, thick, joyful, sorrowful, exorbitant, exact, indulgent, handsome.

Join suitable adjectives to each of the following nouns:—

Moon, field, fountain, trees, garden, horse, willow, man, woman, pen, ink, day, wood, boys, thoughts, feelings, actions, conduct.

Good writers, however, sometimes compare such adjectives, when they do not take them in their full sense. "Our sight is the *most perfect* of our senses." —*Addison.* This means that it approaches nearer, than the rest, to perfection. "And love is still an *emptier* name."—*Goldsmith.*

Is the word which the adjective qualifies or limits, always expressed?

It is not; but, in parsing, it must be supplied.

Ex.—"These apples are better than those" [apples]. "The idle [persons] are generally mischievous." "Nearly all [the soldiers] were captured."

5. VERBS.

If we look into the world, we shall find, that, to the many different beings and things denoted by nouns and pronouns, belong not only many different qualities, denoted by adjectives, but also many different motions, actions, and states of existence, which are expressed by certain words called *verbs;* as, John reads, *writes, runs,* and *plays.* What, then, is a *verb,* or what is its chief use in language?

A **verb** is a word used to affirm something of a subject.

Ex.—The wind *blows.* The rose *blooms.* The tree *is* dead. Brutus stabbed Cæsar. Cæsar *was* stabbed by Brutus. *Do* you not *study?* Do (you) *study* diligently. (For the meaning of the word *affirm,* see page 4.)

What must every verb denote?

Some kind of action or state.

When verbs are actually used to express affirmations, they are called *finite* verbs; but there are two forms of the verb which do not express affirmations, and which are called the *participle* and the *infinitive:* as, *Writing, written, being written, having written, having been written; to write, to have written, to be written, to have been written.*

Exercises.

The verbs, and why:—

The sun rises. Saddle your horse. Bees collect honey. Honey is collected by bees. The bird flutters. The workmen have built the house. Pinks are fragrant. The thunder was rolling. The problems should have been solved. The mill can not grind with the water that has passed. Riches are got with pain, kept with care, and lost with grief. Drunkenness makes a man's eyes red, bloats his face, empties his purse, wastes his property, poisons his blood, destroys his digestion, blunts his feelings, corrupts his body and mind, disgraces his family, and shortens his life.

Words Explained.*—Verb* means *word,* or, pre-eminently, *the word*: grammarians have called this part of speech so, because it makes the chief part of every grammar, or because it is the chief word of language. *States of existence,* how things are. *Finite verb,* a verb that must be affirmed of a nominative.

What, then, is a *participle?*

A **participle** is a form of the verb, that merely assumes the act or state, and is generally construed like an adjective.

A tree, *bending* with fruit. (A tree, *full* of fruit.) The man was found *imprisoned.* (The man was found *dead.*) John is *studying.* (John is *studious.*)

What is an *infinitive?*

An **infinitive** is a form of the verb, that begins generally with *to*, and expresses no affirmation.

Ex.—An opportunity *to study.* He is obliged *to sell.* It is too dark *to travel.* He seems *to have been disappointed.*

Of how many words may a verb consist?

Of as many as four.

Ex.—Eagles *soar.* The house *was built.* The mail *may have arrived.* These lessons *should have been learned.* *To have been writing.*

Almost every verb may be expressed in a great variety of ways or forms; thus, from W R I T E we have *writing, wrote, written, writes, writeth, writest, to write, to have written, to be written, to have been written, to be writing, to have been writing, having written, having been written, is written, was written, should be written, is writing, was writing, can write, must write, will write, shall write, would write, should write, may write, might write, may be written, may be writing, may have been writing, might have been written, mightst have been writing,* etc., etc.

Now, that we may be enabled to master all these different forms,—understand their meanings, and thus be enabled to use them correctly,—grammarians have found it best to divide verbs into certain *classes*, and also to regard them as having certain *properties.*

How are verbs classified? [form.

Into *regular* and *irregular*, with reference to their

Into *transitive* and *intransitive*, with reference to their meaning or use.

What is a *regular* verb?

A **regular** verb takes the ending *ed*, to form its preterit and its perfect participle.

Ex.—Present *play*, peterit *played*, perfect participle *played*; move, *moved, moved*; regret, *regretted, regretted.* (See page 153.) In stead of *preterit,* the pupil may also say *past,* a less appropriate but more euphonic word.

Words Explained.—*Par'ticiple,* partaking of; having the nature of a verb and of an adjective or a noun. *Con'strued like an adjective,* arranged in the same way with other words of a sentence. *Infin'itive,* from *in,* not, and *finitus,* bounded; not bound, free, not obliged to have a nominative. *Regular,* according to rule, like most of its kind. *Euphon'ic,* agreeable in sound.

What is an *irregular* verb ?

An **irregular** verb does not take the ending *ed*, to form its preterit and its perfect participle.

Ex.—Present *see*, preterit *saw*, perfect participle *seen*; speak, *spoke*, *spoken*.

Which are the *principal parts* of the verb, or those from which all the other parts can be formed ?

The principal parts are the *present*, or the simplest form given in a dictionary; the *preterit*, or the simplest form that affirms a past fact; and the *perfect participle*, or the form that makes sense with the word *having* or *being*.

Ex.—Present, *walk*, *write*; pret., (I) *walked*, (I) *wrote*; perf. part., having *walked*, being *written*. To the *principal parts* given, may be added the *present participle*; which, since it ends always with *ing*, is too well known to need mentioning. It may be mentioned, however, before the perfect participle.

List of Irregular Verbs.*

The following catalogue shows the principal parts of all the irregular verbs. When the pupil has learned these, he will also know the principal parts of all the other verbs, which must be regular. He must not infer, however, from the word *irregular*, that these words are a mere straggling offshoot from the language; for they are really the very core or pith of it.

I. The Two Past Forms Different.

Present.	Preterit, or Past.	Perfect Part.	Present.	Preterit, or Past.	Perfect Part.
Arise,	arose,	arisen.	Beat,	beat,	beaten, beat.
Awake,	awoke, R.,	awaked, awoke.*	Become,	became,	become.
Be *or* am,	was,	been.	Befall,	befell,	befallen.
Bear (*bring forth*),	bore, bare,	born.	Beget,	begot, begat,*	begotten, begot.
Bear (*carry*),	bore,	borne.	Begin,	began,	begun.

Words Explained.—*Pret'erit*, from the Latin *præter*, past, and *itus*, gone; gone by or past. *Perfect*, from the Latin *per*, through, and *fectus*, made; made throughout, finished. The **present** is either the *present indicative*, or the *present infinitive* without *to*. According to Greek and Latin dictionaries, it is the former; according to Teutonic or old English dictionaries, it is the latter. *Reg'istered*; put in order, so as to be easily found. *Cat'alogue*, a regular list. *Ancient*, used long ago. *Poet'ic*, used by poets. *Defective*, wanting. *Re-dun'-dant*, overflowing, having more than enough. *Be* was formerly used for *am, are, is*, etc.

* In using irregular verbs, we are liable to error for the most part only in the use of those whose preterit and whose perfect participle are not alike. Those verbs have therefore been given first, and separate from the rest, that they may be learned perfectly. R. denotes that the regular form may also be used in stead of the other. * denotes that the form under it is seldom used, being either ancient, poetic, or of late introduction. The form supposed to be of the best present usage, is placed first. The second form of some verbs is preferable, when applied in a certain way; as, "*freighted* with spices and silks," "*fraught* with mischief;" "*thunderstruck*," "*sorrow-stricken*."—Commit to memory the unmarked forms only.

VERBS.

Present.	Preterit, or Past.	Perfect Part.	Present.	Preterit, or Past.	Perfect Part.
Bid,	bid, bade,	bid, bidden.	Heave,	heaved, hove,	heaved, hoven.*
Bite,	bit,	bitten, bit.	Hew,	hewed,	hewn, R.
Blow,	blew,	blown.	Hide,	hid,	hidden, hid.
Break,	broke, brake,*	broken, broke.*	Hold,	held,	held, holden.**
Chide,	chid,	chidden, chid.	Know,	knew,	known.
			Lade (load),	laded,	laden, R.
Choose,	chose,	chosen.	Lie (repose),	lay,	lain.
Cleave (adhere),	cleaved, clave,ª*	cleaved.	(Lie, speak falsely; regular.)		
			Mow,	mowed,	mown, R.
Cleave (split),	cleft, clove, clave,	cleft, cloven.	Prove,	proved,	proved, proven.*
Come,	came,	come.	Rend,	rent,	rent, R.ᵈ*
Crow,	crowed, crew,	crowed.	Ride,	rode,	rode, ridden.
Dare (venture),	dared,ᵇ durst,	dared.	Ring,	rang, rung,	rung.
(Dare, challenge; regular.)			Rise,	rose,	risen.
			Rive,	rived,	riven, R.*
Dive,	dived, dove,*	dived.	Run,	ran,	run.
			Saw,	sawed,	sawn, R.
Do (principal verb),	did,	done.	See,	saw,	seen.
Draw,	drew,	drawn.	Seethe,	seethed, sod,	seethed, sodden.
Drink,	drank,	drunk, drank.*	Shake,	shook,	shaken.
Drive,	drove,	driven.	Shape,	shaped,	shaped, shapen.*
Eat,	ate, ĕat,	eaten, ĕat.*	Shave,	shaved,	shaved, shaven.
Fall,	fell,	fallen.			
Fly,	flew,	flown.			
Forbear,	forbore,	forborne.	Shear,	sheared, shore,*	shorn, R.
Forget,	forgot,	forgotten, forgot.	Show,	showed,	shown, R.
Forsake,	forsook,	forsaken.	Shrink,	shrunk, shrank,	shrunk, shrunken.*
Freeze,	froze,	frozen.			
Freight,	freighted,	freighted, fraught.	Slay,	slew,	slain.
Get,	got,	got, gotten.	Slide,	slid, R.,	slidden, slid, R.
Give,	gave,	given.	Smite,	smote,	smitten, smit.
Go,	went,	gone.			
Grave,	graved,	graven, R.	Sing,	sung, sang,	sung.
Grow,	grew,	grown.			

(a.) My tongue *clave* to the roof of my mouth.—*Dickens*. (b.) This line he *dared* not cross.—*Macaulay*. (c.) Beholden; withholden.* (d.) Come as the winds come when forests are *rended*.—*W. Scott*.

VERBS.

Present.	Preterit, or Past.	Perfect Part.
Sink,	sunk, sank,	sunk.
Sow (scatter),	sowed,	sown, R.
Speak,	spoke, spake,*	spoken.
Spin,	spun, span,*	spun.
Spit,	spit, spat,*	spit, spitten.*
(Spit, pierce with a spit; regular.)		
Spring,	sprung, sprang,	sprung.
Steal,	stole,	stolen.
Stride,	strode, strid,	stridden, strid.
Strike,	struck,	struck, stricken.
Strive,	strove, R.,*	striven, R.*

Present.	Preterit, or Past.	Perfect Part.
Strow,	strowed,	strown, R.
Swear,	swore, sware,	sworn.
Swell,	swelled,	swollen.
Swim,	swum, swam,	swum.
Take,	took,	taken.
Tear,	tore,	torn.
Thrive,	thrived, throve,	thrived, thriven.
Throw,	threw,	thrown.
Tread,	trod, trode,*	trodden, trod.
Wax (grow),	waxed,	waxed, waxen.*
Wear,	wore,	worn.
Weave,	wove, R.,*	woven, R.*
Write,	wrote,	written.

2. The Two Past or the Three Forms Alike.

Present.	Preterit, or Past.	Perfect Part.
Abide,	abode,	abode.
Behold,	beheld,	beheld.
Belay,	belaid, R.,	belaid, R.
Bend,	bent, R.,	bent, R.
Bereave,	bereft, R.,	bereft, R.
Beseech,	besought,	besought.
Bet,	bet, R.,	bet, R.
Betide,	betided, betid,*	betided. betid.*
Bind,	bound,	bound.
Bleed,	bled,	bled.
Blend,	blended, blent,*	blended, blent.*
Bless,	blessed, blest,	blessed, blest.
Breed,	bred,	bred,
Bring,	brought,	brought.
Build,	built, R.,	built, R.
Burn,	burned, burnt,	burned, burnt.
Burst,	burst,	burst.
Buy,	bought,	bought.

Present.	Preterit, or Past.	Perfect Part.
Cast,	cast,	cast.
Catch,	caught, R.,*	caught, R.*
Cling,	clung,	clung.
Clothe,	clothed, clad,	clothed, clad.
Cost,	cost,	cost.
Creep,	crept,	crept.
Cut,	cut,	cut.
Deal,	dealt, R.,*	dealt, R.*
Dig,	dug, R.,	dug, R.
Dwell,	dwelt, R.,	dwelt, R.
Dream,	dreamed, dreamt,	dreamed, dreamt.
Dress,	dressed, drest,*	dressed, drest.*
Feed,	fed,	fed.
Feel,	felt,	felt.
Fight,	fought,	fought.
Find,	found,	found.
Flee,	fled,	fled.
Fling,	flung,	flung.
Gild,	gilded, gilt,	gilded, gilt.

VERBS.

Present.	Preterit, or Past.	Perfect Part.
Gird,	girt, R.,	girt, R.
Grind,	ground,	ground.
Hang,	hung, R.,	hung, R.ᵃ
Have (principal verb),	had,	had.
Hear,	heard,	heard.
Hit,	hit,	hit.
Hurt,	hurt,	hurt.
Keep,	kept,	kept.
Kneel,	knelt, R.	knelt, R.
Knit,	knit, R.,	knit, R.
Lay,	laid,	laid.
Lead,	led,	led.
Lean,	leaned, leant,	leaned, leant.
Leap,	leaped, leapt,*	leaped, leapt.*
Learn,	learned, learnt,	learned, learnt.
Leave,	left,	left.
Lend,	lent,	lent.
Let,	let,	let.
Light,	lighted, lit,	lighted, lit.
Lose,	lost,	lost.
Make,	made,	made.
Mean,	meant,	meant.
Meet,	met,	met.
Pass,	passed, past,*	passed, past.ᵇ
Pay,	paid,	paid.
Pen (fence in),	penned, pent,	penned, pent.
(Pen, write; regular.)		
Plead,	pleaded, plead, pled,	pleaded, plead, pled.
Put,	put,	put.
Quit,	quit, R.,	quit, R.
Rap, .	rapped, rapt,	rapped, rapt.ᶜ
Read,	read,	read.

Present.	Preterit, or Past.	Perfect Part
Reave,*	reft,	reft.
Rid,	rid,	rid.
Roast,	roasted,	roasted, roast.ᵇ
Say,	said,	said.
Seek,	sought,	sought.
Sell,	sold,	sold.
Send,	sent,	sent.
Set,	set,	set.
Shed,	shed,	shed.
Shine,	shone, R.,*	shone, R.*
Shoe,	shod,	shod.
Shoot,	shot,	shot.
Shred,	shred,	shred.
Shut,	shut,	shut.
Sit,	sat,	sat.
Sleep,	slept,	slept.
Sling,	slung,	slung.
Slink,	slunk,	slunk.
Slit,	slit, R.,	slit, R.
Smell,	smelt, R.,	smelt, R.
Speed,	sped, R.,*	sped, R.*
Spell,	spelled, spelt,	spelled, spelt.
Spend,	spent,	spent.
Spill,	spilt, R.,	spilt, R.
Split,	split, R.,*	split, R.*
Spoil,	spoiled, spoilt,*	spoiled, spoilt.*
Spread,	spread,	spread,
Stay,	staid, R.,	staid, R.ᵈ
String,	strung,	strung, B.ᵉ
Stave,	stove, R.,	stove, R.
Stand,	stood,	stood.
Stick,	stuck,	stuck.
Sting,	stung,	stung.
Stink,	stunk, stank,*	stunk.
Sweat,	sweat, R., swet,	sweat, R. swet.
Sweep,	swept,	swept.

(a.) Hang, hanged, hanged; *to suspend by the neck with intent to kill*. but the distinction is not always observed. (b.) *Past* is used as an adjective or as a noun. (c.) Rap, rapt, rapt; *to seize with rapture*. (d.) Stay, stayed, stayed; *to cause to stop*. (e.) *Stringed* instruments.

Present.	Preterit, or Past.	Perfect Part.	Present.	Preterit, or Past.	Perfect Part.
Swing,	swung,	swung.	Beware,	—	—
Teach,	taught,	taught.	Can,	could,	—
Tell,	told,	told.	Do (auxil'y)	did,	—
Think,	thought,	thought.	Have, "	had,	—
Thrust,	thrust,	thrust.	May,	might,	—
Wake,	woke, R.,	woke, R.	Must,	must,	—
Wed,	wedded, wed,*	wedded, wed.*	Ought, —	ought, quoth,	— —
Weep,	wept,	wept.	Shall,	should,	—
Wet,	wet, R.,	wet, R.	Will, "	would,	—
Win,	won,	won.	(Will, wish, bequeath; regular.)		
Wind,	wound,	wound.	Wit,		
Work,	worked, wrought,	worked, wrought.	Wot,* Wis,*	wot,* wist,*	
Wring,	wrung,	wrung.	Weet,*	wote,*	

What are the last few verbs usually called?

Defective, because some of the parts are wanting; and verbs having more parts than are absolutely necessary, are termed *redundant*, as *bereave, slide, swim*.

How are formed the principal parts of verbs derived from other verbs by means of prefixes?

Generally in the same way as those of their primitives.

Ex.—Take, *took*, *taken*; mistake, *mistook*, *mistaken*; undergo, *underwent*, *undergone*. But *behave*, *engrave*, and *welcome*, are regular.

Exercises.

Give the principal parts; and tell whether the verb is regular or irregular, and why:—

Form, attack, strip, deny, bow, sow, grow, sew, sin, win, spin, rise, despise, moralize, skim, swim, heal, steal, fling, bring, spread, dread, fold, hold, uphold, close, lose, choose, blind, find, fine, spurn, burn, reel, feel, blend, send, tend, lend, loan, tent, need, feed, blight, fight, wink, drink, slink, squeak, speak, steep, sleep, cleave, weave, leave, reach, teach, fret, get, let, whet, smut, pût, agree, free, see, flee, fly, cry, spite, bite, write, take, make, bake, bare, dare, stray, pay, slay, may, trick, click, stick, call, fall, fell, bind, bound, grind, ground, heat, eat, roam, come, welcome, hive, strive, live, give, forgive, undo, undergo, counteract, say, gainsay, will, till, shall, cull, have, shave, land, stand, am, be, rise, raise, tell, toll, quell, die, lie, lay, fit, hit, sit, scat, set.

What is a *transitive* verb?

A transitive verb is a verb that has an object.

Ex.—John *struck* James. (Struck whom?) Cats *eat* rats and mice. (Eat what?) I *know* him. The house *has* a portico. *To run* a race.

A transitive verb always implies both a doer and an object, and either can be made its subject. If the object is made the subject, the verb must be expressed in what is called the *passive voice*, and is then often called a *passive verb*. (See next page.)

Describe an *intransitive* verb?

An **intransitive** verb does not have an object.

Ex.—John *walks*. The child *cries*. The rose *blooms*. Webster *was* eloquent. Webster *was* an orator. Alice *reads* and *writes* well.

A few of the intransitive verbs, as, *be, lie, remain*, etc., imply no action or exertion, and are frequently called *neuter verbs*, as being *neither* active nor passive. *Be* is the chief neuter verb, and extends alone farther than all the active verbs together; for existence is a more general idea than action.

What properties have verbs?

Voices, moods, tenses, persons, and **numbers.**

Exercises.

The verbs, and why; whether transitive or intransitive, and why; and if intransitive, whether neuter, and why?

Men build houses. Dogs bark. The horse kicked the man. The horse kicks. He talks well. He talks nonsense. I knew him, but he did not know me. The crew captured and sold a whale. We are gathering plums and cherries. She grieves and weeps. The picture hung on the wall. Then arose Lord Chatham. Such as I am I have always been, and always shall be. Spare superfluities, to supply necessaries. You might have assisted us. He seated himself. He sat in a corner. He set a trap for a rat. Lay the book where it lay before. Having written his letter, he sealed it. Give him a knife. The fields look fresh and green. Soft eyes looked love to eyes which spake again. Boys like to play. (Like what?) Children do not consider how much has been done for them by their parents. (Consider what?) Who knows who he is?

Words Explained.—*Transitive*, from the Latin *trans*, over, and *itus*, gone; going or passing over: a transitive verb generally denotes an act that passes over from the subject to the object. *Intran'sitive*, from *in*, not, and *transitive*; not transitive. *Passive*, suffering or receiving. *Voice*—the voice expresses tone, and thereby our state, whether as acting or as suffering. *Id'iom*, a mode of expression peculiar to a language. *Classic languages;* the Latin, Greek, and similar languages.

n. A transitive verb can generally be expressed in two different ways; as, "John *struck* James," "James *was struck* by John;" and hence transitive verbs are said to have two voices. What, then, is *voice?*

Voice is a property of transitive verbs that shows whether the subject does or receives the act.

There are two voices; the *active* and the *passive.*

What does the *active* voice denote?

The **active** voice represents the subject as acting, or the verb as relating to an object.

Ex.—David *slew* Goliath.   John *resembles* his father.

What does the *passive* voice denote?

The **passive** voice represents the subject as acted upon, or the verb as having the object for its subject.

Ex.—Goliath *was slain* by David.   This farm *was owned* by them.

When a transitive verb is made *passive*, the object no longer remains the object, but becomes the subject. Voice, unlike the other properties of verbs, does not extend through all verbs, but belongs to transitive verbs only. A few intransitive verbs, however, are sometimes *passive in form*, but they are *not passive in sense;* as, "He *is gone.*—*Scott.* "The melancholy days *are come.*"— *Bryant.* This is an imitation of a French idiom, in which *be* is used for *have.* On the other hand, verbs are sometimes *active in form* but *passive in sense;* as, "This timber *saws* well"—*capacity to receive the act in a certain way.* "Your poem *reads* smoothly." "We could easily see what *was doing* on the other side of the river." So, "Virgil describes some spirits as *purging* in fire, to recover the primitive beauty of their nature."—*Addison.* "You may be sure he has an ax *to grind.*"—*Franklin.* This is an imitation of an idiom in the Classic languages.

In the following, the object of the preposition is made the subject: "Col. Butler *was* accordingly *written to,* and ordered to hasten forward with the volunteers."—*Irving.* (Compound passive verb.)

Exercises.

The verbs, and why; whether in the active voice or in the passive, and why:—

The water turns the wheel.   The wheel is turned by the water. The horse carries his rider.   The horse was hitched to the buggy. Mary is reading her book.   The book is read.   Most people are influenced by their neighbors.   You could have learned the lesson. The lesson might have been learned by you.   Having taught, having been taught, to have taught, to have been taught, to have been teaching.   Since these men could not be persuaded, it was determined to persecute them.   The workmen are building the house.   The house is building.   Green maple saws well.   He was never heard of afterwards.

b. If I say, "I *write*," I express a matter of fact; "I *may* or *can write*," I express what is not matter of fact, yet may become such; "If I *were writing*," I express a mere supposition; "*Write*," I request it to be done; "*To write*," "*Writing*," I simply speak of the act. These different modes of expressing the verb, grammarians call *moods*. What, then, does *mood* express?

Mood expresses the manner of assertion.

Most grammarians reckon *five* moods; the *indicative*, the *subjunctive*, the *potential*, the *imperative*, and the *infinitive*.

How does the *indicative* mood express the act or state?

The **indicative** mood affirms something as an actual occurrence or fact.

Ex.—God *created* this beautiful world. The guilty *are* not happy.

"If I *am deceived*," "If I *was deceived*," are still in the indicative mood, and not in the subjunctive; for they assume something as *matter of fact*.

How does the *subjunctive* mood express the act or state?

The **subjunctive** mood affirms something as a future contingency, or as a mere supposition, wish, or conclusion.

If it *rain* to-night, our plants will live. Were I a lawyer, I should not like to plead a rogue's case. (But I am not.) O, *had* I the wings of a dove.—*Cowper*. But if I *asked* [*should ask*] your papa, he would only say you *had* better [to] stay [it *would be* better for you *to stay*] at home.—*Bulwer*. If conscience *had had* as strong a hold on his mind as honor, he *had* still *been* [*would* still *have been*] innocent.—*British Essayists*. Some of these forms are good old rather than good modern English.

Exercises.

Change the following sentences so as to make the active verbs passive, and the passive verbs active:—

The sun adorns the world. Indolence produces misery. My neighbor has planted some apple-trees. The dog bit the stranger. The distance was measured by a surveyor. Morse invented the telegraph. The boat was built by Ericsson. Can the river be forded, at this place, by a man on horseback? He paid for the carriage. The ministers speak of peace. He was expected to strike.

Words Explained.—*Mood*, manner, state of mind; mood affirms the act or state as *real, ideal, contingent,* or *willed,* or else merely assumes it in an abstract or modifying sense. *Indic'ative,* pointing out, declaring; *subjunctive,* joined to; *poten'tial,* having power; *imper'ative,* commanding; *infin'itive,* left free. *Subjunctive,* joined to; because the clause in which this mood occurs, is always joined to another, or depends upon it for complete sense. *Supposition,* what is merely in the mind. *Contin'gency,* that which depends on something else, that which may or may not take place. *Conclusion;* a thought drawn from others, that generally ends the matter.

VERBS. 37

What words often precede this mood, or indicate it?
If, though, that, lest, except, unless, provided, etc.

What does a verb in the subjunctive mood suggest, when it refers to present or past time?
That the contrary of what is supposed, or something different, is the true state of the case. See p. 36.

What other mood does the subjunctive resemble in its form, and what one in its meaning?
In its form, the indicative; but in meaning, the potential, with which it is also most frequently associated in sentences. See p. 36.

What does the *potential* mood affirm of the subject?
The **potential** mood affirms merely the power, liberty, liability, necessity, will, duty, or a similar relation of the subject, in regard to the act or state.

Ex.—God *can destroy* this world. You *may play.* They who *would be* happy, *must be* virtuous. Children *should obey* their teachers.

How can this mood be known, or what words are used to express it?
May, can, must, might, could, would, and *should.*

What does the *imperative* mood express?
The **imperative** mood expresses command, exhortation, entreaty, or permission.

Ex.—John, *study* your lessson. (Command.) *Go* where glory waits thee. (Exhortation.) Oh! then *remember* me. (Entreaty.) *Return* to your friends.

What is the subject of every verb in the imperative mood?
Thou, you, or *ye,* usually understood.

Ex.—"Know thyself"—Know *thou* thyself. "My young friends, be pure

Exercises.

The verb, and why; then the mood, and why:—
William is writing. The rosemary nods on the grave, and the lily lolls on the wave. He caught a fish. It will rain this evening. I may command, but you must obey. He could and should have assisted us, but he would not. I wish to go, but I can not.

***Words Explained.**—Potential,* implying the power only; expressing what causes the act, but not that the act is produced. *Liability,* what may be. *Necessity,* what must be. *Duty,* what ought to be. *Exhortation,* advice and persuasion to do good. *Entreaty,* beseeching; humble yet urgent request. We *command* inferiors, *exhort* equals, *entreat* superiors, and *permit* in compliance with the will of others. *Expressed,* put down in the book; *understood,* not put down, but to be supplied by the mind.

and cautious"—My young friends, be *ye* pure and cautious. A verb in this mood sometimes has a subject of the 1st or 3d person; as, "*Seek we* now some deeper shade." "*Lead he* the way who knows the spot."

How does the *infinitive* mood express the act or state?

The **infinitive** mood does *not affirm* the act or state. It comprises the infinitive and the participle.*

Ex.—Be careful *to avoid* the danger. The clouds *dispersing*. See p. 28.

Which of the moods can be used interrogatively?

The indicative and the potential.

Ex.—Who *is* my friend? *Must* I *endure* all this?

How are they made interrogative?

By placing the subject after the verb, or after some part of it.

Ex.—"Thou art he;" "Art *thou* he?" "Can *you* help us?"

---

c. Time may naturally be divided into *present, past*, and *future;* and we may consider an act or state as simply taking place in each of these periods, or as completed: thus, "I *write*, I *have written*;" "I *wrote*, I *had written*;" "I *shall write*," "*I shall have written*"—Present, present-perfect; past, past-perfect; future, future-perfect. Hence verbs have what grammarians call *tenses*. How, then, would you define *tense*?

Tense is the form and meaning of the verb to distinguish time.

Exercises.

Do not value a gem by what it is set in. If William study, he will soon know his lesson. If wishes were horses, beggars would ride. Train up a child in the way he should go; and when he is old, he will not depart from it. The violet soon will cease to smile, the whippoorwill to chant. May you be happy. O, that he were wiser! If you are disappointed, blame not me. If you be disappointed, blame not me. This government will fall, if it lose the confidence of the people. This government would fall, if it lost the confidence of the people. This government would have fallen, had it lost the confidence of the people. Let us now turn to another part. Turn we now to another part. Somebody call my wife. (Imperative.)

---

* The infinitive mood is tolerated, only as we tolerate a neuter gender. It implies the absence of all assertion rather than any particular mode of assertion. Prof. Gibbs, of Yale, says, "The infinitive mode so called is the crude form of the verb. It is the verb divested of all modality. It is no mode at all." In this book, we practically ignore this mood; or, when we call a verb a participle or an infinitive, the mood is implied. And we include under the infinitive mood, *participles* with infinitives, just as zoölogists include under the cat genus not merely cats, but also lions, tigers, leopards, etc.

There are six tenses; the *present*, the *past*, the *future*, the *perfect*, the *pluperfect*, and the *future-perfect*. In stead of *perfect* and *pluperfect* the words *present-perfect* and *past-perfect* may also be used.

What does the *present* tense express?

The **present** tense expresses present acts or states.

Ex.—I *am writing*. It *snows*. You *may commence*. *Let* me *see* it.

This tense is also used to express what is always so from the very nature or condition of things.

Ex.—Heat *melts* ice. Traveling *is* expensive. People *must die*.

Sometimes the present tense is used to express past or future events more vividly; as, "The combat *deepens*. On, ye brave!" "The guard never *surrenders: it dies!*" Also in speaking of the dead, when judged by their existing works; as, "Seneca *moralizes* well."

How does the *past* tense express the act or state?

The **past** tense refers the act or state simply to past time.

Ex.—Bonaparte *was banished* to St. Helena. She *died* this morning. I soon *saw* that he *could* not *see*. The ship *arrived* before day.

This tense is usually called the *imperfect* tense, but inappropriately. It may be well to call it the *aorist* or *indefinite* tense, in the subjunctive and the potential mood, whenever it does not denote past time.

How does the *future* tense express the act or state?

The **future** tense refers the act or state simply to future time.

Ex.—The cars *will come* this evening. Merit *will be rewarded*.

How does the *perfect* tense express the act or state?

The **perfect** tense represents something as past, but still connected with present time.

Ex.—This magnificent city *has been built* within one hundred years. I *have* just *sold* my horse. The mail *may have arrived*. This house appears *to have been* a church. I *have* often *read* Virgil. (*Subject* still remaining.) Thus *has* it *flowed* for ages. (*Act* still remaining.) Cicero *has written* orations. (*Object*, or result, still remaining.)

How does the *pluperfect* tense express the act or state?

The **pluperfect** tense represents something as finished or ended by a certain past time.

Ex.—I *had* already *sent* my trunk to the river, when I received your letter. A fish *had been* on the hook. A fish *might have been* on the hook.

Words Explained.—*Tense*, from the French *temps*, Latin *tempus*, time. *Pe'riod*, a going round, as a year; a portion of time. *A'-o-rist*, from the Greek *a*, not, and *oristos*, marked out; indefinite. *Plu'perfect*, from the Latin *plus*, more, and *fectus*, finished; that is, farther back in time than what is only now finished.

How does the *future-perfect* tense express the act or state?

The **future-perfect** tense represents something as finished or ended by a certain future time.

Ex.—The flowers *will have withered*, when winter returns.

The three perfect tenses are sometimes called the *relative* tenses, because they relate from one point of time to another; and the other three tenses, which have not this relation, are called the *absolute* tenses.

Every perfect tense, except sometimes a participle, must have what two parts?

Have, or some one of its variations, and the perfect participle of some verb.

Ex.—Have written; having written; to have written; may have written; has been writing; shall have written; should have been writing; had written.

How does the present, the past, or the future tense, sometimes express the act or state?

As something habitual or customary in present, past, or future time.

Ex.—He *chews* tobacco. People *go* to church on Sunday. There *would* he *spend* his earnings. The wolf also *shall dwell* with the lamb.

When the act or state is expressed as ideal rather than real, as in the subjunctive mood, and frequently in the potential, what may be observed of the tenses, in respect to the time of the event?

That they move forward, one tense or more, in time.

Ex.—"If I *am*"—now; "If I *be*"—hereafter. "If I *was*"—at any past time; "If I *were*"—now. "I *had been* there"—before a certain past time; "*Had* I *been* there"—at a certain past time. "I *had paid* you"—before a certain past time; "I *might have paid* you"—at a certain past time. "Such governments *could* not *last*, if they *contained* ever so much wisdom and virtue."—*P. Henry.* At any time. See second definition of present tense.

The present and the perfect indicative are sometimes carried into future time, by the words *when, as soon as, whoever*, etc.; as, "*When he comes home*, send for me;" "*When he has done the work*, I will pay him."

In most of the tenses, a verb may be expressed in several different ways: as, "He *strikes;*" "He *does strike;*" "He *is striking;*" "He *is struck;*" "He *striketh.*" Grammarians usually distinguish these, by calling them, emphatically, the FORMS *of the verb*—better, *the forms of the tenses.*

What is the *common* form?

The **common** form is the verb expressed in the most simple and ordinary manner.

Ex.—He *went* home. Time *flies*. No man *has* ever *been* too honest.

Words Explained.—*Future-perfect* literally means *future-finished*. *Habit'ual*, what a person does often. *Cus'tomary*, what is done by many people. *Ide'al*, merely in the mind. *Progres'sive*, from *pro*, forth, and *gressive*, stepping; going forth or on.

What is the *emphatic* form?

The **emphatic** form has *do* or *did* as a part of the verb, to give it greater force.

Ex.—I *did say* so. Really, it *does move*. *Do come* to see me.

Do and *did* are also generally used to express propositions negatively or interrogatively; but they do not make such propositions emphatic.

What is the *progressive* form?

The **progressive** form is *be*, or some variation of it, combined with the participle that ends in *ing*.

This form denotes continuance of the act or state.

Ex.—I wrote; I *was writing*. He *is drinking* wine. (*Drinks*—habit.)

What is the *passive* form?

The **passive** form is *be*, or some variation of it, combined with the perfect participle.

This form is generally passive in sense.

Ex.—The oak *was shattered* by lightning. The melancholy days *are come*.

What is the *ancient* form, or *solemn* style?

The **ancient** form has the ending *t*, *st*, or *est*, for the second person singular; and *th* or *eth*, in stead of *s* or *es*, for the third person singular; and generally uses *thou* or *ye* in stead of *you*.

This form occurs often in Scriptural or poetic style.

Ex.—Thou *barb'dst* the dart. Adversity *flattereth* no man. Who *chooseth* me, must hazard all he *hath*. *Ye* are the salt of the earth.

Doth is used for the auxiliary *does*, and *doeth* for the verb *does*. *Hath* and *saith* are contractions of *haveth* and *sayeth*.

d. When I say, "I *am*, thou *art*, he *is*;" "I *write*, thou *writest*, he *writes*;" you see that the verb varies with the *person* of its subject: and when I say, "He *is*, they *are*;" "He *writes*, they *write*;" you see that the verb varies with the *number* of its subject. Hence the verb is said to have *person* and *number*; that is, it is so expressed as to indicate the person and number of its subject, and

Exercises.

The verb, and why; then the form, and why:—

Twilight is weeping o'er the pensive rose. It fell instantly. It does amaze me. Ye know not what ye say. Learning taketh away the barbarity of men's minds. The apples are gathered and sold. Our chains are forging. The improved rifles are being introduced into the army. Thou art the man.

The tenses being more difficult, the exercises on them are deferred till the Conjugation has been learned.

thereby the subject itself. What, then, is meant by the *person* and *number* of a verb?

The **person** and **number** of a verb are its form as being suitable to the person and number of its subject.

The term, "*a form of the verb*," signifies, in its widest sense, any mode of expressing it.

When is a verb *singular?* and when *plural?*

It is *singular*, when its form is proper for predicating of a singular subject; and *plural*, when proper for predicating of a plural subject.

Ex.—The NIGHT *was* serene, and all the STARS *were shining*.

Define *singular* subjects and *plural* subjects.

A *singular* subject denotes one object, or more objects taken singly or separately; a *plural* subject denotes more than one, but not taken as one single thing.

Ex.—*Singular:* "*The boy* | is studious;" "*Every tree* | is known by its fruit;" "*John, James, or Joseph,* | is studying;" "*Neither John, James, nor Joseph,* | is studying;" "*The crowd* | was large." *Plural:* "*The boys* | are studious;" "*John, James, and Joseph,* | are studious;" "*The people* | are fickle."

Singular subject: Singular nominative; singular nominatives, joined by *or* or *nor*; singular nominative or nominatives, modified by *each, every, either, neither, many a*, or *no*; singular nominatives, joined by *and*, but denoting only one object; collective noun, presenting all the objects as one thing.

Plural subject: Plural nominative; singular nominatives, joined by *and*; collective noun, presenting the objects individually.

In correct discourse, of what person and number is the verb always said to be?

Of the same as its subject or nominative.

Ex.—" I am." Here *am* is said to be of the first person and singular number, because its subject, *I*, is of this person and number.

Exercises.

The verb, and why; then of what person and number, to agree with——:—

I study. We write. He stutters. Grass grows. They were. You might improve. Thou art he. It is. It is I. It is they. Is it he? Thou hast been. The wind has risen. Cows are lowing. The cricket chirps. Sing, heavenly Muse. Seek we the shade. I myself saw him. The general himself was slain. The public are respectfully invited. The country was harassed by civil war. Many a man has been ruined by speculation. Either your horse or mine is gone. Both your horse and mine are gone. Neither the woman nor her child was hurt. Thou or I am to blame. He, as well as I, is to blame.

How is the verb varied, to express person and number?

The third person singular of the present indicative is generally expressed, like the plural of nouns, by adding *s* or *es*. In most other cases, the verb itself remains unchanged.

Ex.—He *plans*; he *marches*; he *tarries*. I *write*; we *write*; they *write*.

PARTICIPLES AND INFINITIVES.

What is a participle? What is an infinitive? See p. 28.

Participles and infinitives perform three offices in language: they are participles and infinitives proper; they combine with the auxiliaries to make most parts of the verb; they become words of other parts of speech.

How many and what participles are there, and how many and what infinitives?

Two of each,—the *present* and the *perfect;* and also a third participle, the *compound*.

How does the *present participle* represent the act or state?

The **present participle** represents the act or state as present and continuing at the time referred to.

Ex.—We saw the moon *rising*. Who goes *borrowing*, goes *sorrowing*.

How does the *present infinitive* represent the act or state?

The **present infinitive** represents the act or state as present, but more often as future, at the time referred to.

Ex.—He seems *to study*. Man never is, but always *to be*, blest. I intended *to say* less; for I was *to speak* again.

How does the *perfect* participle or infinitive represent the act or state?

The **perfect participle** or **infinitive** represents the act or state as past or ended at the time referred to.

Ex.—A fox, *caught* in a trap. The river appears *to have risen*.

The perfect participle is sometimes *present* in sense; as, "He lives *loved* by all." The present infinitive sometimes denotes simply the act or state; and the perfect infinitive, the completed act or state.

What is a *compound* participle?

A **compound participle** consists of two or more participles; and it is in sense generally a *perfect*, but sometimes a *present*, participle.

Ex.—*Having purchased* a farm, he retired to the country. The terms *being settled*, he produced the cash. He, *having been* previously *engaged*, and *being* then *engaged*, in making coast surveys, was appointed.

How is the participle sometimes used?

As an adjective, and then called a *participial* adjective.

Define a participial adjective.

A **participial adjective** ascribes the act or state to its subject as a quality.

Ex.—"A *leaping* and *murmuring* rivulet." "*Written* laws." A participial adjective usually stands before the noun which it qualifies. A word is a participle or participial adjective, only when it is derived directly from a verb of the same meaning. *Writing* and *written* are formed from the verb *write:* but *unknown, situated, enterprising,* are merely adjectives; for there is no such verb as *unknow, situate,* or *enterprise.*

Participles and infinitives are frequently used as what other parts of speech?

As **nouns**, and then often called **verbal** nouns.

When should a participle or an infinitive be considered a noun?

When it evidently takes the place, and is used in the sense, of a noun.

Ex.—"*To live* without *being annoyed*, is pleasant." What is pleasant? without what?—*Life* without *annoyance* is pleasant. "Successful *studying* requires exertion." "*To have learned* so beautiful an art, will be ever a pleasure to me." "He made no secret of my *having written* the review."—*Irving.* "His *being* there, was the ground of suspicion." "Boys like *to play.*" (Boys like *apples.*) "*To love* is *to obey.*"

AUXILIARY VERBS.

No complete verb in our language can express all its properties, or be expressed in all its forms, without the aid of certain other little verbs. Thus, to express "strike" in future time, we say, "*shall* or *will* strike;" in the potential mood, "*may, can, must, might, could, would,* or *should* strike;" in the passive voice, "*is* struck, *was* struck, *being* struck," etc. These little *helping* verbs are therefore called *auxiliary* verbs. *Auxiliary* means *helping.*

How, then, would you define an auxiliary verb?

An **auxiliary** verb helps another verb to express its meaning in a certain manner or time.

Which are the auxiliary verbs?

Be, and all its variations; *do, did; can, could; have, had; may, might; must; shall, should; will, would.*

Words Explained.—*Verbal,* formed from a verb, like a verb. *Possibil'ity,* what can be. *Probabil'ity,* what is likely to be. *Rea'sonableness,* the state of being proper. *Injunction,* request, command. *Compulsion,* force. *Adap-ta'-tion,* fitness, suitableness. *Pre'fix;* some letter or letters put to the beginning of a word, to vary its meaning. *Exem'plified,* shown by examples.

For what are the auxiliaries *be* and its variations used?
They are used to express the verb progressively or passively.
Ex.—The farmer *is ploughing* his field. The field *is ploughed.*

For what are the auxiliaries *do* and *did* used?
They are used to express the verb with emphasis, and often negatively or interrogatively.
Ex.—I *do believe* it. He *did say* so. He *did* not *go.* *Did* you *go?*

What do *can* and *could* imply?
Power or ability.
Ex.—I *can lift* the stone. I *can learn* the lesson. I *could* not *give* my consent.

What do *have* and *had* imply, and for what are they used?
They imply possession, and are used to express the act or state as finished or ended at the time referred to.
Ex.—I *have gathered* the plums which the wind *had blown* down.

What meaning is conveyed by *may* and *might?*
Permission, possibility, or probability; sometimes reasonableness.
Ex.—You *may go* to play. But remember the horse *may die.* It *may rain* this evening. But the question *might be asked,* Is the tax legal?

What do *must, shall,* and *should* denote?
Duty or injunction: but *shall,* more frequently compulsion; and *must,* generally necessity.
Ex.—We *should care* for others. Thou *shalt* not *swear.* He *shall go.* You *must* not *look* for me before next week. Pupils *must obey.*

What do *will* and *would* denote?
Willingness, adaptation, or tendency.
Ex.—He *would pay* if he could. This *will do.* Weeds *will grow* where there is no cultivation. Roses *will fade.*

Generally speaking, **shall** *foretells* in the first person, and *threatens* in the second and third persons; **will** *promises* or *consents* in the first person, and *foretells* in the second and third persons. In dependent or interrogative propositions, these words often reverse or vary their meanings.

For what purpose are all the auxiliaries more or less used?
To express the verb interrogatively. For this purpose, they are placed before the nominative.
Ex.—"You are wounded;" "*Are* you wounded?" "*Does* he know you?"

CONJUGATION AND SYNOPSIS.

What is it, to *conjugate* a verb?

To conjugate a verb is to show, in a regular way, how some or all of its parts are correctly expressed.

Ex.—*Be* and *write* in the present tense, indicative mood.

	Singular.	Plural.
First Person.	I am,	1. We are,
Second Person.	You are,	2. You are,
Third Person.	He, she, *or* it, is;	3. They are.
	1. I write,	1. We write,
	2. You write,	2. You write,
	3. He *or* she writes;	3. They write.

What is it, to *give the synopsis* of a verb?

To give the synopsis of a verb, is to express it correctly, in a single person and number, or in a particular form, through some or all of its moods and tenses.

Ex.—Synopsis of *write*, with *I*, through the indicative mood: Present, *I write*; past, *I wrote*; future, *I shall* or *will write*; perfect, *I have written*; pluperfect, *I had written*; future-perfect, *I shall* or *will have written.*

Most parts of the verb consist of auxiliaries combined with participles and infinitives. *To*, the sign of the infinitive, is omitted when this is combined with auxiliaries; it is also generally omitted after *bid, make, need, hear,* | *let, see, feel,* and *dare,* in the active voice, because these verbs have acquired to some extent the meaning of auxiliaries. From the **p r e s e n t**, all the parts of a regular verb can be easily formed; when the verb is irregular, the three principal parts must be given.

Exercises.

The verb, and why; then the auxiliary, what it implies, and what mood and tense it expresses:—

John can read. Mary may write. Die I must. He does improve rapidly. Do you know him? The sun has risen. The thief had left the tavern when his pursuers came. I have a knife, and it is sharp. You shall obey me. Ye will not come that ye may have life. I will come if I can. He would not remain, if he were sent. Whoever would desert, should be hanged. Did not you go too? May God ever protect the right.

Words Explained.—*Conjugation,* from the Latin *con,* together, and *jugum,* a yoke; a yoking-together. *Conjugation* signified, in old times, the joining of various endings and prefixes to the chief parts of verbs called the roots; but, with us, the word rather signifies the joining of the various forms of the verb to their nominatives. *Synopsis* means a *look at the whole;* and as we are apt to see only the chief or most striking parts, by looking at all at once, the word has come to signify the chief parts, or the outline, of the whole of a thing. *Paradigm;* a display of the variations of a word, or of a class of words.

Formation of the Tenses.

Present participle: Present + *ing;* i. e., the *present* combined with the ending *ing*.
Perfect participle: Present + *ed;* or, irregular and given. See pp. 29–33.
Compound participle: *Being, having,* or *having been* + perfect participle.
Present infinitive: *To* + present. See p. 29.
Perfect infinitive: *To have* + perfect participle.
Present indicative: Present; or *do* + present infinitive (without *to*).
Past indicative: Present + *ed;* or, *did* + present infinitive; or, irregular
Future indicative: *Shall* or *will* + present infinitive. [and given. See pp. 29–33.
Perfect indicative: *Have* + perfect participle.
Pluperfect indicative: *Had* + perfect participle.
Future-perfect indicative: *Shall* or *will* + perfect infinitive.
Present subjunctive: Same as present indicative; but *be* in stead of *am*.
Past subjunctive: Same as past indicative; but *were* in stead of *was*.
Pluperfect subjunctive: Same as pluperfect indicative.
Present potential: *May, can,* or *must* + present infinitive.
Past potential: *Might, could, would,* or *should* + present infinitive.
Perfect potential: *May, can,* or *must* + perfect infinitive.
Pluperfect potential: *Might, could, would,* or *should* + perfect infinitive.
Present imperative: Same as present indicative.
PROGRESSIVE FORM: Corresponding tense of the verb *be* + present participle.
PASSIVE FORM: Corresponding tense of the verb *be* + perfect participle.

To express the progressive passive sense, the ordinary progressive form is sometimes used, when the subject can not be considered the doer, and when the common passive verb would denote completion; as, "The fortress *was building.*" —*Irving.* *Being* is sometimes put into the common passive verb, for the same purpose; as, "The men *are being enrolled.*"—*Newspaper.*

CONJUGATION EXEMPLIFIED.

I have here presented to you the very irregular verb *be,* the regular verb *row,* and the irregular verb *take,* in all the forms in which they can be expressed. Like them, or by their means, may all other verbs be expressed in all their forms; and for *I, you, he, she, it, we, you,* and *they,* can be used any other nominatives having the same person and number, that is, all nominatives whatsoever; so that the following conjugation is sufficient to teach all the correct forms of all the verbs, for all the propositions that have been spoken or written, and all that can be spoken or written, in the English language.

Be.   Row.   Take.

Principal Parts.

Present.	*Preterit, or Past.*	*Perfect Participle.*
Be *or* am,	was,	been.
Row,	rowed,	rowed.
Take,	took,	taken.

INDICATIVE

ABSOLUTE

Present

	First Person.	Singular. Second Person.	Third Person.
	I	You	He, She, or It,
	am,	are,	is;
C.	row,	row,	row s;
E.	do row,	do row,	does row;
Pr.	am row ing,	are rowing,	is rowing;
P.	am row ed,	are rowed,	is rowed;
C.	take,	take,	take s;
E.	do take,	do take,	does take;
Pr.	am tak ing,	are taking,	is taking;
P.	am tak en,	are taken,	is taken;

Past

		Singular.	
	I	You	He
	was,	were,	was;
C.	row ed,	rowed,	rowed;
E.	did row,	did row,	did row;
Pr.	was row ing,	were rowing,	was rowing;
P.	was row ed,	were rowed,	was rowed;
C.	took,	took,	took;
E.	did take,	did take,	did take;
Pr.	was tak ing,	were taking,	was taking;
P.	was tak en,	were taken,	was taken;

Future

		Singular.	
	I	You	He
		shall or will—	
	be,	be,	be;
C.	row,	row,	row;
Pr.	be row ing,	be rowing,	be rowing;
P.	be row ed,	be rowed,	be rowed;
C.	take,	take,	take;
Pr.	be tak ing,	be taking,	be taking;
P.	be tak en,	be taken,	be taken;

* Recite the following paradigm across both pages; and the synopsis with *thou*, down the page. The entire paradigm can also be recited down the page, as well as across; thus, First person singular, com. form, *I row;* emphatic form, *I do row*, etc. The parts in italics show what auxiliary matter must be put to the root of the verb, or what change must be made in

MOOD.*

TENSES.

Tense.

First Person.	Plural. Second Person.	Third Person.
WE	YOU	THEY
are,	are,	are.
row,	row,	row.†
do row,	*do* row,	*do* row.
are rowing,	*are* rowing,	*are* rowing.
are rowed,	*are* rowed,	*are* rowed.
take,	take,	take.
do take,	*do* take,	*do* take.
are taking,	*are* taking,	*are* taking.
are taken,	*are* taken,	*are* taken.

Tense. (IMPERFECT.)

	Plural.	
WE	YOU	THEY
were,	were,	were.
rowed,	rowed,	rowed.
did row,	did row,	did row.
were rowing,	were rowing,	were rowing.
were rowed,	were rowed,	were rowed.
took,	took,	took.
did take,	did take,	did take.
were taking,	were taking,	were taking.
were taken,	were taken,	were taken.

Tense. (FIRST-FUTURE.)

	Plural.	
WE	YOU	THEY
	shall or *will*.	
be,	be,	be.
row,	row,	row.
be rowing,	be rowing,	be rowing.
be rowed,	be rowed,	be rowed.
take,	take,	take.
be taking,	be taking,	be taking.
be taken,	be taken,	be taken.

It, to express the mood, tense, form, person, and number. *C.* stands for *Common Form*; *E.*, for *Emphatic Form*; *Pr.*, for *Progressive Form*; and *P.*, for *Passive Form*.

† Observe that the verb, like the nouns and pronouns in their declension, remains sometimes unchanged, is sometimes partly changed, and is sometimes wholly changed, to express its different properties; and that it sometimes calls in the help of the auxiliary verbs.

VERBS.

RELATIVE

Perfect

Singular.

	First Person.	*Second Person.*	*Third Person.*
	I	You	He
	have—	*have—*	*has—*
	been,	been,	been;
C.	row *ed*,	rowed,	rowed;
Pr.	*been* row *ing*,	been rowing,	been rowing;
P.	*been* row *ed*,	been rowed,	been rowed;
C.	tak *en*,	taken,	taken;
Pr.	*been* tak *ing*,	been taking,	been taking;
P.	*been* tak *en*,	been taken,	been taken;

Pluperfect

Singular.

	I	You	He
		had—	
	been,	been,	been;
C.	row *ed*,	rowed,	rowed;
Pr.	*been* row *ing*,	been rowing,	been rowing;
P.	*been* row *ed*,	been rowed,	been rowed;
C.	tak *en*,	taken,	taken;
Pr.	*been* tak *ing*,	been taking,	been taking;
P.	*been* tak *en*,	been taken,	been taken;

Future-Perfect

Singular.

	I	You	He
		shall or *will have—*	
	been,	been,	been;
C.	row *ed*,	rowed,	rowed;
Pr.	*been* row *ing*,	been rowing,	been rowing;
P.	*been* row *ed*,	been rowed,	been rowed;
C.	tak *en*,	taken,	taken;
Pr.	*been* tak *ing*,	been taking,	been taking;
P.	*been* tak *en*,	been taken,	been taken;

VERBS.

TENSES.

Tense. (PRESENT-PERFECT.)
      Plural.
 First Person. *Second Person.* *Third Person.*
WE   YOU   THEY
have—   *have—*   *have—*
been,   been,   been.
rowed,   rowed,   rowed.
been rowing, been rowing, been rowing.
been rowed, been rowed, been rowed.
taken,   taken,   taken.
been taking, been taking, been taking.
been taken, been taken, been taken.

Tense. (PAST-PERFECT.)
      Plural
WE   YOU   THEY
     had—
been,   been,   been.
rowed,   rowed,   rowed.
been rowing, been rowing, been rowing.
been rowed, been rowed, been rowed.
taken,   taken,   taken.
been taking, been taking, been taking.
been taken, been taken, been taken.

Tense. (SECOND-FUTURE.)
      Plural.
WE   YOU   THEY
   shall or *will have—*
been,   been,   been.
rowed,   rowed,   rowed.
been rowing, been rowing, been rowing.
been rowed, been rowed, been rowed.
taken,   taken,   taken.
been taking, been taking, been taking.
been taken, been taken, been taken.

SUBJUNCTIVE

Present

Singular.

First Person.	Second Person.	Third Person.
IF I	IF YOU	IF HE
be,	be,	be;
C. row,	row,	row;
E. *do* row,	*do* row,	*do* row;
Pr. *be* row*ing*,	*be* rowing,	*be* rowing;
P. *be* row*ed*,	*be* rowed,	*be* rowed;
C. take,	take,	take;
E. *do* take,	*do* take,	*do* take;
Pr. *be* tak*ing*,	*be* taking,	*be* taking;
P. *be* tak*en*,	*be* taken,	*be* taken;

Past

Singular.

IF I	IF YOU	IF HE
were,	were,	were;
C. row*ed*,	rowed,	rowed;
E. *did* row,	*did* row,	*did* row;
Pr. *were* row*ing*,	*were* rowing,	*were* rowing;
P. *were* row*ed*,	*were* rowed,	*were* rowed;
C. took,	took,	took;
E. *did* take,	*did* take,	*did* take;
Pr. *were* tak*ing*,	*were* taking,	*were* taking;
P. *were* tak*en*,	*were* taken,	*were* taken;

Pluperfect

Singular.

IF I	IF YOU	IF HE
had—		
been,	been,	been;
C. row*ed*,	rowed,	rowed;
Pr. *been* row*ing*,	*been* rowing,	*been* rowing;
P. *been* row*ed*,	*been* rowed,	*been* rowed;
C. tak*en*,	taken,	taken;
Pr. *been* tak*ing*,	*been* taking,	*been* taking;
P. *been* tak*en*,	*been* taken,	*been* taken;

We can also say, "Were I," "Were you," "Were he," etc., "Had I been," "Had you been," etc., "Be it ever so fine, 1

MOOD.
Tense.

Plural.

First Person.	Second Person.	Third Person.
IF WE	IF YOU	IF THEY
be,	be,	be.
row,	row,	row.
do row,	do row,	do row.
be rowing,	be rowing,	be rowing.
be rowed,	be rowed,	be rowed.
take,	take,	take.
do take,	do take,	do take.
be taking,	be taking,	be taking.
be taken,	be taken,	be taken.

Tense. (IMPERFECT.)

Plural.

IF WE	IF YOU	IF THEY
were,	were,	were.
rowed,	rowed,	rowed.
did row,	did row,	did row.
were rowing,	were rowing,	were rowing.
were rowed,	were rowed,	were rowed.
took,	took,	took.
did take,	did take,	did take.
were taking,	were taking,	were taking.
were taken,	were taken,	were taken.

Tense. (PAST-PERFECT.)

Plural.

IF WE	IF YOU *had—*	IF THEY
been,	been,	been.
rowed,	rowed,	rowed.
been rowing,	been rowing,	been rowing.
been rowed,	been rowed,	been rowed.
taken,	taken,	taken.
been taking,	been taking,	been taking.
been taken,	been taken,	been taken.

would not buy it;" for, "If I were," "If you were," "If I had been," "Though it be ever so fine, I would not buy it."

POTENTIAL

Present

	Singular.	
First Person.	*Second Person.*	*Third Person.*
I	You	He

may, can, or *must—*

	First Person	Second Person	Third Person
	be,	be,	be ;
C.	row,	row,	row ;
Pr.	be row*ing,*	be rowing,	be rowing ;
P.	be row*ed,*	be rowed,	be rowed ;
C.	take,	take,	take ;
Pr.	be tak*ing,*	be taking,	be taking ;
P.	be tak*en,*	be taken,	be taken ;

Past

	Singular.	
I	You	He

might, could, would, or *should—*

	First Person	Second Person	Third Person
	be,	be,	be ;
C.	row,	row,	row ;
Pr.	be row*ing,*	be rowing,	be rowing ;
P.	be row*ed,*	be rowed,	be rowed ;
C.	take,	take,	take ;
Pr.	be tak*ing,*	be taking,	be taking ;
P.	be tak*en,*	be taken,	be taken ;

Perfect

	Singular.	
I	You	He

may, can, or *must have—*

	First Person	Second Person	Third Person
	been,	been,	been ;
C.	row *ed,*	rowed,	rowed ;
Pr.	been row*ing,*	been rowing,	been rowing ;
P.	been row*ed,*	been rowed,	been rowed ;
C.	tak *en,*	taken,	taken ;
Pr.	been tak*ing,*	been taking,	been taking ;
P.	been tak*en,*	been taken,	been taken ;

Does the subjunctive mood vary, in its forms, through the different persons and numbers?

MOOD.

Tense.

First Person.	Plural. Second Person.	Third Person.
WE	YOU	THEY
	may, can, or *must—*	
be,	be,	be.
row,	row,	row.
be rowing,	be rowing,	be rowing.
be rowed,	be rowed,	be rowed.
take,	take,	take.
be taking,	be taking,	be taking.
be taken,	be taken,	be taken.

Tense. (IMPERFECT.)

	Plural.	
WE	YOU	THEY
	might, could, would, or *should—*	
be,	be,	be.
row,	row,	row.
be rowing,	be rowing,	be rowing.
be rowed,	be rowed,	be rowed.
take,	take,	take.
be taking,	be taking,	be taking.
be taken,	be taken,	be taken.

Tense. (PRESENT-PERFECT.)

	Plural.	
WE	YOU	THEY
	may, can, or *must have—*	
been,	been,	been.
rowed,	rowed,	rowed.
been rowing,	been rowing,	been rowing.
been rowed,	been rowed,	been rowed.
taken,	taken,	taken.
been taking,	been taking,	been taking.
been taken,	been taken,	been taken.

Can you show how some of the forms of the subjunctive mood differ from the corresponding forms of the indicative mood?

Pluperfect

Singular.

First Person.	Second Person.	Third Person.
I	You	He

might, could, would, or *should have—*

	been,	been,	been;
C.	row *ed*,	rowed,	rowed;
Pr.	*been* row *ing*,	been rowing,	been rowing;
P.	*been* row *ed*,	been rowed,	been rowed;
C.	tak *en*,	taken,	taken;
Pr.	*been* tak *ing*,	been taking,	been taking;
P.	*been* tak *en*,	been taken,	been taken;

IMPERATIVE MOOD.

Present Tense.

Singular.	Plural.
C. Be, *or* be thou;	be, *or* be ye.
E. Do be, *or* do thou be;	do be, *or* do ye be.
C. Row, *or* row thou;	row, *or* row ye.
E. Do row, *or* do thou row;	do row, *or* do ye row.
Pr. Be rowing, *or* be thou rowing;	be rowing, *or* be ye rowing.
P. Be rowed, *or* be thou rowed;	be rowed, *or* be ye rowed.
C. Take, *or* take thou;	take, *or* take ye.
E. Do take, *or* do thou take;	do take, *or* do ye take.
Pr. Be taking, *or* be thou taking;	be taking, *or* be ye taking.
P. Be taken, *or* be thou taken;	be taken, *or* be ye taken.

Exercises.

The verb, and why; then the tense, and why:—

The tree blossoms, has blossomed; blossomed, had blossomed; will blossom, will have blossomed; may blossom, might blossom.

The moonlight is glimmering on the water. Hushed now are the whirlwinds that ruffled the deep. The storm had ceased before we reached a shelter. The storm ceased before we reached a shelter. He who is a stranger to industry, may possess, but he can not enjoy. Men must be taught as if you taught them not. How bright yon pearly clouds reposing lie! He sank exhausted on the

How many and what tenses has the *indicative* mood?—the *subjunctive*?—the *potential*?—the *imperative*? What *participles are there*?—what *infinitives*?

In what mood and tense do you find *do*?—*did*?—*have*?—*had*?—*shall* or *will*?—*shall* or *will have*?—*may, can,* or *must*?—*may, can,* or *must have*?—*might, could, would,* or *should*?—*might, could, would,* or *should have*?

VERBS.

Tense. (PAST-PERFECT.)
Plural.

First Person.	Second Person.	Third Person.
WE	YOU	THEY

might, could, would, or *should have—*

been,	been,	been.
rowed,	rowed,	rowed.
been rowing,	been rowing,	been rowing.
been rowed,	been rowed,	been rowed.
taken,	taken,	taken.
been taking,	been taking,	been taking.
been taken,	been taken,	been taken.

INFINITIVE MOOD.

Present Infinitive.
    To be.
C. To row.
Pr. To be rowing.
P. To be rowed.
C. To take.
Pr. To be taking.
P. To be taken.

Perfect Infinitive.
To have been.
To have rowed.
To have been rowing.
To have been rowed.
To have taken.
To have been taking.
To have been taken.

Present Participle.
Being.
Rowing.
Taking.

Perfect Participle.
Been.
Rowed.
Taken.

Compound Participle.
Neuter. Having been.
Active. Having rowed.
Passive. Being rowed.
Passive. Having been rowed.
Active. Having taken.
Passive. Being taken.
Passive. Having been taken.

Exercises.

bloody field. It would have pleased me to have heard from you. Strike! for the green graves of your sires. I may have made some mistakes. I had heard that the spirit of discontent was very prevalent here; but with pleasure I find that I have been grossly misinformed. Had the whole Turkish empire risen in opposition, it could not, at that moment, have deterred them. Your character will have been formed at the age of twenty. She seems to study. He is supposed to have written the book. As soon as I have learned my lesson, I will play with you.

ANCIENT FORM, OR SOLEMN STYLE.—THOU.

INDICATIVE MOOD.

Present.	Past.	Future.	Perfect.	Pluperfect.	Future-Perfect.
THOU	THOU	THOU	THOU	THOU	THOU
	shalt or wilt—	hast—	hadst—	shalt or will have—
art;	wast or wert;	be;	been;	been;	been;
C. rowest,	rowedst,	row,	rowed,	rowed,	rowed,
E. dost row,	didst row,				
Pr. art	wast	be	been	been	been
rowing,	rowing,	rowing,	row,ing,	rowing,	rowing,
P. art rowed;	wast rowed;	be rowed;	been rowed;	been rowed;	been rowed;
C. takest,	tookst,	take,	taken,	taken,	taken,
E. dost take,	didst take,				
Pr. art taking,	wast taking,	be taking,	been taking,	been taking,	been taking,
P. art taken.	wast taken.	be taken.	been taken.	been taken.	been taken.

SUBJUNCTIVE MOOD.

Present.	Past.	Pluperfect.
IF THOU	IF THOU	IF THOU
		hadst—
be;	wert or were;	been;
C. row,	rowed,	rowed,
E. do row,	did row, or didst row,	
Pr. be rowing,	wert rowing,	been rowing,
P. be rowed;	wert rowed;	been rowed·
C. take,	took,	taken,
E. do take,	did take, or didst take,	
Pr. be taking,	wert taking,	been taking,
P. be taken.	wert taken.	been taken.

We can also say, "*Wert* thou," "*Wert* thou *rowed*," "*Hadst* thou *been*," "*Hadst* thou *rowed;*" for, "*If* thou *wert*," "*If* thou *hadst been,*" etc.

POTENTIAL MOOD.

Present.	Past.	Perfect.	Pluperfect.
THOU	THOU	THOU	THOU
mayst, canst,	mightst, couldst,	mayst, canst,	mightst, couldst, wouldst,
or must—	wouldst, or shouldst—	or must have—	or shouldst have—
be;	be;	been;	been;
C. row,	row,	rowed,	rowed,
Pr. be rowing,	be rowing,	been rowing,	been rowing,
P. be rowed;	be rowed;	been rowed;	been rowed;
C. take,	take,	taken,	taken,
Pr. be taking,	be taking,	been taking,	been taking,
P. be taken.	be taken.	been taken.	been taken.

6. ADVERBS.

If I say, "He reasons *correctly,* speaks *fluently,* and persuades *earnestly;*" "Walk *up,* walk *down,* walk *in;*" "*Very* tall, *horribly* ugly, *surprisingly* abrupt, *more* ingenious, *most* eloquent, *very powerfully, quite fast;*" you see that the slanting words tell *how, when, where,* or *to what degree,* a thing is done; also *how* or *in what degree* a quality or property exists; and being most generally applied or *added to verbs,* these words are called *adverbs.* What, then, is an *adverb ?*

An **adverb** is a word used to modify the meaning of a verb, an adjective, or an adverb. See above.

Some entire phrases—as, *long ago, in vain, to and fro, by and by, the more, the less, sooner or later*—are generally used as adverbs, and called *adverbial phrases,* or simply *adverbs.* Adverbs, indeed, are but shorter expressions for phrases or clauses. *Gracefully—in a graceful manner; never—at no time; occasionally—as occasion requires.*

Do adverbs always strictly modify verbs, adjectives, or adverbs only ?

An adverb sometimes relates to a phrase or proposition, and sometimes it modifies a word with reference to a substantive or phrase.

Ex.—" He sailed *nearly* | *round the world.*" " He was so young, so generous, *so* | *every thing that we are apt to like in a young man.*"—*Irving.* "'Twas better so to close, than longer wait *to part entirely foes.*"—*Byron.* "None

---

Exercises.

Give, in the order of the conjugation, the participles, then the infinitives :—
Move, rise, spring, degrade, drown, invigorate, overwhelm, bleed.
Change into the other tenses of the same mood :—
I write, I may write, If I write, If I be writing, To write.
Conjugate fully the verbs RULE, PERMIT, CARRY, STRIKE, SEE.
The verb; regular or irregular; transitive or intransitive; mood, tense, and form; person and number,—and why :—
He is reading law. We have slept. She died. Were we surpassed. You had sent him. Take care, lest you lose it. My time might have been improved better. The corn was ripening.
*Conjugate each of the following verbs, beginning with the first person singular, and stopping with the subject :—*The boy learns. (Thus: SINGULAR, 1st person, *I learn;* 2d person, *You learn;* 3d person, *He,* or *the boy, learns.*) The leaves are falling. Flowers must fade. Jane reads. Jane and Eliza read. Jane or Eliza reads.
*Tell of what mood and tense, then conjugate throughout the tense, beginning with the first person singular :—*I imagine. He suffered. We have lost it. I had been ploughing. I will visit. Were I. Had I been. If he were. Were I invited. Had I been invited. If I be invited. They shall have written. I lay. We read. It may pass. You should have come. We may have been robbed. I was speaking. It is rising. You might be preparing. Had you been studying. Do you hope? Did she smile? If I do fail. If thou rely. Thou art. Art thou? He forgiveth. Dost thou not forgive? It must have happened. They are gone. Thou art going.
Predicate each of the following verbs correctly of THOU; *then of* HE, *and of* THEY: —Am, was, have been, would have been, are deceived, had been, do say, did maintain, gave, touched, cast, amass, recommend, be discouraged, shall have been, will pardon, may have been rejoicing, was elected, should have been elected.

are perfect, *no*, not one." (*No*, like an adverb of emphasis, strengthens the negative proposition.) "*But chiefly* Thou, O Spirit .... instruct me."—*Milton.* "John *only* | bought the horse." "Can *not* you go?" differs from "Can you *not* go?" "Hannibal sailed for Cadiz; and, on his *arrival* | *there*, the population came out to greet him." (When he had arrived there.) *There* seems to modify the verb lurking in the noun. "The *fame* | *hereof* went abroad."— *Bible.* (The fame *of this.*) "From *stars* | *above* to *flowers* | *below.* From *yonder* stars to *these* flowers.) Adjuncts—adjectives or adverbs, and can therefore be modified by adverbs. Predicates and participial or infinitive phrases resemble verbs, and can be modified in the same way. When the adverb, as in the last three examples, has the sense of an adjective adjunct, it is probably best to parse it as an adjective.

From what are most adverbs derived?

From adjectives, by adding *ly.*

Ex.—Bad, *badly;* careful, *carefully;* merry, *merrily.*

How can you tell, in doubtful cases, whether the adjective or the adverb should be used?

To express manner or describe the act, the adverb should be used; to describe the object, the adjective.

Ex.—" *Things* look *favorable* this morning." (*Are* favorable.) "He *looks* | *skillfully* at the moon, through his telescope." "We arrived *safe.*" (We *were safe*, when we arrived.) When the verb can be changed to the neuter verb *be* or *become*, the adjective is required.

If adverbs describe or limit as well as adjectives, can they also be compared?

Adverbs, like adjectives, admit of comparison; but a smaller proportion of adverbs can be compared, and they are more frequently compared by *more* and *most.*

Ex.—Thus, we can say, "*Slow, slower, slowest; lively, livelier, liveliest;*" but we must say, "*So, more so, most so; wisely, more wisely, most wisely.*"

What do most adverbs express?

Manner, Place, Time, or Degree.

Ex.—Thus, well, merrily, gayly; here, there; now, then; very, more, most.

List of Adverbs.

Since it is not unfrequently difficult to determine whether a given word is an adverb or not, or to what class of adverbs it should be referred, a large catalogue is given below, which should be carefully and thoroughly studied. The classification, too, is more minute than it usually is; because it is supposed that the nature and various powers of the adverbs can be better learned by this means.

MANNER, MODE, or QUALITY. *How?*

So, thus, well, ill, how, wisely, foolishly, justly, somehow, anyhow, however, howsoever, otherwise, else, likewise, like, alike, as, extempore, headlong, lengthwise, across, aslant, astride, adrift, amain, apace, apart, asunder, amiss, anew, fast, together, separately, aloud, accordingly, agreeably, necessarily, in vain, in brief, at once, in short, foot by foot, so so, so and so, helter-skelter, hurry-skurry, namely, suddenly, feelingly, surprisingly, trippingly, lovingly, hurriedly, mournfully, proportionally, exactly, heavily, lightly; and many others ending with *ly*, and formed from *adjectives* or *present participles.*

ADVERBS.

PLACE. *Where? Whence? Whither?*

Of place absolute: Here, there, yonder, where, everywhere, somewhere, universally, nowhere, wherever, anywhere, herein, therein, wherein, hereabouts, thereabouts, whereabouts, hereabout, thereabout, abed, aground, on high, all over, here and there.

Of place reckoned FROM *some point:* Whence, hence, thence, elsewhere, away, far, afar, far off, out, remotely, abroad, above, forth, below, ahead, aloof, outwards, about, around, beneath, before, behind, over, under, within, without, from within, from without.

Of place reckoned TO *some point:* Whither, thither, hither, in, up, down, upwards, downwards, forwards, hitherward, homeward, aside, ashore, afield, aloft, aboard, aground, nigh.—The forms *upward, downward, backward,* etc., are also used as adverbs.

Of order: Firstly, secondly, thirdly, etc., next, lastly, finally, at last, in fine.

TIME. *When? How long? How often? How soon? How long ago?*

Of time absolute: Ever, never, always, eternally, perpetually, constantly, forever, incessantly, everlastingly, evermore, aye.

Of time relative; i. e., *reckoned with, to, or from some other time:* When, whenever, then, meanwhile, meantime, as, while, whilst, till, until, after, afterward, afterwards, subsequently, before, ere, late, early, betimes, seasonably.

Of time repeated: Again, often, sometimes, occasionally, seldom, rarely, frequently, now and then, ever and anon, daily, weekly, hourly, monthly, yearly, anew, once, twice, thrice, four times, etc.

Of time present: Now, to-day, nowadays, at present, yet (—heretofore and now), as yet.

Of time past: Yesterday, heretofore, recently, lately, of late, already, formerly, just, just now, anciently, since, hitherto, long since, long ago.

Of time future: Hereafter, henceforth, soon, to-morrow, shortly, erelong, by and by, presently, instantly, immediately, straightway, forthwith, not yet, anon.

DEGREE. *How much? How little? To what extent?*

Adverbs of degree are not easily classified; for adverbs from several other classes, especially when they are to modify adjectives or adverbs, may be used to express degree. The following adverbs, to the dash-line, are not all strictly adverbs of degree.

Adverbs showing how much, to what extent, or in what degree: Much, more, most, greatly, far, further, very, too, little, less, least, extra, mostly, entirely, chiefly, principally, mainly, generally, commonly, usually, in general, fully, full, completely, totally, wholly, perfectly, all, altogether, quite, exceedingly, immeasurably, immensely, excessively, boundlessly, infinitely, clear, stark, nearly, well-nigh, partly, partially, intensely, scarcely, scantily, precisely, enough, exactly, even, everso, just, equally, sufficiently, the, as, so, how, however, somewhat, at all.

Of exclusion or emphasis: Merely, only, but, alone, simply, barely, just, particularly, especially, in particular.

Adverbs implying something additional to what has been mentioned, or something beyond what might be expected, and often with emphasis: Also, besides, else, still, yet, too, likewise, withal, moreover, furthermore, however, extra, eke, even, nevertheless, anyhow.

Adverbs implying cause or means: Why, wherefore, therefore, hence, thence, consequently, accordingly, whereby, hereby, thereby.

Of negation: Not, nay, no, nowise, noway, noways, by no means.

Of affirmation, admittance, or emphasis: Truly, doubtless, undoubtedly, unquestionably, forsooth, indeed, well, very well, well then, yes, yea, ay, verily, surely, certainly, really, assuredly, amen, of course, to be sure.

Of doubt or uncertainty: Perhaps, probably, possibly, perchance, peradventure, haply, mayhap, may-be.

The adverbs of the last three classes are sometimes termed *modal* adverbs;

because they show, it is said, "the *manner* of assertion." They have a more direct reference to the mind of the speaker than the others have. We may deny or refuse, hesitate, consent; disbelieve, doubt, believe; pass from strong negation through doubt into strong positive assertion, and *vice versa.*

EXPLETIVE ADVERBS. *These serve merely to begin sentences, in order to render them less blunt or more sprightly; as,* There, well, why.

CONJUNCTIVE ADVERBS. *These connect as well as modify. They are usually adverbs of time, place, or manner; as,* When, where, while, till, as, etc.

INTERROGATIVE ADVERBS. *These are those adverbs of the foregoing classes, which are used to ask questions; as,* Why? where? when? how? whither?

From the foregoing list, it may be seen that the same word may sometimes be referred to one class of adverbs, and sometimes to another, according to its meaning. "I have *just* come." (*Time.*) "It is *just* full;" i. e., neither more nor less. (*Extent or degree.*)

The pupil, after having carefully studied the foregoing catalogue, will probably be able to refer any adverb not in it to its proper class. In parsing, when an adverb can not be easily referred to some special class, or for the sake of saving time, it will be sufficient to refer the adverb to the general class to which it belongs,—to call it simply an adverb of *manner, place, time,* or *degree.*

Will you mention six adverbs of manner?—three of place where?—three of place whence?—three of place whither?—three of order?—three of time absolute?—three of time relative?—three of time repeated?—three of time present?—three of time past?—three of time future?—six of degree?—three implying exclusion?—three implying something additional?—three of cause?—three of negation?—three of affirmation?—three of doubt? —three expletive adverbs?—six conjunctive adverbs?—one interrogative adverb of manner, one of place, and one of time?—six adverbial phrases?

7. PREPOSITIONS.

When I say, "The horses are *in* the ferry-boat, the ferry-boat is *on* the river, and the river is *between* the hills;" you see that the words *in, on,* and *between,* show how different objects are relatively situated. These little words are called *prepositions;* because *preposition* means *placing before,* and prepositions must generally be placed before nouns, to make the latter capable of being used as descriptive words. What, then, is a *preposition?*

A **preposition** is a word used to govern* a noun or pronoun, and show its relation to some other word.

Ex.—In, on, under, above, over, around, at, from, to, through. A rabbit *in* a hollow tree. (What in what?) How sweetly bloom the violets *on* yonder bank!

Two prepositions are sometimes combined, and some phrases are constantly used in the sense of prepositions. The former expressions may be called *complex prepositions;* the latter, *prepositional phrases;* or both may be termed simply *prepositions.* See the List.

Exercises.

The adverbs, and why; of what kind, and what they modify:—

Wisely, now, here, very. The horse runs swiftly. God is everywhere. Never before did I see her look so pale. These things have always been so. I have been too idle heretofore, but henceforth I will study more diligently. Your book is more beautiful. He was lately here. You do not know him as well as I do. The hall was brilliantly illuminated, and densely crowded with hearers.

Compare late, soon, early, much, little, well, ill, long, far, proudly, heroically.

* *Govern,* to have such influence upon as to cause the case or form of.

PREPOSITIONS.

What does a preposition usually join to some other word or part of the sentence?

A substantive denoting the place, time, possessor, cause, means, manner, or some other circumstance.

Ex.—The apples hang ON the *tree*. We have snow IN *winter*. He was stabbed BY a *volunteer*, WITH the *sword* OF a *Kentuckian*. To write WITH *ease*.

What is an *adjunct*?

An **adjunct*** is a preposition with its object, or with the words required after it to complete the sense.

Ex.—The wind glides *in waves* | *over the bristling barley*.

How are adjuncts related to adjectives, adverbs, and possessives?

They are their equivalents; they often relieve them, or supply their deficiency; and they are probably the richest group of descriptive expressions in language.

Ex.—" A man *of wisdom and virtue*"—A *wise* and *virtuous* man. "To stand here"—To stand *in this place*. "The beauty *of Absalom*"—*Absalom's* beauty. " A land *of liberty*." No adjective. "To sail *to New England*." No adverb. Adjuncts show *where, when, how, how long, of what kind, by whom*, etc.

Is the preposition always expressed?

It is sometimes understood.

Ex.—"Give him his book"—Give his book *to* him. "I stood near him"—I stood near *to* him. "He is like his father"—He is like *to* or *unto* his father.

A preposition without its object becomes an adverb, sometimes an adjective. See p. 60. A preposition is sometimes so blended with a verb or participial noun, as to become a part of it; as, "He was laughed | at," i. e., *ridiculed*." "Our country is worth *fighting* | *for*."

List of Prepositions.

A,	bating,	ere,	respecting,	up,	atween,
aboard,	before,	except,	round,	upon,	atwixt,
about,	behind,	excepting,	save,	versus,	cross,
above,	below,	for,	saving,	with,	dehors,
across,	beneath,	from,	since,	within,	inside,
after,	beside, }	in,	through,	without,	maugre,
against,	besides, }	into,	throughout,		minus,
along,	between,	notwith-	till,	NOT COMMON.	outside,
amid, }	betwixt,	standing,	to,		plus,
amidst, }	beyond,	of,	touching,	Abaft,	sans,
among, }	but,	off,	toward, }	adown,	than,
amongst, }	by,	on,	towards, }	afore,	thorough,
around,	concerning,	over,	under,	aloft,	via,
aslant,	despite,	past,	underneath,	alongside,	withal,
at,	down,	pending,	until,	aloof,	withinside.
athwart,	during,	per,	unto,	aneath,	

Aboard of,	as for,	from before,	from out,
according to,	as to,	from betwixt,	from under,
contrary to,	because of,	from beyond,	out of,
along with,	from among,	from off,	round about.

Can you repeat the prepositions that begin with a ?—b ?—c ?—d ?—e ?—f ?—i ?—n ?—o ?—p ?—r ?—s ?—t ?—u ?—v ?—w ?

* *Ad'junct*, from the Latin *ad*, to, and *junctus*, joined ; what is joined to something else.

8. CONJUNCTIONS.

When I say, "John *and* James write;" "John writes *and* ciphers;" "John spilt his ink on the desk *and* on the floor;" "John writes twice every day, *and* I generally look at his writing;" you see that the word *and* brings on something more to what has been said, or joins together two *words*, two *phrases*, or two *propositions;* and as *conjunction* means *joining together*, this word, and others like it, have been called *conjunctions*. What definition, then, may be given of a *conjunction?*

A **conjunction** is a word used to connect other words, and show the sense in which they are connected.

Ex.—Grain will be cheap, *and* perhaps unsalable. Grain will be cheap, *for* the harvest is abundant. He rides, *if* he is sick. He rides, *though* he is sick. He rides, *because* he is sick.

Two conjunctions are sometimes combined, and certain phrases are sometimes used in the sense of conjunctions: as, "His health, *as well as* his estate, is ruined; *and yet* he still persists in his course." The former expressions may be called *complex conjunctions;* and the latter, *conjunctive phrases;* or both may be termed simply *conjunctions*.

What is a *coördinate* conjunction?

A **coördinate** conjunction connects parts of equal rank, or parts of which one does not modify the other.

Ex.—And, but, or. "The woods are sprouting, *and* the dove is cooing." Here *and* connects clauses which do not depend on each other, and therefore they are said to be *coördinate*, which means *of equal rank*.

What is a *subordinate* conjunction?

A **subordinate** conjunction connects parts of unequal rank, or parts of which one modifies the other.

Ex.—If, that, since, because. "I will work for you, *if* you pay me." Here *if* connects two clauses, of which one depends on the other, and therefore the dependent one is said to be *subordinate*, which means *ranking under*.

Exercises.

Mention the corresponding adverb:—

True, new, sure, good, (well,) glaring, studious, ardent, bad, patient, noble, lazy, profuse, slavish, richer, (more richly,) richest, plainer, severest, necessary, graphic, critic, order, grammar, history, arithmetic, geography.

With vigor; in a careless manner; without care; in what place; from what cause; in this place; in that place; at all times; at the present time; in the lowest degree; at that time; one time; from instinct; by the year.

The prepositions, and why; and between what they show the relation:—

Flowers are growing along the rivulet. I saw him, through a window. The bear was attacked by the dogs, and chased through a cane-brake into the river. My dinner is in my basket under the bench. Beneath the oak lie acorns in abundance. The hog never looks up to him who threshes down the acorns. By assisting me you will confer a favor on me. It happened since morning, and before eleven o'clock. They were rowing up the river; but we, down.

What is a *corresponding* or *correlative* conjunction?

A **corresponding** conjunction suggests another conjunction, and assists it in connecting the same parts.

Ex.—I will *neither* buy *nor* sell. *Though* he reproves me, *yet* I esteem him.

By examining the beginning of this section, what words would you infer may be connected by conjunctions?

Words of almost any part of speech.

Where are conjunctions mostly used?

In connecting the parts of long sentences.

Are conjunctions ever understood?

Sometimes they are; and other words are generally understood after them.

Ex.—"Rout, [and] ruin, [and] panic, scattered all." "I knew [that] he had lost it." "You may first read this sentence, and then [you may] parse it."

How may adverbs, prepositions, and conjunctions be distinguished, or what is the chief characteristic of each class?

Adverbs modify or limit; *prepositions* govern substantives in the objective case; and *conjunctions* connect.

Ex.—"He took *but* one apple"—*adverb*. "I saw all *but* him"—*preposition*. "I saw him, *but* he would not come"—*conjunction*.

List of Conjunctions.

1. *Conjunctions implying continuance or addition, simply or emphatically:* And, as well as, again, also, besides, both, moreover, furthermore, even, nay, so (—also). (*Copulative conjunctions.*)

2. *Separation or choice:* Or, nor, either, neither, or else. (*Alternative or disjunctive conjunctions.*)

3. *Contrariety, restriction, or reservation:* But, yet, still, however, howsoever, nevertheless, notwithstanding, unless (—but not... if), except, that, save. (*Adversative or restrictive conjunctions.*)

4. *Comparison:* Than, as. (*Comparative conjunctions.*)

5. *Concession:* Although, though, even if, even though, notwithstanding, albeit; *and perhaps, what though* (—although). (*Concessive conjunctions.*)

6. *Condition or doubt:* If, unless (—if not), whether, provided, provided that, in case that, so, except, lest. (*Conditional or contingent conjunctions.*)

7. *Cause or reason:* Because, for, since, as, seeing, inasmuch as, forasmuch as, whereas. (*Causal conjunctions.*)

8. *Consequence or inference:* Then, so, therefore, wherefore. (*Illative conjunctions.*)

9. *Purpose, motive, or statement:* That, so that, in order that, lest, so as.

10. *Corresponding conjunctions:* Either—or; neither—nor; whether—or; if—then; though, *or* although—yet; both—and; as—so; as—as.

Conjunctions are sometimes accumulated, or take adverbial particles, merely to strengthen or to modify slightly the connection between the parts. Sometimes, phrases even, or adverbial particles, may be treated simply as conjunctions, unless great accuracy is required; or else they may be analyzed more rigidly otherwise, especially by supplying such words as can be reasonably supposed to have been omitted.

The conjunctions of the first three classes are chiefly *coördinate;* the others, to the tenth class, *subordinate.* The former rather indicate the movements and turns of thought; the latter subjoin parts that are used more or less in the sense of parts of speech.

Can you mention two copulative conjunctions?—two alternative? (Pass thus through the list.)

9. INTERJECTIONS.

In every language, there are certain words used when the mind is suddenly or greatly excited, in order to give vent to some strong feeling or sudden emotion; as, *Oh! alas!* These words are called *interjections,* a word that means *thrown among;* because interjections are so loosely combined with the other words of a sentence, that they seem *thrown among* them, or seem to be thrown into discourse by the force of passion, without regard to syntax.

What is an *interjection?*

An **interjection** is a word that expresses an emotion only, and is not connected in construction with any other word.

Ex.—Alas! fie! O! oh! hurrah! hail! adieu! O Grave! where is thy victory! Ah! Terentia, I am worn out with grief. *Pshaw!* never mind it.

As the heart is susceptible of many different emotions or feelings, the interjections may be divided into various classes.

List of Interjections.

1. *Of sorrow, grief, or pity:* Oh! alas! ah! alack! hoo! welladay

2. *Of earnestness or joy:* O! eigh! hey! eh! ha!

3. *Of surprise, wonder, or horror:* Hah! ha! what! h'm! heigh! strange! indeed! hey-dey! la! whew! zounds! eh! ah! oh! hoity-toity!

4. *Of contempt or aversion:* Pshaw! pish! tut! tush! poh! foh! bah! humph! faugh! whew! off! begone! avaunt!

5. *Of exultation or approbation:* Aha! ah! hey! huzzah! hurrah! good! bravo!

6. *Of attention or calling:* Ho! lo! behold! look! see! hark! la! heigh-ho! soho! hollo! halloa! hoy! hold! whoh! halt! 'st!

7. *Of silence:* Hush! hist! whist! 'st! aw! mum!

8. *Of interrogating:* Eh? hem, or h'm? (The opposite of the preceding class.)

9. *Of detection:* Aha! oho! ay-ay!

10. *Of laughter:* Ha, ha, ha! he, he, he!

11. *Of saluting or parting:* Welcome! hail! all-hail! adieu! good-by! and perhaps good-day! good-night! good-morning! good-evening!

It is difficult to make a satisfactory classification of interjections; for some of them are used in various senses. When the learner meets with an interjection, it is perhaps best that he should determine its meaning from the spirit of the sentence or discourse.

Can you mention two interjections of grief?—two of joy? (Pass thus through the List.)

If a man cultivates the earth, he may be styled a *farmer;* if the same man should engage in the business of buying and selling goods, a *merchant;* if in preaching the gospel, a *preacher:* even so the same word, according to its use, is sometimes of one part of speech, and sometimes of another.

Ex.—" A *black* horse ;" " To *black* boots ;" " *Black* is a color." See p. 152.
The first *black* is an adjective; the second, a verb; and the third, a noun.

10. RULES OF SYNTAX.

THE RELATIONS OF WORDS TO ONE ANOTHER, IN THE STRUCTURE OF SENTENCES.

Words are used to express thoughts; but every thought requires two or more words to be associated or grouped together, in order to express it. Almost every word, therefore, is so made or modified, or is of such a nature, that it looks to some other word for complete sense, and would be as unmeaning and useless by itself as a detached piece of a steam-engine.

Ex.—" The white house gleaming on yonder hill, was built long ago for me and my family to live in it." *The* relates to *house,* showing that some particular one is meant; *white* relates to *house,* describing it; *house* relates to *was built,* tho thing said of it; *gleaming* relates to *house,* describing it; *on* relates to *gleaming* and *hill,* showing where; *hill* relates to *on,* showing on what; *was built* relates to *house,* showing what is said of it; *long ago* relates to *was built,* showing when; *for* relates to *was built* and *me and my family,* showing the purpose; *me and my family* relates to *for;* and connects *me* and *family,* showing that the two are to be taken together; *my* relates to *family,* showing what family ; *to live* relates to *me* and *family,* showing what we do; *in* relates to *it* and *to live,* showing where; and *it* relates to *house* as the thing meant, and to *in* as denoting where. This illustration may teach you, to some extent, what the following Rules mean.

☞ The teacher may show the relations of words in sentences still better, by writing the foregoing sentence, and the most suitable of the following sentences, on the blackboard, and then joining the related words by connecting lines drawn above and below.

Exercises.

The conjunctions, what they imply, and what they connect:—
Him and her we know; but who are you? It ran around the house, and under the floor. You must study, if you would be wise. He is neither educated, nor naturally wise. I will either come or send.

The interjections, and why; then of what kind:—
O! oh! alas! welcome! ho! ah! tush! hurrah! Deluded hopes!—oh, worse than death! Tut! such aristocracy! Adieu! adieu! dear native land.

Supply the words omitted:—
A man and woman were drowned. You may write, and then cipher. Give him his book. He is like you. A book of my sister's. John knows more than Rufus. The first tree and the fourth are dead. I have lost the letter you wrote. Who bets, should be willing to lose. The door opens to whoever knocks. (—*any one who—*) Here are the marbles: take which is yours. Let it be. Arm, soldiers! How now, Tubal; what news from Genoa? Sweet the pleasure, rich the treasure. Strange indeed. Soon ripe, soon rotten.

Change the position of the words, without changing the meaning:—
After a painful struggle, I yielded to my fate. Sweet songs were heard the leafy dells along. Me glory summons to the martial scene. Various, sincere, and constant are the efforts of men to attain happiness. Gone, for ever gone, are the happy days of youth. (See Gray's Elegy, 4th stanza, p. 131.)

Rule I.—Nominatives.

*A **noun** or **pronoun** used as the subject of a finite verb, must be in the nominative case.*

I* am. *We* are. *He* is. (*Who* is?) *They* are. Were *I*. Shall *you* go? Go *thou* hence. *Thou* dar'st not. *She* sings well. Yonder comes the powerful *king* of day. Come *ye* in peace here, or come *ye* in war? There is a *calm* for those *who* weep. *Wheat, corn,* and *tobacco,* are the principal productions. Large *quantities* of hides and tallow are exported. The *man who* is industrious, can earn what *he* needs. (Who can earn? Observe that the nominative relative is the subject of the verb next to it; and its antecedent, of the verb beyond.) Who is *he?* (He is who?) Art *thou* that traitor angel, art *thou* he, *who* first broke peace in Heaven? *I* have less than *he* [has]. *Talent* is full of thoughts; but *Genius,* full of thought. *To lie* is disgraceful. *That liars are not believed when they tell the truth,* is a just part of their punishment.

* *I* is a pronoun, in the nominative case to *am,* according to Rule I. (Repeat it. Pass thus through all the examples under each Rule; and, at some future time, parse the words.)

Rule II.—Nominatives.

*A **noun** or **pronoun** used independently or absolutely, must be in the nominative case.*

Independent.—*By direct address*: Go, *Tubal,** go. *Plato,* thou reasonst well. *By exclamation:* Three thousand *ducats!* 'tis a good round sum. *To be*—or not *to be,*—that is the question! (*Life* or *death,*—that is the question!) *By pleonasm or specification:* The Pilgrim *Fathers,*—where are they? My *banks* they are furnished with bees. Worcester's *Dictionary,* Unabridged. (Title.)

Absolute.†—*Before a participle:* The *rain* having ceased, the sun reappeared. The *steed* [being] at hand, why longer tarry? (*Being* is often understood.) *After a participle or an infinitive:* The vanity of being a *belle.* To be a good *Christian,* was his highest ambition. No one suspected his being a *foreigner.*

* *Tubal* is a noun; and it is in the nominative case independent, by direct address, according to Rule II. † "Since *you are* alone, I will return;" "He *has become a lieutenant;*" "There is no doubt that he *is a patriot;*" "There is no doubt that he *is patriotic,*" etc. Change these *finite verbs* into *participles* and *infinitives,* and the Italic words are *absolved,* or set free, from their former dependence.

Rule III.—Possessives.

*A **noun** or **pronoun** that limits the meaning of another by denoting possession, must be in the possessive case.*

John's* horse. (That is, not any horse, but the one that belongs to John.) *Sir Walter Scott's* works. *Whose* book is it, if not *mine* [—*my* book]? *Fulton's* invention. (See p. 18.) *Boys'* clothing. *Smith's* [store] and *Barton's* store. *Smith, Allen,* and *Barton's* store. Call at *Smith's,* the *bookseller.*† (That is, at Smith's house or store.) The *captain* of the Neptune's wife. (Whose wife,—the captain's or the Neptune's? See p. 89.) Evidence of *their* having quarreled.

* *John's* is a noun, in the possessive case, governed by *horse,* according to Rule III. † *Bookseller* is in the possessive case, and agrees with *Smith's,* according to Rule VII.

Rule IV.—Objectives.

*A **noun** or **pronoun** used as the object of a transitive verb, must be in the objective case.*

I caught *them.** He shot a *deer.* The soil produces *cotton, rice,* and *sugar.* I saw *him,* and he saw *me.* "*Whom* did you hit?—*John.*" (Supply "I hit.") *Whom* therefore ye ignorantly worship, *him* declare I unto you. I hid *myself*

Teach *us*. Teach *us grammar*. (See Comp. Gram., pp. 148, 149.) Teach *me to feel* another's woe. Give us our daily *bread*. (Supply *to*.) They crowned *him* king. (See Rule VII.) The lightnings flashed a brighter *curve*. He talked *himself* hoarse. Having made the *law*, enforce *it*. By reading good *books*, you will improve. To see green *fields*, is pleasant. I knew *him* well, and every truant knew. He rode the *horse*; and I, the *mule*. Most children like *to play*—like *sleighing* and *skating*. Do you know *when to send?* No one knows *how much the fellow is in debt.* The sentry cried out, "*Who goes there?*". "Has Mary come?—How can I tell?" (Supply "*whether she has come.*")

* *Them* is a pronoun, in the objective case, being the object of the verb *caught*, according to Rule IV.

Rule V.—Objectives.

A noun or pronoun used as the object of a preposition, must be in the objective case.

It was sent by *me** to *him*. (That is, we could not say, when speaking correctly, "It was sent by *I* to *he.*") A melon for three *pears* and five *peaches*. By *reading* in good *books*, you will improve. Come, walk with *me* the *jungle* through. Lend *me* your knife. (Supply *to*.) Here he had need all *circumspection*. "Of *whom* did you buy it?—*Jones.*" The river flowed from under the *palaces*. She never comes except *to scold*. The question of *what are to be the powers of the crown*, is superior to that of *who is to wear it*.

* *Me* is a pronoun, in the objective case, governed by the preposition *by*, etc.

Rule VI.—Objectives.

A noun or pronoun used without a governing word, but limiting like an adjunct or adverb some other word, must be in the objective case.

The street is a *mile** long, and forty *feet* wide. (Long and wide to what extent?) He remained five *days*. (*During* five days. A preposition can generally be supplied. These objectives are abridged adjuncts without the preposition, just as *in vain, in short,* etc., are abridged adjuncts without their objects.) The horse ran six *miles*. It is a *ton* heavier. I do not care a *straw*. The milk is a *little* sour. The knife is worth a *dollar*. (Here *worth* is an adjective—*valuable to the extent of a dollar.*) He went *home*. I was taught *music*, and she was taught *it*. "He has been here five *times*." And perhaps, "Five times *four* are twenty."

Most nouns under this Rule denote some estimate of *space, time, weight,* or *value*.

* *Mile* is a noun, and in the objective case, limiting *long*, according to Rule VI.

Rule VII.—Same Cases.

A noun or pronoun used for explanation or emphasis, by being predicated of another, or put in apposition with another, must be in the same case.*

This Rule embraces two kinds of construction: SAME CASE, by *predication;* and SAME CASE, by *apposition*. When two substantives refer to the same person or thing, and an intransitive or passive verb joins them, the latter or explanatory substantive is said to be predicated of the other, and is called a *predicate nominative* or *substantive*; as, "Jackson was the *general* who was elected *President.*" When no verb joins them, the substantives are said to be in *apposition*, or the latter is called an *appositive*; as, "Jackson, the *general*, was at Lake *Pontchartrain.*"

Miscellaneous: Taxes, endless *taxes*, are the *consequences* of corruption. He, being the eldest *son*, inherited the estate. She looks a *goddess*, and she walks a *queen*. They made him *captain*. He was made *captain*. If we whip the enemy, it is a *victory*; if we do not, we call it *strategy*. Tea is the dried *leaves* of a Chinese shrub. Our liberties, our greatest *blessing*, we shall not surrender. I

4

am the *man*. Hail, Sabbath! thee I hail—the poor man's *day*. Yo *scenes* of my childhood. Explain the terms *reason* and *instinct*. They bore *each* [*one*] a banner. They regard winter as 'the *season* of domestic enjoyment. I *myself* went. It was *I*. *What* is he? (He is what?) *Whom* do you take me to be? Which is *which?* (Which is the right one?) IT is easy *to spend* money. IT is not known *how the Egyptians embalmed their dead.*

* One Rule. Compare with "A *good* boy," "The boy is *good*"—also one Rule. † *Hudson* is a noun, in the objective case, to agree with *river*, according to, etc.

Rule VIII.—Two Cases.

*The relative **what**, or a like term when its form allows them, may supply two cases.**

I took *what* suited me.† *Whoever* sins, shall suffer. I will employ *whomsoever* you recommend. Take *whichever horse* you like. The lion will kill *whatever man* touches him.

* This Rule is merely a convenience; for it can be dispensed with, by applying *two* other Rules. † *What* is a relative pronoun, representing *thing* and *which;* and it is used here as the object of *took* and the subject of *suited*, according to Rule VIII.

Rule IX.—Pronouns.

*A **pronoun** must agree with its antecedent, in gender, person, and number.**

Mary lost *her* book.† The best throw with the dice, is to throw *them* away. Liberty has God on *her* side. John and James know *their* lessons. (What makes a singular or plural subject, makes also a singular or plural antecedent. See p. 42.) Neither John nor James knows *his* lesson. Every heart best knows *its* own sorrows. You, Henry, and I, must weed *our* garden. Pupils, obey *your* teachers. The people and *their* rulers The mob and *its* leader. And there *her* brood the partridge led. (The antecedent sometimes follows the pronoun.) Too low they build, *who* build beneath the stars. (A relative may refer to a different pronoun as its antecedent.) Who *that* knows him, would trust him? You are very sick, and I am sorry for *it*. (The antecedent may be a phrase or clause.) You wrote to me, *which* was all you did. Said Joseph to *his* brother, "I will go with you."

* This Rule is applied, only when it is definitely known what the antecedent is. † *Her* is a personal pronoun, of the feminine gender, 3d person, and singular number, to agree with *Mary*, etc.

Rule X.—Articles and Adjectives.

*An **article** or an **adjective** belongs to the noun or pronoun to which it relates.*

ARTICLES.—Bring *a** | *rose* from the | garden. *A* | *gardener's* wages. Once upon *a* summer's day. *A* | *noun* and pronoun. (Supply *a*.) *The* | *house* and lot. *An* | *industrious people*, having a | *great many curious inventions*. (The article relates to the entire phrase after it.)

ADJECTIVES.—*This* apple is *ripe*. I am *sorry* that you are not *better*. The clay burned *white*. The story is *interesting*. A *thick stone* wall. *Every* | *seven* days. (*Every* relates to the phrase.) The truly *good* [people] are *happy*. To live comfortably, is *desirable*. (What is desirable?)

NOTE X.—*An adjective is sometimes used absolutely after a participle or an infinitive.*

To be *good* is to be *happy*. (Goodness is happiness.) The way to be *happy*, is to be *good*. The dread of being *poor*. (This Note can often be dispensed with, by regarding the phrase as a noun, or by supplying a noun. See Comp. Gram., p. 188.)

* *A* is an article, and belongs to *rose*, according to Rule X.

Rule XI.—Finite Verbs.

*A **finite verb** must agree with its subject, in person and number.*

He *is*.* (Who is?) They *are*. Thou *art*. I *am*. Tea and silk *are brought*† from the East. (See p. 42.) A week or a month soon *passes*‡ away. Every horse and mule *was taken*. You, he, and I, *are allowed*§ to go. (We.) You or I *am mistaken*. (You are, etc.) Our people *are*‖ enterprising. No nation *is* at war with us. Down *went* the ship and her gallant crew. Down *went* the ship, with her gallant crew. The saint, the father, and the husband, *prays*. (One person.) The "Pleasures of Hope" *was written* by Campbell. (One thing.) To turn and fly *was* now impossible. For thine *is* the kingdom, and the power, and the glory. (Repeat *thine is*.) John, as well as his brother, *was drafted*. *Believe* [thou] and *obey*. *Read*, John. He that *seeketh, findeth*. To write ten lines a day, ‖ *is* sufficient. That so many *are ruined* in large cities, ‖ *is* owing to bad examples. All work and no play, *makes* Jack a dull boy. (To have all, etc.)

* *Is* is a verb, in the 3d p., s. n., to agree with *He*, according to, etc. † Say,—"and in the 3d pers., plur. n., to agree with *Tea* and *silk*, a plural subject," etc. ‡ Say,—"to agree with *week* or *month*, a singular subject," etc. § Say,—"to agree with *You*, *he*, and *I*, equivalent to *We*." ‖ Say,—"to agree with *people*, a collective noun that expresses a plural idea," etc.

NOTE XI.—*In a few peculiar expressions, finite verbs are used without a suitable subject, or without any subject.*

Ex.—"*Methinks*." And perhaps, "God said, *Let* us make man in our image."
"Forthwith on all sides to his aid *was run*
By angels many and strong."—*Milton's P. L., B. VI.*

Rule XII.—Participles and Infinitives.

*A **participle** relates to the noun or pronoun which is the subject of the act or state.*

*An **infinitive** relates to an expressed or indefinite subject ; and it may besides modify the meaning, or complete the construction, of some other part of the sentence.*

The last clause of this Rule often applies also to participles. The subject of a participle or an infinitive, is the noun or pronoun denoting the object to which the act or state belongs ; and it may be in the objective case, as well as in the nominative.

Columbus became *wearied** and *disheartened* by impediments *thrown* in his way. The Passions oft, *to hear* her shell, thronged around her magic cell. We walked out *to see* the moon *rising*. Now is the time *to sell*. A mountain so high as *to be* perpetually *covered* with snow.

* *Wearied* is a participle, and it relates to *Columbus*, according to, etc. † *To hear* is an infinitive that relates to *Passions* as its subject, and to *thronged*, as showing the purpose, according to, etc. ‡ *To sell* relates to an indefinite or unexpressed subject, and modifies *time*,—by showing what time it is,—according to, etc.

NOTE XII.—*A participle or an infinitive is sometimes used absolutely or independently.*

To go prepared, is necessary. Generally *speaking*, young men are better for business than old men are. *To go* about, *seeking* employment, is irksome. But, *to proceed :* It has been frequently remarked, etc. Every man has, so *to speak*, several strings by which he may be pulled. (Suitable words can generally be supplied, to avoid the necessity of using this Note.)

[The infinitive is the most irksome element in syntax. I therefore offer to teachers the following Rule for trial, as one that will reach all constructions of participles and infinitives, and whose truthfulness most examples strikingly attest.

RULE XII.—*A **participle** or an **infinitive**, being a part of the verb, relates to an expressed or indefinite subject ; and it may besides have the sense of a noun, an adjective, an adverb, or a clause.*]

Rule XIII.—Adverbs.
*An **adverb** belongs to the word or words which it modifies.*

A *most** beautiful horse galloped *very* | *rapidly* up the road. *There* was nothing *there* that I wanted. *When* will you go? *The* cooler the water, *the better* I like it. "Did you see him?—*No.*" (*No* relates to the question. See p. 59.) I consulted him *once* or *twice, not* | *oftener*. (Supply words.) *Secondly*, we could wait *no* | *longer*. "Will you go *there*?—I go *there*? *Never*." You have *perhaps not* noticed *quite* all the adverbs in the sentence which I have *just* read.

* *Most* is an adverb of degree, modifies *beautiful*, and belongs to it, according to, etc.

NOTE XIII.—*A conjunctive adverb joins on something that usually expresses the time, place, or manner; or that is used in the sense of an adverb, an adjective, or a noun.*

Ex.—"Go *when* you please." "The grave *where* our hero was buried." (What grave?) "I know *how* you got it." (Know what?) "He did *as* I said." (How?) In stead of this Note, the Rule can be applied, by parsing the adverb as relating to the verbs in both propositions.

REMARK XIII.—*An adverb appears to be sometimes used independently.*

Ex.—"*Well*, I really don't know what to do." "*Why*, that is a new idea." Adverbs thus used partake somewhat of the nature of both conjunctions and interjections. *Yes, nay, amen*, etc., are usually parsed as being independent, though they nearly always relate to the preceding sentence or discourse.

Rule XIV.—Prepositions.
*A **preposition** shows the relation between two terms, and governs the latter in the objective case.*

The *antecedent term* may be a *noun*, a *pronoun*, an *adjective*, a *verb*, an *adverb*, or even a *phrase;* the *subsequent term* must be a *substantive*.

A man | *of** | wisdom spoke. The man spoke | *of* | wisdom. Parrhasius stood gazing *up on* the canvas. (What upon 'what?) The trees most *beautiful in* spring, blossomed *along* the bank *on* the other side *of* the river. He took the slate *from* him and me, and gave it *to* her *for* whom he had bought it. Oranges grow, like apples, *on* small trees. He is too old *for* service. He came *from beyond* Jordan. *Through* glades and glooms the mingled measure stole. (Terms inverted.) She has nothing to live *for*. (For *which* to live.)

* *Of* is a preposition, and shows the relation between *spoke* and *wisdom*, etc. Analysis will always help to show between what words the preposition shows the relation.

Rule XV.—Conjunctions.
***Conjunctions** connect clauses or sentences; and also words or phrases in the same construction.*

Weeds | *a n d* | briers now grow in the field, *because* it is not cultivated. A long *and* cordial friendship had existed between him *and* me. *If* you desire it, I will *both* write to him *and* speak to him about the matter. *And* so it may be *that* infancy is a happier period *than* manhood, *and* manhood *than* old age. (Supply words.)

Rule XVI.—Interjections.
***Interjections** have no grammatical connection with other words.*

Ah me! (Ah! woe to me!) *Oh!* luckless [am] I. *Aha!* caught at last.

Can *you* repeat Rule 1st?—2d?—3d?—4th?—5th?—6th?—7th?—8th?—9th?—10th?—11th?—12th?—13th?—14th?—15th?—16th?

SUMMARY OF PARSING.

1. A **noun** is a name.

—— is a proper, common, or collective noun; of the masculine, feminine, common, or neuter gender; the first, second, or third person; the singular or plural number; and the nominative, possessive, or objective case. Rule I, II, III, IV, V, VI, VII, or VIII.

2. A **pronoun** is a word that supplies the place of a noun.

—— is a personal, relative, or interrogative pronoun;* of the masculine, feminine, common, or neuter gender; the first, second, or third person; the singular or plural number; (Rule IX, if the pronoun has an antecedent;) (declension;) and in the nominative, possessive, or objective case. Rule I, II, III, IV, V, VI, VII, or VIII.

* There may also occur *demonstrative, distributive, indefinite,* or *reciprocal* pronouns.

3. An **article** is a word placed before a noun, to show how the noun is applied.

—— is the definite or indefinite article. Rule X.

4. An **adjective** is a word used to qualify or limit the meaning of a noun or pronoun.

—— is a descriptive or a definitive adjective; (compare it, if it can be compared;) in the positive, comparative, or superlative degree. Rule X.

5. A **verb** is a word used to affirm something of a subject.

—— is a regular or an irregular verb; transitive or intransitive; (if transitive) in the active or the passive voice; in the indicative, subjunctive, potential, or imperative mood; the present, past, future, perfect, pluperfect, or future-perfect tense, and the common, emphatic, progressive, or ancient form; (conjugation;) in the first, second, or third person, and the singular or plural number. Rule XI.

A *participle* is a form of the verb, that merely assumes the act or state, and is generally construed like an adjective.

—— is a transitive or an intransitive, active or passive (if transitive), present or perfect, or compound present or perfect participle, from the verb ——. Rule XII.

An *infinitive* is a form of the verb, that begins generally with *to*, and expresses no affirmation.

—— is a transitive or an intransitive, active or passive (if transitive), present or perfect infinitive, from the verb ——. Rule XII.

6. An **adverb** is a word used to modify the meaning of a verb, an adjective, or an adverb.

—— is an adverb of manner, place, time, or degree. Rule XIII.

7. A **preposition** is a word used to govern a noun or pronoun, and show its relation to some other word.

—— is a preposition, showing the relation between ——. Rule XIV.

8. A **conjunction** is a word used to connect other words, and show the sense in which they are connected.

—— is a copulative, adversative, alternative, distributive, comparative, conditional, corresponding, etc., conjunction, or a conjunction expressing purpose, conclusion, statement, etc.; and it connects ——. Rule XV.

9. An **interjection** is a word that expresses an emotion only, and is not connected in construction with any other word.

—— is an interjection of grief, joy, surprise, contempt, etc. Rule XVI.

INTRODUCTORY EXERCISES.

Analysis is the resolving of a sentence into its clauses, phrases, and words, according to the sense in which they are put together.

Parsing is the resolving of a sentence into its parts of speech, and telling their grammatical properties.

Sentence Building.

Sentences are made of words. The core or chief combination of words, in making sentences, is *predication*.

1. Simplest Combination of Subject and Predicate.

Soldiers fight.* Dogs bark. Time flies. Wolves howl. Hens cackle. Doves coo. Jewels glitter. Bells are tolling. Bees were humming. Mary was chosen. We shall return.

ANALYSIS.—* This is a simple sentence. The subject is *Soldiers*, and the predicate is *fight*. (The teacher should ask such questions, and require such reasons to be given, as he may deem most instructive to the pupil.)

PARSING.—*Soldiers* is a common noun; of the masculine gender, third person, plural number; and in the nominative case to *fight*, according to Rule I. (Repeat the Rule.) *Fight* is an irregular intransitive verb; its principal parts are, present *fight*, past *fought*, present participle *fighting*, perfect participle *fought*; and it is in the third person, plural number, to agree with its subject *Soldiers*, according to Rule XI. *We* is a personal pronoun; of the common gender, first person, plural number; and in the nominative case to *shall return*, according to Rule I.

2. Object added to the Predicate-Verb.

Dogs bite strangers.* Wolves catch lambs. Lightning strikes trees. Raccoons steal corn. Misers love gold. Merchants sell goods. Horses draw carriages. I shall see him.

ANALYSIS.—* This is a simple sentence. The subject is *Dogs*. The entire predicate is *bite strangers*; the predicate-verb is *bite*, which is limited by the object *strangers*. (Bite what? A word limits or modifies another, when it completes or fixes its meaning. A modifying word or expression is called a *modifier*.)

PARSING.—*Dogs* is a common noun; of the masculine gender, third person, plural number; and in the nominative case to the verb *bite*, according to Rule I. *Bite* is an irregular transitive verb; its principal parts are *bite*, *bit*, *biting*, *bitten*; etc., as above. *Strangers* is a com. noun; of the c. g., 3d p., p. n.; and in the objective case—because it is the object of the verb *bite*—according to Rule IV.

3. Article or Adjective added to the Subject or the Object.

The vessel was wrecked.* John found a knife. Leaves cover the ground. Sweet music rose. The young lady wrote a good composition. Tall and beautiful poplars fringe the river.

ANALYSIS.—* This is a simple sentence. The entire subject is *The vessel*; the subject-nominative is *vessel*, which is modified by the article *The*. *Was wrecked* is the predicate.

PARSING.—*The* is the definite article; and it belongs to *vessel*, according to Rule X. (Parse *vessel* like *Dogs* above.) *Was wrecked* is a regular verb, in the passive voice; principal parts, *wreck*, *wrecked*, *wrecking*, *wrecked*; and it agrees with *vessel*, in the third person and singular number, according to Rule XI.

Sweet is a descriptive adjective, in the positive degree; positive *sweet*, comparative *sweeter*, superlative *sweetest*; and it belongs to *music*, according to Rule X.

And is a copulative conjunction, connecting *tall* and *beautiful*, according to Rule XV.

4. Adjective or Nominative added to the Predicate-Verb.

Lead is heavy.* Most people are ambitious. A bad companion is dangerous. The wind blew cold. Flies are insects.* The rose is a famous flower. It was you.

ANALYSIS.—* This is a simple sentence. *Lead* is the subject. *Is heavy* is the predicate; *is* is the predicate-verb, and it is limited, or has its construction completed, by the adjective *heavy*. Or say, *Is* is the predicate-verb, and it is limited by *heavy*, an attribute of the subject. See p. 116. (Analyze *are insects* in like manner.)

PARSING.—(Parse *Lead* like *Soldiers*.) *Is* is an irregular intransitive verb; its principal parts are *be* or *am, was, being, been;* and it agrees with its subject *Lead*, in the 3d p. and s. n., according to Rule XI. *Heavy* is a descriptive adjective, in the positive degree; (compare it;) and it belongs to *Lead*, according to Rule X.
(Parse *Flies* and *are* like *Lead* and *is* above.) *Insects* is a common noun; of the c. g., 3d p., p. n.; and in the nominative case, to agree with *Flies*, according to Rule VII.

5. Adverb added to the Predicate-Verb.

John comes frequently.* Good pupils study diligently. The procession moved slowly. The eagle flew round and upwards. Flowers are peeping out everywhere. I was there.

ANALYSIS.—* This is a simple sentence. The subject is *John*. The entire predicate is *comes frequently; comes* is the predicate-verb, and it is modified by the adverb *frequently*.

PARSING.—*Frequently* is an adverb of time; and it belongs to *comes*, according to Rule XIII.

6. Adjunct added to the Predicate-Verb.

The mountain is clothed with evergreens.* The wind glided over the grass. Our troubles are aggravated by imaginary evils. My cousin went to your house, at noon, in a carriage.

ANALYSIS.—* This is a simple sentence. The entire subject is *The mountain;* the subject-nominative is *mountain*, which is limited by the article *The*. *Is clothed with evergreens* is the entire predicate; *is clothed* is the predicate-verb, which is modified by the adjunct *with evergreens*.

PARSING.—*With* is a preposition, showing the relation between *is clothed* and *evergreens*, according to Rule XIV. *Evergreens* is a common noun; of the n. g., 3d p., p. n.; and in the objective case—it is the object of the preposition *with*—according to Rule V.

7. Adjunct added to the Subject or the Object.

A wreath of rose-buds encircled her head.* She brought a basket of fruit. The old oak is loaded with a flock of singing blackbirds. The path through the woods is cool and pleasant.

ANALYSIS.—* This is a simple sentence. The entire subject is *A wreath of rose-buds;* the subject-nominative is *wreath*, which is limited by the article *A* and the adjunct *of rose-buds*. *Encircled her head* is the entire predicate; *encircled* is the predicate-verb, which is limited by the object *head*, and *head* is limited by the possessive *her*.

PARSING.—*Of* is a preposition; showing the relation between *wreath* and *rose-buds*, according to Rule XIV. *Rose-buds* is a c. n.; of the n. g., 3d p., p. n.; and in the objective case—it is the object of the preposition *of*—according to Rule V.

8. Possessive or Appositive added to the Subject or the Object.

My hat is new.* Mary's eyes are blue. Our neighbor's bees left their hive. Rogers the poet was a banker.† Lake Erie is a beautiful sheet of water. We visited Rome, the capital of Italy.

ANALYSIS.—* This is a simple sentence. The entire subject is *My hat;* the subject-nominative is *hat*, which is modified by the possessive *My*. (Analyze *is new* like *is heavy* above.)
† This is a simple sentence. The entire subject is *Rogers the poet;* the subject-nominative is *Rogers*, which is limited by the appositive *poet*, and *poet* is modified by the article *the*.

PARSING.—*My* is a personal pronoun; of the common gender, first person, singular number; and in the possessive case, limiting *hat*, according to Rule III. *Poet* is a c. n.; of the m. g., 3d p., s. n.; and in the nominative case, to agree with *Rogers*, according to Rule VII.

11. PARSING.

General Formula.—The part of speech, and why; the kind, and why; the properties, and why; the relation to other words, and according to what Rule.

Articles.

Formula.—An *article*, and why; $\left. \begin{array}{l} \textit{definite,} \\ \textit{indefinite,} \end{array} \right\}$ and why; to what it belongs, and according to what Rule.

"The river."

" *T h e* " is an *article*,—a word placed before a noun to show how it is applied; *definite,* it shows that some particular river is meant; and it belongs to " *river,*" according to Rule X : " *An article belongs to the noun to which it relates.*"*

ABRIDGED.—*The* is the definite article; and it belongs to *river,* etc.

" *R i v e r* " is a noun, it is a name; *common,* it is a name that can be applied to every object of the same kind ; *neuter gender,* it denotes neither a male nor a female ; *third person,* it represents an object as spoken of; *singular number,* it means but one.

ANALYSIS.—*The river* is a phrase. The principal word is *river,* modified by the article *The.* (All the following exercises may be first analyzed, and then parsed, if the teacher deems it best to do so.)

In like manner parse the following phrases :—

The man.	The men.	A rose.	An arrow.
The horse.	The horses.	A melon.	An island.
The child.	The children.	A university.	An uncle.

"A man's hat."

" *A* " is an *article*,—a word placed before a noun to show how it is applied; *indefinite,* it shows that no particular man is meant; and it belongs to " *man's,*" according to Rule X. (Repeat it.)

ABRIDGED.—*A* is the indefinite article; and it belongs to *man's,* etc.

" *M a n ' s* " is a *noun,* it is a name; *common,* it is a name common to all objects of the same kind ; *masculine gender,* it denotes a male ; *third person,* it represents an object as spoken of; *singular number,* it means but one ; and in the *possessive case,* it limits the meaning of " *hat,*" according to Rule III. (Repeat it.)

" *H a t* " is parsed like " *river.*"

ABRIDGED.—*Man's* is a common noun, of the masculine gender, third person, singular number ; and in the possessive case, governed by *hat,* according to Rule.

ANALYSIS.—*A man's hat* is a phrase. The principal word is *hat,* modified by *man's,* showing what hat; and *man's* is modified by *A,* showing that no particular man is meant.

In like manner parse the following phrases :—

A neighbor's farm. The boy's book.
An Indian's hatchet. The boys' books.
The sun's splendor. Women's fancies.

Adjectives.

Formula.—An *adjective*, and why; $\left. \begin{array}{l} \textit{descriptive,} \\ \textit{definitive,} \end{array} \right\}$ and why; whether compared or not, and how; the *degree,* and why; to what it belongs, and according to what Rule.

---

* It is not necessary, in parsing, to repeat more of a Rule than the example requires.

PARSING.

"A beautiful morning, with a refreshing breeze."

"*Beautiful*" is an *adjective*,—a word used to qualify or limit the meaning of a noun; *descriptive*, it describes or qualifies the morning; *compared* pos. *beautiful*, comp. *more beautiful*, superl. *most beautiful*; in the *positive degree*, it expresses the quality simply; and it belongs to "*morning*," according to Rule X. (Repeat it.)

ABRIDGED.—*Beautiful* is a descriptive adjective, in the positive degree (pos. *beautiful*, comp. *more beautiful*, superl. *most beautiful*); and it belongs to *morning*.

"*Refreshing*" is an adjective,—a word, etc. * * * *participial*, it ascribes the act to its subject as a quality; and it belongs to "*breeze*," according to Rule X. (Repeat it.)

ABRIDGED.—*Refreshing* is a participial adjective, from the verb *refresh*; and it belongs to *breeze*, according to Rule X. (Repeat it.)

ANALYSIS.—*A beautiful morning, with a refreshing breeze*, is a phrase. (Give definition.) The principal word is *morning*, which is modified by the article *A*, the adjective *beautiful*, and the adjunct *with a refreshing breeze*. *Breeze* is modified by the article *a*, the adjective *refreshing*, and joined to *morning* by the preposition *with*.

Descriptive Adjectives.

A[a] ripe melon.	A whiter rose.	The fairest lady.
A dark night.	Purling streams.	The black-winged redbird.
An early riser.	Ground corn.	The red-winged blackbird.
Delightful scenery.	The best gift.	
Flowery meadows.	A most[o] ingenious story.	
Mahogany[b] furniture.	The least[o] troublesome servant.	
A more[o] beautiful day.	Webster's most[o] eloquent speech.	
John's bay horse.	The obedient, cheerful, and industrious pupil.	
The worst condition.		
A good boy's mother.	A man bold, sensible, sensitive,	
A large, threatening cloud.	proud, and[o] ambitious.	

"All men."   "Five dollars."

Formula.—An *adjective*, and why; the *kind*, and why; to what it belongs, and according to what Rule.

"*All*" is an *adjective*,—a word used to qualify or limit the meaning of a noun, *definitive*, it limits or modifies the meaning of "*men;*" and it belongs to "*men*," according to Rule X. (Repeat it.)

ABRIDGED.—*All* is a definitive adjective, and belongs to *men*, according to, etc.

"*Five*" is an adjective,—a word, etc. * * * *numeral*, and of the *cardinal* kind, because it expresses number and shows how many; and it belongs to "*dollars*," according to Rule X. (Repeat it.)

ABRIDGED.—*Five* is a numeral adjective, of the cardinal kind, and belongs to *dollars*, according to Rule X.

Definitive Adjectives.

Yonder house.	These trees.	Every fourth man.
This tree.	Each pupil.	Those two benches.
That barn.	Such a person.	The lawyer's own case.

Twelve Spartan virgins, noble, young, and[o] fair,
With[o] violet wreaths adorned[o] their[o] flowing hair.—*Dryden*.

(*a.*) "*A*" shows that no particular "ripe melon" is meant. (*o.*) To be omitted in parsing.
(*b.*) Say, in stead of comparison, "It can not be compared with propriety."

Nouns.

Formula.—A *noun*, and why; *proper, common,* and why; *collective,* and why; *gender,* and why; *person,* and why; *number,* and why; *case,* and Rule.

"Snow is falling."

"*Snow*" is a noun, it is a name; *common*, it is the common name of a substance; *neuter gender*, it denotes neither male nor female; *third person*, it represents an object as spoken of; *singular number*, it means but one; and in the *nominative case*—it is the subject of the verb *is falling*—according to Rule I. (Repeat it.)

ABRIDGED*.—*Snow* is a common noun, of the neuter gender, third person, singular number; and in the nominative case to *is falling*, according to Rule I.

ANALYSIS.—*Snow is falling,* is a simple declarative sentence. *Snow* is the subject, and *is falling* is the predicate.

Parse the articles, the adjectives, and the nouns:—

David slew Goliath[a].
Cattle eat grass.
Cats catch mice.
In golden ringlets[b].
With Sarah's pen.
Edward Everett's[c] orations.
Allen's[d] and Brown's store.
Allen and Brown's store.

Jones[e] the saddler's[f] wife.
The Duke of Wellington's[g] forces.
Mr. Smith taught Ida[a] music[a].
Give John[h] the book.
James the coachman[i] is sick.
George is a gentleman[i].
Bancroft the historian was made chairman[j].

Alice[k], bring your books, slate, and paper.
The boy[l]—O! where was he?
My mother[m] being sick, I remained at home.
To become[n] a scholar[m] requires mind and labor.
The canal is 4 feet[o] deep, and 36 feet wide.
To advance[n] was now utterly impossible.
Thou shalt not steal[p], is the eighth commandment.

Sweet clime of my kindred, blest land of my birth!
The fairest[r], the brightest, the dearest on earth!

(*a.*) "*Goliath*" is a noun, it is a name; *proper*, it is the name of a particular person, to distinguish him from other persons, etc. *** and in the objective case—it is the object of the verb "*slew*"—according to Rule IV. (*b.*) "*Ringlets*" is a noun, etc. *** and in the objective case—it is the object of the preposition *In*—according to Rule V. (*c.*) "*Edward Everett's*" is a proper noun. (*d.*)—and in the possessive case—it limits the meaning of *store*, understood—according to Rule III. (*e.*)—and in the *possessive* case—it limits the meaning of "*wife*," by showing whose wife she is—according to Rule III. (*f.*)—and in the *possessive* case—to agree with "*Jones*"—according to Rule VII. (*g.*)—and in the *objective* case—it is the object of the preposition "*of*"—according to Rule V. (*h.*)—and in the *objective* case—it is the object of the preposition *to*, understood—according to Rule V. (*i.*)—and in the *nominative* case—to agree with *James*—according to Rule VII. (*j.*)—and in the *nominative* case—to agree with "*Bancroft*"—according to Rule VII. (*k.*)—and in the *nominative* case independent, by direct address, according to Rule II. (*l.*) Rule II. (*m.*)—and in the *nominative* case absolute, according to Rule II. (*n.*) "*To become*" is an infinitive, used here as a noun of the neuter gender, 3d person, singular number, and nominative case to "*requires,*" according to Rule I. (*o.*)—and in the *objective* case, limiting "*deep,*" according to Rule VI. (*p.*) *Thou shalt not steal,* is a clause, used here as a noun of the neuter gender, 3d p., s. n.; and in the nominative case to *is*, according to Rule I. Parse each word. (*r.*) Supply *land.*

* Parsing is usually abridged, by simply omitting the reasons.

Pronouns.

Formula.—A *pronoun*,—definition; *personal, relative, interrogative,* and why; *gender*, and why; *person*, and why; *number*, and why; *case*, and Rule.

"I myself saw John and his brother."

"*I*" is a *pronoun*,—a word that supplies the place of a noun; *personal*, it is one of the pronouns that serve to distinguish the three grammatical persons; of the *common gender*, it may denote either a male or a female, *first person*, it denotes the speaker; *singular number*, it means but one; and in the *nominative case*—it is the subject of the verb "*saw*"—according to Rule I. Nom., *I*; poss., *my* or *mine*, etc.

ABRIDGED.—*I* is a personal pronoun, of the common gender, first person, singular number; and in the nominative case to the verb *saw*, according to Rule I.

"*Myself*" is a *pronoun*,—a word that supplies the place of a noun; *compound*, it is compounded of *my* and *self*; *personal*, etc. * * * and in the *nominative case*, to agree with "*I*," according to Rule VII.

ABRIDGED.—*Myself* is a compound personal pronoun, of the common gender, etc.

"*His*" is a *pronoun*,—a word that supplies the place of a noun; *personal*, it is one of the pronouns that serve to distinguish the three grammatical persons; of the *masculine gender*, *third person*, and *singular number*, to agree with "*John*," according to Rule IX; (repeat it;) and in the *possessive case*, it limits the meaning of "*brother*," according to Rule III. (Repeat it.)

ABRIDGED.—*His* is a personal pronoun, of the masculine gender, 3d pers., s. n., to agree with *John*, according to Rule IX; (repeat it;) and in the possessive case, governed by *brother*, according to Rule III.

ANALYSIS.—This is a simple declarative sentence. The entire subject is *I myself*; *I* is the subject-nominative, which is modified by the emphatic appositive *myself*. *Saw John and his brother*, is the entire predicate; *saw* is the predicate-verb, which is modified by the objects *John* and *brother*, which are connected by *and*, and the latter of which is modified by *his*. (For Analysis, henceforth, see pp. 108-11.)

Parse the articles, the adjectives, the nouns, and the pronouns:—
Personal Pronouns.

We caught him.*
Albert dressed himself³&⁴.
With me⁵.
Among themselves.
Thou² majestic Ocean⁷.
Ye golden clouds.

Art thou¹ the man⁷!
Martha and Mary have recited ⁹their³ lessons.
A dutiful son is the delight⁷ of his parents.
John, ⁹you⁴ are wanted.

* In these and all future parsing lessons, a number placed over a word, indicates the Rule to be applied to it; and a caret (∧) shows where words are to be supplied.

"Read thy doom in the flowers, which fade and die."

"*Which*" is a *pronoun*,—a word that supplies the place of a noun; *relative*, its clause relates to and describes a preceding word, and is dependent; of the *neuter gender*, *third person*, and *plural number*, to agree with "*flowers*," according to Rule IX; (repeat it;) and in the nominative case—it is the subject of the verbs "*fade*" and "*die*"—according to Rule I.

ABRIDGED.—*Which* is a relative pronoun, of the neuter gender, third person, and plural number, to agree with *flowers*, according to Rule IX; and in the nominative case to the verbs *fade* and *die*, according to Rule I.

"James reads what pleases him."

"*What*" is a *pronoun*—a word that supplies the place of a noun; *relative*, it makes its clause dependent on another; of the *neuter gender*, it denotes neither a male nor a female; *third person*, it represents an object as spoken of; *singular num-*

ber, it means but one; and it is here used as the object of "*reads*" and the subject of "*pleases*,"—because it takes the place of *that which* or *thing which*,—according to Rule VIII: "*The relative* WHAT *may supply two cases.*"

ABRIDGED.— *What* is a relative pronoun, of the neuter gender, third person, singular number; and it is here used as the object of *reads*, etc.

"Nature deigns to bless whatever man will use her gifts aright."

"*Whatever*" is an *adjective*,—a word that qualifies or limits the meaning of a substantive; *definitive*, it limits or modifies the meaning of "*man*," and it belongs to "*man*," according to Rule X.

"*Man*" is a *noun*, it is a name; *common*, it is a generic name, etc. * * * and it is used here as the object of "*to bless*" and the subject of "*will use*,"—because the phrase *whatever man* takes the place of *any* or *every man that*,—according to Rule VIII.

ABRIDGED.—*Man* is a common noun, of the m. g., 3d p., s. n., and is here used as the object, etc.

"I do not know what he is doing."

"*What he is doing*," is a clause used in the sense of a noun, of the neuter gender, third person, singular number; and in the objective case—it is the object of "*do know*"—according to Rule IV.

"*What*" is a *pronoun*,—a word that supplies the place of a noun; *relative*, it makes its clause dependent on another; of the *neuter gender*, it denotes neither a male nor a female; *third person*, it represents an object as spoken of; *singular number*, it means but one; and in the *objective case*—it is the object of the verb *is doing*—according to Rule IV.

ABRIDGED.— *What* is a responsive relative pronoun, of the n. g., 3d p., s. n.; and in the objective case, governed by *is doing*, according to Rule IV.

Relative Pronouns.

I saw your brother[4], who[9 & 1] was well.
She [*]who[1] studies her[3] glass, neglects her heart.
He was such a talker [*]as[1 *] could delight us all[10].

It was I[7] [*]that[1 b] went.
What[8] costs nothing, is worth[10] nothing[8].
Take whatever[9] you like.
We shall leave what is useless.
I am his[3] [9]who[1 c] created me.

(*a.*) —" was such a talker as"—was a talker *that*, or *who*—. (*b.*) *That=who* ; hence a *relative* pronoun. (*c.*) That is,—"*his property, who* created me;" or, "the property of *him who*," etc.

"Whom did you see?"

"*Whom*" is a *pronoun*,—a word that takes the place of a noun; *interrogative*, it is used to ask a question; of the *common gender*, it may denote either a male or a female; *third person*, it represents an object as spoken of; *singular number*, it means but one; and in the *objective case*—it is the object of the verb "*did see*"— according to Rule IV.

ABRIDGED.— *Whom* is an interrogative pronoun, of the common gender, third person, singular number; and in the objective case, governed by *did see*, etc.

"The Gaul offered his own head to whoever should bring him that of Nero." "The old bird feeds her young ones." "These horses I received for the others."

"*Whoever*" is a *pronoun*,—a word that supplies the place of a noun; *compound* it is compounded of *who* and *ever ; relative* it makes its clause dependent on another; of the *common gender, third person, singular number*, to agree with "*person*," or "*any person*,"—understood before it,—according to Rule IX; and in the *nominative case*—it is the subject of the verb "*should give*"—according to Rule I.

ABRIDGED.— *Whoever* is a compound relative pron., of the c. g., 3d p., s. n., etc.

"*That*" is a *pronoun*,—a word that supplies the place of a noun; it is here used in place of "*the head*," and is therefore of the *neuter gender, third person, singular number ;* and in the *objective case*—being the object of the verb "*should bring*"—according to Rule IV. ("*Ones*" and "*others*" are parsed in a similar way.)

ABRIDGED.—*That* is a demonstrative pronoun, used here in place of the phrase *the head*, and is therefore of the n. g., 3d p., s. n.; and in the objective case, governed by *should bring*, etc.

Interrogative Pronouns.

^aWho⁷ was Blennerhasset¹?   Who¹ can tell what⁷ democ-
^bWho¹ is my neighbor⁷?   racy¹ is?

Miscellaneous Examples.

Your horse trots well, but mine^c paces.   Others may be more intelligent, but none¹ are more amiable, than she is.   Whoever⁸ gives to the poor, lends to the Lord.   From their abhorrence of each other^d.

I hope^e what^e I say will have an effect upon him, and prevent the impression which what⁸ he says may have upon others.

Hereditary bondsmen! know ye not,
Who would be free, themselves⁷ must strike the blow?

(*a.*) "Who was Blennerhasset?"—Blennerhasset was who? (*b.*). To apply Rule VII to "*who*," would give a different meaning to the sentence. (*c.*) Say, "*Mine*" is here used for "*my horse.*" *My* is a pronoun, etc. (Parse the two words as usual.) (*d.*) "*Each other*" is a *pronoun*,—a word that supplies the place of a noun; *compound*, it consists of two words; of the com. gen., etc. (*e.*) "*Hope*" has the entire member after it as its object. (Hope what?)

Verbs.

Finite Verbs.

Formula.—A *verb*, and why; *principal parts;* $\left. \begin{array}{c} \textit{regular,} \\ \textit{irregular,} \end{array} \right\}$ and why; $\left. \begin{array}{c} \textit{transitive, with voice,} \\ \textit{intransitive, or neuter,} \end{array} \right\}$ and why; the *mood*, and why; the *tense*, and why,— with *form* (emphatic or progressive), and why; the *person* and *number*, to agree with its subject ———, according to Rule XI.

"My father is ploughing the field which was bought last year."

"*Is ploughing*" is a *verb*,—a word used to affirm something of a subject; *principal parts*,—pres. *plough*, past *ploughed*, perf. part. *ploughed ; regular*, it assumes the ending *ed ; transitive*, it has an object (*field*),—and in the *active voice*, because it represents its subject as acting ; *indicative mood*, it affirms something as an actual occurrence or fact ; *present tense*, it expresses the act in present time,— and progressive form, it represents it as continuing; *third person* and *singular number*,—to agree with its subject *father*,—according to Rule XI. (Repeat it.)

ABRIDGED.—*Is ploughing* is a regular transitive verb, from the verb *plough ;* (principal parts,—pres. *plough*, past *ploughed*, perf. part. *ploughed ;*) in the indicative mood, present tense, progressive form ; and in the third person and singular number, to agree with its subject *father*, according to Rule XI. First person, I am *ploughing ;* second person, You *are ploughing*, etc.

"*Was bought*" is a verb,—a word used to affirm something of a subject; *principal parts*,—pres. *buy*, past *bought*, perf. part. *bought ; irregular*, it does not assume the ending *ed ; transitive*, but in the *passive voice*, because it affirms the act of the object acted upon ; *indicative mood*, it asserts something as an actual occurrence or fact ; *past tense*, it refers the act simply to past time ; *third person* and *singular number*,—to agree with its subject *which*,—according to Rule XI.

ABRIDGED.—*Was bought* is an ir. pass. verb, from the verb *buy ;* (principal parts,—pres. *buy*, past *bought*, perf. part. *bought ;* in the ind. m., past t., and c. f. ; and in the 3d p., s. n., to agree, etc.

Parse the articles, adjectives, nouns, pronouns, and verbs :—

Regular Verbs.
Columbus discovered America.
John regretted his loss.
Fortune worries men.

Irregular Verbs.
They struck me.
Birds fly. It was I[7].
Joseph has lost his hat.

Transitive Verbs.
Horses eat corn.
The Indians shunned us.
We armed ourselves.

Voices.
She broke the pitcher.
The pitcher is broken.
They named her[4] Mary[7].
She was named Mary[7].

Intransitive Verbs.
Bright leaves quivered.
Rivers flow, and winds blow.
John will become rich.
Horace struts a dandy[7]

Neuter Verbs.
The rose is beautiful.
Fierce was the conflict.
The house stands firm[10].

Moods.
Robert sold his horse.
Were he rich, he would be lazy.
Can you spell *"phthisic"*?
Be sincere. (Be thou sincere.)
Man is made to mourn.

Tenses.
The distant hills look blue.
Have you been sick?
The soldiers will be attacked.
Your coat will have been finished.
You must write a composition.
We should love our neighbors.
Did you go?
The apples might have been eaten.
The lady may have been handsome.
Had I but known it.
Do you venture a small fish, to catch a great one.

Forms.
The tall pines are rustling.
I do protest against it.
Thou hast a heart of adamant.

Persons and Numbers.
Reckless youth makes rueful age.
How are the mighty[a] fallen!
The Rhine and the Rhone rise[b] in Switzerland.
Monday or Tuesday was[c] the day.
Yonder lives[d] a hero and patriot.
His family is[e] large.
The multitude pursue[f] pleasure.
Every house has a garden.
You[g] or he is in fault.
You, he, and I, are invited[h].
I say, be your own friend.
To scorn meanness, is heroic.
That weak men should seek strength in cunning, is natural.

(*a.*) Supply *men*, or parse *mighty* as a noun. (*b.*) Say,—" and in the third person, plural number, to agree with '*Rhine* and *Rhone*'—a plural subject, because it consists of two nominatives joined by *and*—according to Rule XI." See p. 42. (*c.*)—and in the third person, singular number, to agree with "*Monday* or *Tuesday*"—a singular subject, because it consists of two singular nominatives joined by *or*—according to Rule XI. (*d.*)—and in the 3d p., s. n., to agree with "*hero* and *patriot*"—a singular subject, because the two words denote but one person—according to Rule XI. (*e.*)—and in the 3d p., s. n., to agree with its subject *family*—a collective noun that expresses the idea of unity, or presents all the objects as one thing—according to Rule XI. (*f.*)—and in the 3d p., p. n., to agree with its subject *multitude*, a collective noun that is plural in idea—according to Rule XI. (*g.*)—and in the nominative case to *are*, understood, according to Rule I. (*h.*)—and in the 1st p., p. n., to agree with its subject "*You, he,* and *I*," equivalent to *We*, according to Rule XI.

Participles and Infinitives.

Formula.—$\left.\begin{array}{l}\text{A } participle, \\ \text{An } infinitive,\end{array}\right\}$ and why; $\left.\begin{array}{l}transitive, \text{ with } voice, \\ intransitive \text{ or } neuter,\end{array}\right\}$ and why;

$\left.\begin{array}{l}present, \\ perfect,\end{array}\right\}$ and why; with *form*, and why; to what it relates, and according to what Rule.

In parsing a present participle, omit *form ;* and in general omit of the Formulas whatever is not applicable.

"The traveler, having been robbed, was obliged to sell his horse."

"*Having been robbed*" is a *participle*,—a form of the verb, that merely assumes the act or state, and is generally construed like an adjective; *compound*, it consists of three simple participles; *passive*, it represents its subject as acted upon; *perfect* in sense, it expresses the act or state as past and finished at the time referred to; and it relates to "*traveler*," according to Rule XII. (Repeat it.)

ABRIDGED.—*Having been robbed* is a compound, passive, perfect participle, from the verb *rob, robbed, robbed;* and it relates to *traveler*, according to Rule XII.

"*To sell*" is an *infinitive*,—a form of the verb, that begins generally with *to*, and expresses no affirmation; *transitive*, it has an object; *active voice*, it represents its subject as doing something; *present*, it denotes the act simply; and it relates to "*traveler*," and completes the sense of "*was obliged*," according to Rule XII.

ABRIDGED.—*To sell* is a transitive, active, present infinitive, from the verb *sell, sold, selling, sold;* and it relates to *traveler* as its subject, and limits *was obliged*, showing as to what, according to Rule XII.

"To betray is base." "I insist on writing the letter."

"*To betray*" is an *intransitive, active, present infinitive*, from the verb *betray, betrayed, betraying, betrayed*. It is here used also as a noun of the *neuter gender, third person, singular number;* and in the *nominative case*—being the subject of the verb *is*—according to Rule I.

"*Writing*" is a *transitive, active, present participle*, from the verb *write, wrote, written*. It is here used also as a noun of the *neuter gender, third person, singular number;* and in the *objective case*—being the object of the preposition *on* —according to Rule V.

"It affords us pleasure to have seen the rising sun attended by so many beautiful clouds."

"*To have seen*" is a *transitive, active, perfect infinitive*, from the verb *see, saw, seen*. It is here used also as a noun of the *neuter gender, third person, singular number;* and in the *nominative case*, to agree with "*It*," according to Rule VII.

"*Rising*" is an *adjective*,—a word used to qualify or limit the meaning of a substantive; *participial*, it is a participle—from the verb *rise, rose, risen*—ascribing the act or state to its subject as a quality; and it belongs to "*sun*," according to Rule X.

"*Attended*" is a *participle*,—a form of the verb, that merely assumes the act or state, and is generally construed like an adjective; *passive*, it represents its subject as acted upon; *perfect* in form, but present in sense, for it represents the act or state as present and continuing at the time referred to; and it relates to "*sun*," according to Rule XII.

ABRIDGED.—*Attended* is a passive participle, from the regular verb *attend, attended, attended;* it is perfect in form, but present in sense, and relates to, etc.

☞ The second Rule for participles and infinitives, which is given on page 71, can be applied to all the foregoing and all the following participles and infinitives.

Parse all except the adverbs, prepositions, conjunctions, and interjections:—

Participles.

The Indians fled, leaving their mules tied to the bushes. He went trudging[a] on foot, wearying himself, and wasting his time. The machinery, being oiled, runs well. The war[a] being ended, prosperity revived. Time and thinking tame the strongest grief. Of making many books, there is no end.

Infinitives.

And fools, who came to scoff,[b] remained to pray. He is anxious to go.[c] We are never too old to learn.[d] The right of the people to instruct[e] their representatives, is generally admitted.

Here was an opportunity to grow[f] rich. I ordered him[g] to be brought. She is wiser than to believe[h] it. The weather was such as to render[i] any military movement difficult. The story was considered so improbable as to obtain[k] no credit. I ought to have written. In order to do[l] this,[m] it was necessary to travel one hundred and twenty miles. To err[1] is human; to forgive, divine. I forgot to tell[2] him[3] the story. Delightful task! to rear[4] the tender thought. To die,[5]—it is an awful thing. It is knowledge enough for some people, to know[6] how[m] far they can proceed in mischief with impunity.

Miscellaneous Examples.

O silvery streamlet of the fields, that flowest full and free.
Now May, with life and music, the blooming valley fills.
Let Love have[n] eyes, and Beauty will have ears.
It had been[o] useless, had he done[o] it.
That a belle should be vain, is not to be wondered at.

Accordingly, a company assembled[11] armed[12] and accoutred[12], and, having procured[12] a field-piece, appointed[11] Major Harrison commander[7], and proceeded[11] to accomplish[12] their design.

The sun hath set in folded clouds,—
Its twilight rays are gone;
And, gathered in the shades of night,
The storm comes rolling on.

(a.) *Trudging* also modifies *went* adverbially. See remark under Rule XII. (b.) *To scoff* relates to *fools* for its subject, and also limits *came*. (c.) *To go* relates to *he* for its subject, and also modifies *anxious*. (d.) *To learn* relates to *We* for its subject, and also limits *too old*. (e.) *To instruct* relates to *people* for its subject, and also modifies *right*. (f.) *That is,*—" an opportunity *for him* or *any person* to grow rich". *To grow* relates to an indefinite subject, and modifies *opportunity*. In regard to *rich*, see Note X. (g.) The phrase *him to be brought*, is the entire (or logical) object of *ordered ; him* is the grammatical object. *To be brought* relates to *him* for its subject, and it also modifies or limits *ordered*. (h.) *To believe* relates to *she* for its subject, and also completes the construction of *than*. Or parse *to believe* as a verbal noun, the subject of *is wise*, understood. (i.) *To render* relates to *weather* for its subject, and with its modifications completes the construction, or is the complement, of the correlative phrase *such as*. Or say, if greater simplicity is desired, " *To render* relates to *weather* for its subject, and also depends on the correlative phrase *such as*, according to Rule XII." (k.) *To obtain* relates to *story* for its subject, and completes the construction, or is the complement, of the correlatives *so* and *as*. *To obtain no credit*, in this sentence, could also be parsed, though somewhat clumsily, as the subject of *might be considered indicative of its improbability*, understood. (l.) *To do* relates to an indefinite subject, and completes the construction of the phrase *in order*. *In order* serves, in reality, only to strengthen the sense of purpose expressed by *to do ;* and if so parsed, *to do* should be parsed as depending on the predicate *was necessary*. *To travel*, etc., is a phrase explanatory of *it;* Rule VII. *One hundred and twenty* is a numeral adjective. (m.) *How far they can proceed*, etc., is the object of *to know*. See p. 80. (n.) That is, "*Do thou let Love* (to) *have*, etc. *Have* is a transitive, present infinitive, without the sign *to*, because used after *let*. It relates to *Love* for its subject, and depends on *Let*, according to Rule XII. (o.) Subjunctive mood. See p. 34.

Adverbs.

Formula.—An *adverb*, and why; if it can be *compared*, say so, and how; of *what kind ;* to what it belongs, and according to what Rule or Note.

"The trees are waving beautifully."

"*Beautifully*" is an *adverb*, it modifies the meaning of a verb (" are waving"); it can be compared,—pos. *beautifully*, comp. *more beautifully*, superl. *most beautifully*; it is an adverb of manner or quality; and it belongs to the verb "*are waving*," according to Rule XIII. (Repeat of the Rule as much as is applicable.)

ABRIDGED.—*Beautifully* is an adverb of manner, can be compared, modifies the verb *are waving*, and belongs to it according to Rule XIII.

"Gather roses while they bloom."

"*While*" is an *adverb*,—a word used to modify the meaning of a verb, an adjective, or an adverb; it is a *conjunctive* adverb of time; and it belongs to both the verb "*gather*" and the verb "*bloom*," according to Rule XIII. Or say,—

"*While*" is an *adverb*,—a word used to modify the meaning of a verb, an adjective, or an adverb; *conjunctive*, it connects its own clause to another to express the time, according to Note XIII.

ABRIDGED.— *While* is a conjunctive adverb of time, modifying the verbs *gather* and *bloom*, and belonging to them according to Rule XIII. Or say, *While* is a conjunctive adverb of time, that joins a dependent clause to another clause adverbially, or to express the time, according to Note XIII.

"Can not you go too?"

"*Not*" is an *adverb*,—a word used to modify the meaning of a verb, an adjective, or an adverb; it is an adverb of negation; and it modifies the verb "*can go*" with reference to "*you*," and therefore belongs to them, according to Rule XIII. (Repeat it.)

ABRIDGED.—*Not* is a negative adverb, modifying the verb *can go* with reference to its subject *you*, and therefore belonging to them, according to Rule XIII.

Parse the articles, adjectives, nouns, pronouns, verbs, and adverbs:—

1. *Adverbs Modifying Verbs.*

The horse galloped gracefully.
The birds sung sweetly.
God rules everywhere.
Mary sews and knits well.

My father has just come.
The leaves must soon fall.
Lofty mountains successively appear.
Here will I stand.

2. *Adverbs Modifying Adjectives.*

Her child was very young.
The music rose softly sweet.
John is most studious.

He is perfectly honest.
My hat is almost new.
The wound was intensely painful.

3. *Adverbs Modifying Adverbs.*

Some horses can run very fast.
He stutters nearly always.
You must come very soon.

Thomas is not very industrious.
The field is not entirely planted.
She had been writing very carefully.

4. *Miscellaneous Examples.*

Smack[a] went the whip, round went the wheels.
Sadly and slowly we laid him down.[13]
In vain we seek for perfect happiness.[b]
We carved not[b] a line, we raised not a stone.
He lay like a warrior[c] taking his rest.
You have advanced not far enough yet.
These scenes, once so[d] delightful, no[13] longer please him.
Hold up[13] the flag. When will you come?
The dew glitters when the sun rises.
As[a] you sow, so[a] you shall reap.
Study while[c] young. He is almost[f] a poet.

Evens from the tomb the voice of nature cries.
Not even[h] a philosopher can endure the toothache patiently.
Even[i] as[a] a miser counts his gold,
Those hours the ancient timepiece told.—*Longfellow.*
Vainly but well that[10] chief had fought,
He was a captive[7] now;
Yet pride[1] that[4] fortune humbles not,
Was written on his brow.—*Bryant.*

(*a*) Manner. (*b.*) "*Not*" limits the meaning of "*carved*" in respect to "*a line.*" (*c.*) Or Rule VI. (*d.*) Degree. (*e.*) "*While going*"—While you are going. (*f.*) "*Almost*" is an adverb, modifying the predicate "*is a poet.*" (*g.*) "*Even*" modifies the adverbial adjunct "*from the tomb;*" or, rather, it modifies the verb "*cries*" with reference to the phrase "*from the tomb.*" Adjuncts = adverbs or adjectives; hence adverbs can modify them, and not, as some grammarians teach, the preposition only. (See p. 60.) (*h.*) Always consider carefully *on what the meaning of an expression bears,* and dispose of the expression accordingly. Therefore say, The adverbial expression "*Not even*" is used here in the sense of an adjective, modifying "*philosopher*" with reference to other subjects. (Compare with "*No philosopher,*" etc.) Or else follow the parsing of "*Can not you go too?*" given above. Or else say, "*Even*" is an adverb modifying the entire proposition after it; and "*Not*" is an adverb modifying the entire proposition beginning with "*even.*" This last parsing may seem best to rigid disciplinarians in grammar. (*i.*) "*Even*" modifies the entire clause after it; or, rather, it modifies "*told*" with reference to this clause of manner.

Prepositions.

Formula.—A *preposition,*—definition ; between what it shows the relation ; Rule.

"The water flows over the dam."

"*Over*" is a *preposition,*—a word used to govern a noun or pronoun, and show its relation to some other word ; it here shows the relation of "*flows*" to "*dam,*" according to Rule XIV. (Repeat it.)

ABRIDGED.—*Over* is a preposition, showing the relation between *flows* and *dam,* according to Rule XIV.

Parse all the words except the conjunctions:—

I found a dollar in the road. In spring, the leaves come forth. We should not live beyond our means. He struggled, like a hero, against the evils of fortune. An eagle rose near[10] the city, and flew over it far away beyond the distant hills. We went from New York to Washington City, by railroad, in eight hours. As to the policy of the measure, I shall say nothing. The river is washing the soil from under the tree. I caught a turtle in stead of a fish.

There stood a forest on the mountain's brow,
Which overlooked the shaded plains below[10];
No sounding axe presumed those trees to bite,
Coëval with the world, a venerable sight.[7]—*Dryden.*

Conjunctions.

Formula.—A *conjunction,* and why ; its peculiar nature ; what it connects ; Rule.

"The meadow produces grass and flowers."

"*And*" is a *conjunction,*—a word used to connect other words, and show the sense in which they are connected ; it implies simply continuance, or that somthing more is added; and it connects the words *grass* and *flowers*, according to Rule XV.

ABRIDGED.—*And* is a copulative conjunction, connecting *grass* and *flowers*, according to rule XV.

"You must either buy mine or sell yours."

"*Either*" is a conjunction, a word, etc. * * * it corresponds to "*or*," and assists it in connecting two phrases, according to Rule XV.

"*Or*" is a conjunction, etc. * * * it is *alternative*, or allows but one of the things offered, to the exclusion of the rest; it here corresponds to "*either*," and connects two phrases, according to Rule XV.

Parse all the words:—

Words Connected.

Learning refines and elevates the mind. It is our duty to cultivate our hearts and minds. She is amiable, intelligent, and handsome. The silk was light-blue, or sky-colored: it should have been white or black. I, even[15] I', went.

Phrases Connected.

Through floods and through forests he bounded away.
Death saw the floweret to the desert given,
Plucked it from earth, and planted it in heaven.

Clauses or Sentences Connected.

Eagles generally go alone, but little birds go in flocks. Italian music's sweet because 'tis dear. I know he is in debt, for he said so. If it rain to-morrow, we shall have to remain at home. Sin may give momentary pleasure, yet the pain is sure to follow. Again, every man is entitled to compensation for his services. Whether my brother come or not, I will either buy or rent the farm. Though he is poor, yet he is honest. I will pardon you, inasmuch as you repent. He was always courteous to wise and gifted men; for he knew that talents, though in poverty, are more glorious than birth or riches [are].

I have no mother, for she died
When I was very young;
But her memory still around my heart,
Like morning light, has hung.

Interjections.

Formula.—An *interjection*, and why; of what kind; Rule.

"Alas! no hope for me remains."

Alas is an *interjection*, it expresses an emotion only, and is not connected in construction with any other word; it here implies grief or dejection; and it is used independently, according to Rule XVI.

ABRIDGED.—*Alas* is an interjection of grief; and it is used independently, according to Rule XVI.

Parse all the words.

O, young Lochinvar is come out of the West. Ah! few[10], shall part where many[10], meet! O Desdemona[2]! Desdemona! dead? Dead! Oh! oh! oh! (Supply *art thou* and *thou art*.)

12. FALSE SYNTAX.

Nouns and Pronouns.—Rule I.—Nominatives.

Him and me* are in the same class. You and him had a long dispute. Thee art most in fault. Them are my gloves. I have tasted no better apples than them are. Them that seek wisdom, will find it. Him I accuse, has entered. *He whom,* etc. Were you and her at the party? Whom, would you suppose, stands head in our class? He promised to employ whomsoever should be sent. I do not think such persons as him [is] competent to judge. There is no better housekeeper than her [is whom] you have dismissed. Did not you see it, as well as me? He is taller than me, but I am as tall as her. Who made the fire?—John and me [made it]. Who swept the room?—Us girls. Who rode in the buggy?—Him and Jane.
The advice of those whom you think are hearty in the cause, must direct you.—*Washington.* A reward was offered to whomsoever would point out a practicable road.—*Walter Scott.* Truth is greater than us all.—*H. Mann.*
And goodly sons grew by his side,
But none so lovely and so brave
As him who withered in the grave.—*Byron.*

* Incorrect: *him* and *me*, in the objective case, should be *he* and *I*, in the nominative case,—to the verb *are*,—according to Rule 1st. (Repeat it.)

Observation.—The object of the active verb, and not that of the preposition, should generally be made the subject of the passive verb.

I was offered a seat.* He was offered the control of the school. He was left a large estate by his uncle. We were shown a sweet potato that weighed 15 pounds. You were paid a high compliment by the young lady.
Mr. Burke was offered a very lucrative employment.—*Prof. Goodrich.*

* Incorrect: not *I*, but *seat*, should be made the nominative to *was offered*, according to the Observation under Rule 1st. (Repeat it.) The sentence should be, *A seat was offered me.*

Rule II.—Nominatives.

Me* being sick, the business was neglected. Him who had led them to battle being killed, they retreated. Them refusing to comply, I withdrew. And me,—what shall I do? Her being the only daughter, no expense had been spared in her education. There is no doubt of its being him. He had no doubt of its being me. —*that it was I.*
Whose gray top shall tremble, Him descending.—*Milton.*

* Incorrect: *me*, in the objective case, should be *I*, in the nominative case,—being used absolutely before *being*,—according to Rule 2d. (Repeat it, and then always state what the corrected sentence should be.)

Rule III.—Possessives.

A mothers* tenderness and a fathers care are natures gifts for man's advantage. His misfortunes awaken nobody's pity, though no ones ability ever went farther for others good. Six months interest remained unpaid. How do you like Douglas' bill? I like Macaulay much better than Alison's style. He disobeyed his father as well as his mother's advice. Do you use Webster or Worcester's Dictionary? Brown, Smith, and Jones's wife, usually went shopping together. I have no time to listen to either John or Joseph's lesson. He was averse to the nation involving itself in war. His father was opposed to him going to California. (Is it proper to write *it's, her's, our's,* or *their's?*)
His curse be on him. He, who knoweth
Where the lightnings hide.—*Mrs. Sigourney.*

* Incorrect: *mothers* should be *mother's* (with an apostrophe before the *s*), according to Rule 3d. (And state how the possessive case is properly formed.)

Obs. 1.—The possessive sign, and the word *of*, should be used to relieve each other in such a way as will make the sentence most clear and agreeable.

Essex's° death haunted the conscience of Queen Elizabeth. Socrates's life and death. Demosthenes'—Demosthenes's orations. For Herodias' sake, his brother Philip's wife. John's brother's wife's sister married a mechanic. The extent of the prerogative of the King of England. Daniel Boone of Kentucky's adventures. The Governor of Pennsylvania's message. He is Clay the great orator's youngest son. The opinionative man thinks his own opinions better than any one's else opinions—any one else's opinions.

* Incorrect: *Essex's death* should rather be, *The death of Essex*, according to Obs. 1st, under Rule 3d, etc.

Obs. 2.—When two or more words, taken together, denote but one possessor, or when the same object belongs in common to two or more possessors, the possessive sign is annexed but once, and to the word immediately before the word or phrase denoting what is possessed.

These works are Cicero's, the most eloquent of men's.* Jack's the Giant-killer's wonderful exploits. Call at Smith's, the bookseller's. South of Mason's and Dixon's Line. Send me Andrews' and Stoddard's Latin Grammar. Send me Pope and White's Shakespeare. Morrison's and Price's farms are the next two on the road. *Morrison's farm and Price's are*, etc. Bond's, Bushnell's, and Woodward's stores, occupy the next three buildings. It was the men's, women's, and children's lot, to suffer great calamities. Allen's, Thomson's, and Hurdcastle's store is opposite to ours. Allen, Thomson, and Hardcastle's stores, are not joint possessions.

* Incorrect: not *men*, but *Cicero* only, should have the possessive sign, according to Obs. 2d, under Rule 3d. (Repeat it, and state what the corrected sentence should be.)

Rule IV.—Objectives.

Let him send you and I* to the spring. Let thou and I the battle try. Having dressed hisself, he went to church. Who do you want? Who shall we send? She that is idle and mischievous, reprove sharply. He and they we know, but ye we do not know. Who did you mean? Who did you see? But who have we here? They that treat me kindly, I will treat so too. He who is guilty, you should correct; not I, who am innocent.

Who should I meet the other day but my old friend!—*Addison*.

* Incorrect: *I*, in the nominative case, should be *me*, in the objective case,—being one of the objects of the verb *send*,—according to Rule 4th, etc.

Rule V.—Objectives.

There is some pudding left for you and I.* Who is that boy speaking to? *To whom*, etc. Who was it sent to? Who were you talking with? They who much is given to, will have much to answer for. There was no one in the room, except he. I gave it to somebody; I have forgotten who. I do not know who she went with. Who did he send for?—We. Who does he look like in that dress?—*Marlowe*.

* Incorrect: *I*, in the nominative case, should be *me*, in the objective case,—being one of the objects of *for*,—according to Rule 5th, etc.

Rule VII.—Same Cases.

They slew Varus, he* that was mentioned before. They slew Varus, who was him that was mentioned before. It wasn't me; it was him or her. It was them that said so. It could not have been him. I knew it was her. Whom do you think it was? Whom do men say that I am? Who do you take me to be? It is not me he is in love with. —*not I that*— Who was it?—Me. Was it him, or me, that you called? Is it him whom you said it was? I knew it was him. I knew it to be he.

* Incorrect: *he*, in the nominative case, should be *him*, in the objective case, to agree with *Varus*, according to Rule 7th. (Repeat it, and state the corrected sentence, as usual.)

Rule IX.—Pronouns.

(Whatever makes a singular or a plural subject, makes also a singular or a plural antecedent. See p. 42.)

Every person should try to improve their* mind and heart. Nobody will ever entrust themselves to that boat again. A person who is energetic and watchful, will be apt to succeed in their undertakings. Will some one of you lend me your umbrella? Many a man looks back on the days of their youth, with melancholy regret. The generals, each in their turn, walked round the coffin. If you have any victuals left, we will help you eat it. I like molasses, when they are clean. The cuckoo lays his eggs in the nest of other birds. The hen looked very disconsolate, when it saw its whole brood rush into the pond. If we deprive an animal of instinct, he will be no longer able to take care of himself. When a bird is caught in a trap, they of course try to get out. Each of the sexes should keep within their proper bounds. To persecute a truly religious denomination, will only make them flourish the better. The people can not be long deceived by its demagogues. I have no interests but that of truth and virtue. Every herb, every flower, and every animal, shows the wisdom of Him who made them. One or the other must relinquish their claim. If any boy or girl be absent, they will have to go to the foot of the class. —*he or she*— Coffee and sugar are imported from the West Indies; and large quantities of it are consumed annually.

Each occupied their several premises, and farmed their own land.—*Thos. Jefferson.* —*his own*— It is our duty to protect this government and that flag from every assailant, be they whom they may.—*Senator Douglas.*

* Incorrect: *their* should be *his*, to agree with *person*, according to Rule 9th, etc.

Obs. a.—*Who* is applied to persons, and generally to personified objects. *Which* is applied to all objects except persons, and sometimes to persons in asking questions.

That is used in speaking of both persons and things, after the superlative degree, after *same*, after the interrogative *who*, or wherever *who*, *which*, or *what*, would be less proper.

Those which* are rich, should assist the poor and helpless. So I gave the reins to my horse, who knew the way much better than I did. The horse and rider which we saw, fell in the battle. Was it the wind, or you, who shut the door? It is the best which can be got. Moses was the meekest man whom we read of in the Old Testament. It is the same coach which stopped at the church. I am the same as I was. I gave all what I had. I sent every thing what you ordered. Who is she who comes clothed in a robe of light green? Who of those ladies do you like best? Of all the congregations whom I ever saw, this was certainly the largest. (A congregation is a thing rather than a person.) This lubberly boy we call Falstaff, who is but another name for fat and fun. The heroic souls which defended the Alamo. Humility is one of the most amiable virtues which we can possess.

With the return of spring came four martins, who were evidently the same which had been bred under those eaves the previous year.—*U. S. Reader.*

* Incorrect: *which* should be *who*, according to Obs. *a*, under Nouns and Pronouns, etc. (Repeat so much of the Observation as is applicable.)

Obs. b.—Nouns and pronouns should be correctly used in gender and number, according to the sense, and the proper form of the word.

She is administrator.* He was married to a most beautiful Jew. The room is eighteen foot† long, and sixteen foot wide. I measured the log with a pole ten foot long—with a ten-feet pole. The teamster hauled four cord of wood and three ton of hay, in nine hours. Several chimnies were blown down. Some of the first familys. Several potatos. His brother-in-laws were educated at the same college. The Drs. Hunters and the Misses Bartons. The Old and the New Testaments—the Old and New Testament, in one large volume, called the Bible. You may learn the ninth and tenth page—the ninth and the tenth pages, and review the first or second pages. The farm is a long ways from market. We encamped behind a small woods. Let us make a memoranda of it. It was for our sakes that Jesus died upon the cross. Few persons are contented with their lots. The Lee's were distinguished officers in the Revolution.

The heathen are those people who worship idols.—*Webster's Spelling-Book.*

* Incorrect: *administrator*, the masculine word, should be *administratrix*, the feminine,—for it evidently denotes a female,—according to Obs. *b*, under Nouns and Pronouns, etc.
† Incorrect: *foot*, in the singular number, should be *feet*, in the plural number, to agree with *eighteen*, according to, etc. But singular in compound adjectives; as, "A two-*foot* ruler."

Obs. c.—Politeness usually requires, that the speaker shall mention the addressed person first, and himself last.

I, Mary, and you,* are to go next Sunday. If James and you take the horses, I and Martha shall have nothing to ride. Mother said that I and you must stay at home.

* Incorrect: *I, Mary, and you*, should be, *You, Mary, and I*, according to, etc.

Obs. d.—Nouns and pronouns should be so construed with other words as not to leave the case or relation uncertain or ambiguous.

The settler here* the savage slew. (Which slew the other?) I would rather give her to thee than another. If the lad should leave his father, he would die. (Repeat the noun.) John told James that his horse had run away. (Vary the sentence.) Lysias promised his father, that he would never forsake his friends. The king dismissed his minister without inquiry, who had never before been guilty of so unjust an action. Where there is nothing in the sense which requires the last sound to be elevated, a pause will be proper. *Where the sense has nothing that requires*, etc. When a man kills another from malice, it is called murder. —*the deed is called murder.* This rule is not strictly true, and a few examples will show it. —*as a few examples will show.* The law is inoperative, which is not right. —*and that it is so, is not right.* And thus the son the fervent sire addressed.—*Pope's Homer.* The lord can not refuse to admit the heir of his tenant upon his death; nor can he remove his present tenant so long as he lives.—*Blackstone.*

* Incorrect: the sentence is ambiguous. It should be, *Here the savage slew the settler,*—which was the meaning of the writer,—according to, etc.

Articles.

Obs. 1.—Articles should be chosen or omitted with great care, in order that the proper meaning may be expressed.

A common noun, without an article, denotes the class generally, a part indefinitely, or merely the kind of thing.

The shows that all are meant, or that a particular one or part is meant.

A points out but one indefinitely, and implies that there are others.

FALSE SYNTAX.

A pine is a species of a tree.* *The pine is a species of tree.* (For how can one tree be a species, or a species a part of one tree!) What kind of a man is he? Such a man does not deserve the name of a gentleman. The highest officer of a State is styled a Governor. Reason was given to a man to control his passions. The Tennessee, the Missouri, and the Mississippi, are all the names derived from the Indian languages. The whites of America are the descendants of the Europeans; but the blacks are the descendants of the Africans, and the Indians are descendants of the aborig'ines. When a whole is put for the part, or the part for a whole; a genus for the species, or the species for a genus; a singular for a plural, or a plural for a singular,—the figure is called a *synecdoche*. Sometimes one article is improperly put for another. A pronoun is a part of speech used for a noun. A violet is an emblem of modesty. The profligate man is seldom or never found to be the good husband, the good father, or the beneficent neigbor. He received only the fourth part of the estate. A winding stairs led us to the Senate Chamber. *A flight of*, etc. The child was not a three weeks old when it died. The Jews returned to their country after a seventy years captivity in Babylon. —*a captivity of seventy*— The ancients supposed the fire, the air, the earth, and the water, to be the elements of all other material things. Drunkenness makes a man of the brightest parts the common jest of the meanest clown.

The original signification of knave was a boy.—*Webster's Spelling-Book.* A librarian is the person who has charge of a library.—*Id.* The work is designed for persons who may think it merits a place in their libraries.—*Preface of Murray's Grammar.* The violation of this rule never fails to displease a reader.—*Blair's Rhetoric.*

* Incorrect: *pine* here denotes all, or the species; and therefore *the* should be used before it. *Tree* refers to the class generally, and therefore no article should be used before it. (Repeat, of the general Observation, only what is applicable to the example which you are correcting.)

Obs. 2.—*A* should be used before consonant sounds.

(*U* long, *eu, w, o* in *one,* and *y* articulated with a vowel after it, have each a consonant sound.)

An should be used before vowel sounds.

(That is, before *a, e, i, o, u* not equivalent to *yu, y* articulated with a consonant after it, silent *h*, and *h* faintly sounded when the next syllable has the chief accent. See Kerl's Comprehensive Grammar, pp. 173—81.)

He had a interest in the affair.* It is an universal complaint. Argus is said to have had an hundred eyes. There was not an human being on the place. An African or an European. A erroneous conclusion. A adjective belongs to the noun which it qualifies. A humble request. Is it an *i*, or an *u*? I would not use such an one. An hero. A heroic action. A hereditary feud. An hyacinth. A hyper'bole. At — hotel on Broadway. An ubiquitous quack.—*Edgar A. Poe.* An useful exercise.—*N. Y. Teacher.*

* Incorrect: *a* should be *an;* because *interest*—the word immediately after it—begins with a vowel sound, and according to Observation 2d, under Articles, *An should*, etc.

Obs. 3.—When the repetition of the article would suggest more objects than are meant, the article should be omitted.

When the omission of the article would not suggest all the objects that are meant, the article should be repeated.

The Old and the New Testaments.* The Old and New Testament. There is another and a better world. My friend was married to a sensible and an amiable woman. Everett, the scholar, the statesman, and the orator, should

be invited. She is not so good a cook as a washerwoman. Fire is a better servant than a master. The figure is a globe, a ball, or a sphere. The white and black inhabitants amount to several thousands. A beautiful stream flowed between the old and new mansion. Give the possessive and the objective cases of *who*—the possessive and objective case of *who*.
The sick and wounded were left at this place.—*Life of Jackson.*

* Incorrect: *the,* repeated, improperly suggests here, that there are several Testaments, in stead of two; therefore it should not have been repeated, according to, etc. (Vary the formulas whenever the example requires a variaton.)

Obs. 4.—A participial noun generally requires an article before it and *of* after it, or else the omission of both the article and the preposition.

A wise man will avoid the showing any excellence in trifles.* Great benefit may be derived from reading of good books. It is an overvaluing ourselves, to reduce every thing to our own standard of judging. I shall oppose the granting this company any more privileges. —*the granting of any more privileges to—* He left off building of Ramah, and dwelt in Tirzah.—*Bible.* The best business now is the opening farms and rearing stock.—*Agricultural Journal.*

* Incorrect: *showing,* having *the* before it, should also have *of* after it, or else both *the* and *of* should be omitted, according to, etc.

Adjectives.

Obs. 1.—Adjectives implying number must agree, in this respect, with the nouns to which they belong.

You have been playing this two hours.* How do you like those kind of carriages? We have been intimate friends this ten years. I never liked these sort of bonnets. I think that were the very words he used.

* Incorrect: *this* should be *these*, to agree with *hours*, according to, etc.

Obs. 2.—Double and all other improper comparatives or superlatives should be avoided.

A farmer's life is the most happiest.* A more healthier place can not be found. I never before lived in a more healthier and pleasanter neighborhood. She is the most loveliest one of the sisters. Nothing can be more worse— worser. The lesser quantity I remove to the other side. I think the rose is the beautifullest of flowers. It was the curiousest thing I ever saw. Virtue confers the supremest dignity on man, and should be his chiefest desire. Cotton is most principally raised in the Southern States. The heath-peach is more preferable than the Indian peach. —*is preferable to—.*
Against the envy of less happier lands.—*Shakespeare.* After the most strictest sect of our religion I lived a Pharisee.—*Bible.* By silence, many a dunderpate, like the owl, the stupidest of birds, comes to be considered the very type of wisdom.—*Washington Irving.*

* Incorrect: *happiest* is itself a superlative, and *most happiest* would therefore be a double superlative, which is improper, according to, etc.

Obs. 3.—The superlative degree must be used when three or more objects are compared, and the comparative is usually required when but two are compared.

The largest of the two boys goes to school. The youngest of the two sisters is the handsomest. Which is the largest number,—the minuend or the subtrahend? His wife is the best manager; therefore let her rule him. The latter one of the three boys had lost his books. Which do you like best,—tea or coffee?

* Incorrect: *largest*, in the superlative degree, should be *larger*, in the comparative degree,—because but two objects are compared,—according to, etc.

Obs. 4.—The superlative degree represents the described object as being a part of the others.

All comparisons without the superlative degree do not strictly represent the object denoted by one term as being a part of those denoted by the other.

The word *other*, and similar terms, imply two distinct parts and yet but one class.

China has the greatest population of any other country on earth.* Jacob loved Joseph more than all his children. Youth is the most important period of any in life. There is nothing so good for a sprain as cold water. —*nothing else*— He was less partial than any historian that ever wrote on the subject. None of our magazines is so interesting to me as Harper's. *No other one of*, etc. These people seemed to us the most ignorant of any we had yet seen.—*N. Y. Herald.* Noah and his family outlived all the people who lived before the flood.—*Webster's Spelling-Book.* (They could not have outlived themselves.)

* Incorrect: China is here absurdly represented as being one of the countries with which it is compared; therefore *the greatest of* should be *a greater than*, according to Obs., etc.

Verbs.

Obs. 1.—Our own voluntary actions are expressed by *will*, and our contingent ones by *shall*; the contingent actions of others are expressed by *will*, and their compulsory ones by *shall*.

A foreigner, having fallen into the Thames, cried out, "I will be drowned; nobody shall help me."* We will have to take our coats, or we will suffer from cold. Will I find you here when I return? Were I to go with you, I would get a whipping. Would we hear a good lecture, if we would go? Whoever will catch him, will be rewarded. I was afraid I would lose my money. If I wished him to come, I would have to write to him. We will then find that this confiscation bill was impolitic; and we will have to suffer for our folly, in the protraction of this war.—*Crittenden.*

* Incorrect: this sentence implies that he wished to be drowned, and wanted no one to help him; *will* should therefore be *shall*, and *shall* should be *will*, according to, etc.

Obs. 2.—The *preterit* is the proper form for affirming, without an auxiliary verb, past acts or states.

The *perfect participle*, and not the *preterit*, should be used after *have*, *be*, and their variations.

I seen him yesterday.* I had saw it before. I done so. They done the best they could. He has took my hat. He run all the way. They begun well, but ended badly. He drunk but little. They been here a whole day. I seen the boy when he done it. I might have went last Saturday, and ought to have went. The river is froze over. My coat is completely wore out. The tree had fell, and all its branches were broke. The apples were shook off by the wind. I knew he had wrote it; for it was well writ. Write to him.— I have done wrote. —*have already written.*

You have chose the worse.—*Washington Irving.*

* Incorrect: *seen*, the perfect participle, should be *saw*, the preterit, according to the first part of Observation 2d, under Verbs, etc.

FALSE SYNTAX. 95

Obs. 3.—Verbs should not be made transitive, intransitive, or passive, contrary to their general use, or contrary to analogy.

He had fled his native land.* Pharaoh and his host pursued after them. San Francisco connects with the sea, by an entrance one mile wide. It now repents me that I did not go. *I now repent,* etc. Well, I suppose we are agreed on this point. We had just entered into the house. My friend is returned—is arrived. He is possessed of great talents. —*possesses*— His estate will not allow of such extravagance.
It must be so, for miracles are ceased.—*Shakespeare.*

* Incorrect: *fled* is here improperly made transitive; therefore *from* should be used after it, to express its proper relation to *land,* according to, etc.

Obs. 4.—In mood and tense, the verbs of a sentence should properly correspond, and also be consistent with the other words.

The *indicative mood,* in conditional clauses, expresses doubt only; but the *subjunctive mood,* both doubt and future time, or mere suppositions.

In the indicative mood, general truths must be expressed by the present tense.

The *perfect infinitive* denotes something as past at the time referred to; and the *present infinitive,* as present or future.

The Lord hath given, and the Lord hath taken away.* I know the family more than twenty years. I am now two years in this city. Next Christmas I shall be at school a year. He that was dead, sat up, and began to speak. The Glenn family will try and requite the favor. —*try to requite*— I wish I was at home. He talked to me as if I was a widow. If the book be in my library, I will send it immediately. If the book is found in my library, I will send it immediately. If the book was in my library, I would send it immediately. If the book were in my library, some one must have taken it. If these remedies be applied, and the patient improves not, the case may be considered hopeless.

He said it was forty miles from Baltimore to Washington. No one suspected that he was a foreigner. Our teacher told us that the air had weight. Plato maintained, that the Deity was the soul of the universe. A late writer on horses supposed, that a horse could perform the labor of six men.

I intended to have written to him. I hoped to have met several of my friends there, but was disappointed. It was your duty to have assisted your friend. He is supposed to be born about three centuries ago.

This was four years ago next August.—*School Report.* They were not able, as individuals, to have influenced the twentieth part of the nation.—*Jefferson.* The most glorious hero that ever desolated nations, might have mouldered into oblivion, did not some historian take him into favor.—*Irving.*

* Incorrect: the giving and the taking could not have been both at the same time; therefore *hath given* should be *gave,* etc. (Give, also, the definitions of the tenses.)

Obs. 5.—The compound participle should not be needlessly made a part of a compound verb, or used to express the act in the progressive sense.

Wheat is now being sold for a dollar a bushel. —*is now selling*— My predictions are now being fulfilled. Another church was being built in the upper part of the city. My coat is now being made by the tailor. *The tailor is now making.* etc. His anticipations are now being realized. Dramshops are now being closed on Sundays. —*are closed*— More than 20,000 children are being gratuitously educated in this city. —*are receiving gratuitous educa-*

tion— Such a poem is worth being committed to memory. —*committing*— Whatever is worth being done, is worth being done well. [*Magazine.* Here certain chemical mysteries are being secretly carried on.—*Harper's* Remark.—This clumsy form is rather an innovation; but the newspapers of our civil war will probably establish it. With a little care, a better expression can generally be found. Verbs denoting momentary or mental acts, seldom admit the form. The form is used only in the present and past indicative, and in the past subjunctive. It is made by putting the word *being* into the common passive verb, between the auxiliary and the participle.

Ex. (*To be conjugated.*)—INDIC. PRES. *Sing.* 1. I am being defeated, 2. You are being defeated, 3. He is being defeated; *Plur.* 1. We are being defeated, 2. You are being defeated, 3. They are being defeated. PAST. *Sing.* 1. I was being defeated, 2. You were being defeated, 3. He was being defeated; *Plur.* 1. We were being defeated, 2. You were being defeated, 3. They were being defeated. SUBJUNC. PAST. *Sing.* 1. If I were being defeated, 2. If you were being defeated, 3. If he were being defeated; *Plur.* 1. If we were being defeated, 2. If you were being defeated, 3. If they were being defeated.

Rule XI.—Person and Number.

I called at your house, but you was not at home.° Was you there? My outlays is greater than my income.† Thou heard the storm; did thou not? Thou shall go. I always learns my lessons, before I goes to school. There is ten cords of wood in the pile. Every one of the turkeys were caught by a fox. Every ten tens makes one hundred. Not one of us have seen your hat. Wheat and rye is sowed in fall; but oats is sowed in spring. Ashes are always used in the plural number. *Tion* are pronounced *shun.* Two parallel lines denotes equality. Five dimes is half a dollar. Nothing but offices are sought by most politicians. The molasses are excellent. What signifies fair words without good deeds? Six is too many to ride in the canoe at once. Six months' interest are due on the bonds. The sum of twenty thousand dollars have been spent on the bridge. A hundred thousand dollars of revenue is in the treasury. The public is respectfully invited. Generation after generation pass away. Mary and her cousin was at our house last week. Neither Mary nor her cousin were at our house last week. There was hay and corn in plenty. How is your father and mother? Where is your slate and pencil?
Such is the tales his Nubians tell,
Who did not mind their charge too well.—*Byron.*
In Mauchline there dwells six proper young belles.—*Burns.*

° Incorrect: *was* should be *were*, to agree with *you*, according to Rule 11th, etc. † Incorrect: *is* should be *are*, to agree with *outlays*, a plural subject, according to, etc. (See p. 42.)

Obs. 1.—The promiscuous use of different forms of verbs in the same connection, is inelegant.

He giveth, and he takes away.*—*Harper's Magazine.* Does he not behave well, and gets his lessons as well as any other boy? Did you not borrow so much of me, and promised to return it? To profess regard, and acting differently, discovers a base mind. Professing regard, and to act differently, discovers a base mind. Educating is to develop the mind. Spelling is easier than to parse or cipher.
Thou who didst call the Furies from the abyss,
And round Orestes bade them howl and hiss.—*Byron.*

* Incorrect: *giveth* should be *gives*, or *takes* should be *taketh*, according to, etc.

Obs. 2.—*To*, the sign of the infinitive, is omitted after the active verbs *bid, make, need, hear, let, see, feel, dare,* and the auxiliaries; and sometimes after a few other verbs that are like some of these in sense.

If I bid you to study, dare you to be idle? We made her to believe it. To go I could not, but to remain I would not. That old miser was never seen give a cent to the poor. We ought not speak ill of others, unless there is a necessity for it. Will you please answer my letter immediately?

In a few modes of expression, the *to* must be retained; as, "I feel it to be my duty;" "I can not see to write the letter," etc.

Adverbs.

Obs.—*Adjectives* should be used to qualify nouns or pronouns; and *adverbs*, to qualify verbs, adjectives, or adverbs. See p. 64, Exercises.

We landed safely, after all our misfortunes.* She sews good and neat. It is near done. Speak slow and distinct. I am only tolerable well, sir. I never studied grammar; but I can talk just as good as them that talk grammatical. Velvet feels smoothly. I felt bad about the matter. You have behaved very bad. I can easier raise a crop of hemp than a crop of tobacco. Abstract principles are best learned when clearest illustrated.

Hindostan is a remarkable fine country.—*Lord Jeffrey.*

* Incorrect: *safely*, the adverb, qualifies *we* rather than *landed;* and therefore it should be *safe*, the adjective, according to, etc.

Prepositions.

Obs.—In the use of prepositions, great care should be taken to select the most appropriate.

Into, from outside to inside; *in,* inside only; *at,* indefinitely in or about; *in,* definitely within; *between,* two only; *among,* three or more; a taste *of* what is enjoyed, a taste *for* what we wish to enjoy; disappointed *of* what is not obtained, disappointed *in* what fails to answer our expectations after it is obtained; die *of* disease, —*by* an instrument; compare *with,* for ascertaining merits, —*to,* for illustration.

Abhorrence *of;* accuse *of;* adapted *to;* agreeable *to;* aspire *to;* capacity *for;* confide *in;* dependent *on;* independent *of;* derogation *from;* differ, different, *from;* difficulty *in;* diminution *of;* eager *in;* followed *by;* founded *on;* influence *over;* made *of;* need *of;* occasion *for;* omitted *from;* prejudice *against;* profit *by;* quarrel *with;* resemblance *to;* rely *on;* reconcile *with;* swerve *from.*

Do not let the dog come in the house.* These bonnets were brought in fashion last year. He died with the typhoid fever—for thirst—with the sword. He was accused with having acted unfairly. In some of these derivative words, the *e* is omitted. Religion and membership may differ widely with each other. This is a different dinner to what we had yesterday. This case has no resemblance with the other. I have little influence with him. He came of a sudden. The sultry evening was followed with a storm. The soil is adapted for hemp and tobacco. I have been at France. I board in the new hotel. The space between the three lines is the area of the triangle. —*within*— I was disappointed in the pleasure of meeting you.

* Incorrect: *in* should be *into*, because the sense is not "inside only," but from "outside to inside," which is best expressed by *into;* and according to Obs., etc.

Miscellaneous Precepts.

Obs. 1.—When two negatives destroy each other's effect, *one* should be omitted to express denial.

I will never do so no more.* We didn't find nobody at home. I don't know nothing about your affairs. I never said nothing about it. Death never spared no one. She will never grow no taller. Neither you, nor no one else, can walk ten miles in one hour.

No skill could obviate, nor no remedy dispel, the terrible infection.—*Goldsmith.*
> * Incorrect: the two negatives, *never* and *no*, contradict each other; and therefore one should be omitted or changed, to express denial, or the meaning intended, according to, etc.

Obs. 2.—Adjectives, adverbs, and adjuncts, should be so placed in the sentence as to make it correct, clear, and elegant.

The bad position of adjectives and adjuncts is generally improved, by bringing them nearer to what they qualify; and adverbs should generally be placed before the adjectives or adverbs which they modify, after verbs in the simple form, and between the auxiliary and the rest of the verb in the compound form; but they are seldom allowable between *to* and the rest of the infinitive.

I have bought a new pair of shoes and a black bolt of cloth.* The congregation will please to sing the three first and the two last stanzas of the hymn. The dress had rows of silk fancy green buttons. I only recited one lesson. (Only what?) I only bought the horse, and not the buggy. I have borrowed this horse only, yet I intend to buy him. Men contend frequently about trifles. They became even grinders of knives and razors. All that we hear, we should not believe. They were not such as to fully answer my purpose. A lecture on the methods of teaching geography, at ten o'clock. *Wanted*—a young man to take care of some horses, of a religious turn of mind. At that time I wished somebody would hang me a thousand times. After he had gained five thousand dollars, by speculation, he lost more than half of it.

Every man can not afford to keep a coach.—*Webster's Spelling-Book.* An *improper triphthong* is one in which all the vowels are not sounded.—*Butler.*
> * Incorrect: not the pair is new, but the shoes are so, etc.

Obs. 3.—No needless word should be used.

That there apple is better than this here one. He died in less than two hours' time. Where is William at? I was not able for to do it. I have got to go. The passion of anger is the cause of many evils. John he went, James he went, and Mary she went; but the rest they all staid at home. These lots, if they had been sold sooner, they would have brought more money. *If these lots had been sold sooner,* etc. Whatever she found, she took it with her. A child of ten or twelve years old. These savage people seemed to have no other element but that of war. It is equally as good as the other. If I mistake not, I think I have seen you before. Old age will prove a joyless and a dreary season, if we arrive at it with an unimproved or with a corrupted mind.

Our debts and our sins are generally greater than we think for.—*Franklin.*

Obs. 4.—No necessary word should be omitted.

The sale of one farm or several will take place to-day. We were at the fair, and saw every thing there. Yonder is the place I saw it. He was a man had no influence. I approve your plan so far as relates to him. Why do what is not lawful to do? He did it for your and my friend's welfare. Neither my house nor orchard is injured. Both the principal and interest. Money is scarce, and times hard. I never have and never will assist such a man. (A part, relating to two or more before it, must suit each.) They might, and probably were, good. Meadows are always beautiful, but never so much as in the opening of spring. —*so much so*— The remark is worthy the fool that made it. There is nothing to prevent him going. White sheep are much more common than black. There is no situation so good anywhere.

Obs. 5.—All the parts of a sentence should so correspond as to be con-

sistent; and the words and their arrangement should be the most appropriate in which the meaning can be expressed.
The wounded had laid on the ground all night.—*Philadelphia Inquirer.* After laying awhile, he raised up. We were all setting round the fire. What do you ask for them peaches? The business will suit any one who enjoys bad health. It is useless trying. —*to try*— No one likes being in debt. Compromising conflicting opinions will be ever necessary in a republic. *To compromise*, etc. Such cloaks were in fashion five years since. —*ago*— (*Since* properly reckons forward from a past point of time; and *ago*, back from present time. *Since* is daily misused.) A wicked man is not happy, be he never so hardened in sin. Neither our position, or the plan of attack, was known. I will see if it snows or no. —*whether* * * * *or not*. She is such a good woman. —*so good a woman*. The book is not as accurate as I wished it to be. This is none other but the gate of Paradise. —*than*— A corrupt government is nothing else but a reigning sin. A conjunction connects words, phrases, and sentences. There is no doubt but what he is mistaken. —*no doubt that*— There are few things so difficult but what they may be overcome. Cedar is not so hard but more durable than oak. —*so hard as oak, but more durable*. It is different and superior to the old. He confides and depends upon me. I can not find one of my books. A diphthong is where two vowels are united in one sound. —*is the union of*— (For it is not *place*.) A diphthong is when two vowels are united. Fusion is while a solid is converted into a liquid by heat. At the same time that men are giving their orders, God is also giving his. *While men,* etc. He drew up a petition where he too freely represented his own merits. —*in which*— The poor man who can read, and that has a taste for reading, can find entertainment at home. —*and who*— Policy keeps coining truth in her mints—such truth as it can tolerate; and every die except its own, she breaks, and casts away. These evils were caused by Catiline, who, if he had been punished, the republic would not have been exposed to dangers so great. —*the punishment of whom would have prevented the republic from being exposed,* etc.
The horses had scarcely crossed the bridge, than the head of the third battalion appeared on the other side.—*Harper's Magazine*. —*when*— O fairest flower, no sooner blown but blasted!—*Milton*. By intercourse with wise and experienced persons, who know the world, we may improve and rub off the rust of a private education.—*Spectator*. My father had just presented me with a knife.—*N. Y. Teacher*. Prepositions, you recollect, connect words as well as conjunctions; how, then, can you tell the one from the other?—*Smith's Gram.*

We *lay* things, and then they *lie;* we *set* things, or they *sit* or *fit* well; but we ourselves *sit*. Do not say *hadn't ought to* for *ought not to; them books, them cups, them boys,* etc., for *those books, those cups, those boys; had have had* for *had had; guine* for *going; jist* or *jest* for *just; sich* for *such; disremember* for *forget*. Do not say *yourn, hern, hissen, ourn, theirn,* nor write *your's, her's, our's, their's,* for *yours, hers, his, ours, theirs*. Do not say *a great ways, a little ways, somewheres, nowheres, anywheres,* for *a great way, a little way, somewhere, nowhere, anywhere*. Do not say *mighty little, great big, a good deal, a nation deal, in a bad fix,* for *very little, very large, much, in a bad condition*. Do not say *got to go* for *must go; aint* for *am not, is not,* or *are not; chaw* for *chew; a licking* for *a beating; unbeknown* for *unknown; ary one* for *either one* or *any one; nary one* for *neither one* or *no one; shet* for *shut; to get shet of* for *to get rid of*. Do not speak of doing things *a heap* for doing things *much*. Do not say the school *takes up* for *begins;* nor say *used up* for *worn out* or *destroyed;* nor *picked up* for *deceived;* nor *cracked up* for *praised* or *represented;* nor *fixed up* for *repaired, dressed,* or *ready*.

Miscellaneous Examples.

1. To say that a person is *consequential*, is the same thing as saying they are not of much consequence.—*Jane Taylor*. We have simply to go to work, each in our places, and do our work.—*Sec. Chase*. Marius ordered a low temple to be built to Honor, thereby intimating that humility was the true way to honor.— *Lempriere*. Neither of these States are entitled to bounty.—*Hall*. What avails all our toil and care in amassing what we can not enjoy.—*N. Y. Teacher*. It would have been no difficult matter to have compiled a volume of such precedents.—*Cowper*.

2. He is one of the preachers that belongs to the church militant, and takes considerable interest in politics. Every body seemed to enjoy themselves. I thought it to be him, but it was not him. The book is her's. Toasts were [*drank?* or *drunk?*] It was such a sound that I never heard before. It is the same man who stood on the portico. Every thing whatsoever he could spare, he gave away. (Rule VIII.) There is no man knows better how to make money. It is more easier to pull down than to build up. There is the most business done in New York of any city in the Union. He is one of the most influential and richest men in the city. (Apparently, *most richest*. Change the order.) A large reward and pardon has been offered.

3. The least of two evils must be preferred.—*Washington*. I hoped there would have been no further cause of uneasiness.—*Id*. We have been prevented marching to-day by the rains.—*Id*. Some were employed in blowing of glass, others in weaving of linen.—*Gibbon*. We have marched eight days, laid in water, and ate any thing we could get.—*Phil. Press*. A large portion of them continue to secretly cherish a love for the Union.—*Ib*. Which phrase, if it mean any thing, means paper money.—*Atlantic Monthly*. Among these islanders, no feeling is so deep as veneration for the tombs of their ancestors.—*Asiatic Islands*.

4. She looks beautifully in her new silk dress. You did the work as good as I could expect. The offer was no sooner made but he accepted it. I would have been obliged to him, if he had have sent it. The three first classes have recited. He has seen as much, perhaps more, of the world, than I have. (Complete the construction of the first part. —*as much of* * * * *as I have seen, and perhaps more*.) He can and ought to give more attention to his business. The cost of the carriage was added to, and greatly increased, my expense. No one ever sustained such mortifications as I have done to-day. I, you, and he, must go. Do like I did. (*As*, manner; *like*, generally resemblance.)

5. The religion of Christ has taught us to look upon such crimes as were often committed by the Persian kings with horror and disgust.—*Peter Parley*. I shall be happy always to see my friends.—*Ec. Magazine*. Let them the State defend, and he adorn.—*Cowley*. A proper fraction is less than 1, because it has less parts than it takes to make a unit.—*Colburn*. —*fewer*— Three fourths is more than one half.—*Bullions*. An hospital is an asylum for the sick.— *G. Brown*. A word modifying either of the three principal parts of a sentence, is an adjunct. Who ever achieved any thing great in letters, arts, or arms, who was not ambitious?

6. In thee is our hope and strength. Four and two is six, and one is seven. No hope, no power remain. What is its person and number? Every tree and steeple were blown down. Every boy's cap and coat was stolen. Books, and not company, occupies his mind. (Determine which is the subject, and make the verb agree with it.) Company, and not books, occupy his mind. The crown of virtue are peace and honor. His chief occupation and enjoyment were controversy. The father, and his son too,——in the battle. The legislature have adjourned. The railroad company was rather uneasy —were rather unsafe. To advance or to retreat were equally dangerous. (*Equally* requires *and*.) Between him and I.

FALSE SYNTAX. 101

7. Washington was given the command of a division.—*Irving.* The greater part of the forces were retired into winter-quarters.—*Id.* Were Aristotle or Plato to come among us, they would find no contrast more complete than between their workshops and those of New York.—*Bancroft.* (Supply also *that.*) The cunning of the hunter and the old buck were often stationed against one another.—*Hall.* —*that of * * set * * each*— It was not me that you saw. —*Clark.* John arrived as soon as me—a little earlier than me.—*Id.*

8. He should not marry a woman in high life, that has no money. The man brought the whole package, which was more than we expected. Religion will afford us comfort, when others forsake us. We saw the lady while passing down the street. (Who passed?) What do you think of [*us?* or *our?*] going into partnership? (See p. 44.) That very subject which we are now discussing, was lately decided in Kentucky. (*This* implies nearness, or has the sense of *latter; that* implies distance, or has the sense of *former.*) These very men with whom you traveled yesterday, are now in jail. Religion elevates man, irreligion degrades him; that binds him to the earth, this raises him to heaven.

9. The use of which accents [Greek and Roman] we have now entirely lost. —*Blair.* (We never had them to lose. Say, *is lost.*) Our pronunciation must have appeared to them [the Greeks and the Romans] a lifeless monotony.—*Id.* (They never heard it. Say, *would have appeared.*) A large portion of the valley of the Amazon is annually overflown.—*Stephens.* We should like to know whether we will be allowed to retain our arms and flag.—*N. Y. Times.* The United States having thus become the [*proprietor?* or *proprietors?*] of what [*is?* or *are?*] called the public lands, the nation was rescued from many evils. —*Hall.*

10. Please walk in the setting room. Whom shall I say called? Who did you vote for? I doubt if it be true. She looked as though she knew. —*as if*— Let us worship God, he who created and sustains us. Do you thus speak to me, I who have so often befriended you? (Better omit *I* altogether.) It was to your brother, to whom I am most indebted. He insists on it, that he is right. I wonder that none of them never thought of it. I ain't got no book. A participle is a word derived from a verb, and which expresses action or being. If I bid you to study, dare you to be idle? She was made believe it. This measure is taking a bold step. *E* has a long and short sound. A little flowing rivulet. Mr. John Dorriss, Esq. (The latter title supersedes the former.) The neck connects the head and trunk together. Said client believes said judge prejudiced to his cause. My brother's being sick was the cause of his absence. *My brother's sickness was,* etc. The vermins were so numerous that we could raise no fowl. I live to home with my mother. (Error common in New York and New England.)

Disputed.—"To-morrow *will* be Saturday." Correct. "To-morrow *is* Saturday." Allowable; mere predication. Sometimes also the present tense is used to express future events more vividly. "I feel [*bad?* or *badly?*] about the matter." Analogy is in favor of *bad;* but custom is in favor of *badly.* See Kerl's Comp. Gram., p. 248. "On page *twenty-fifth.*" Correct. "On page *twenty-five.*" Allowable. 25 is here a noun, representing, by synecdoche, page, and put in apposition with it. Compare with "The year 1862." In discussing a subject by numerical divisions, whether we should say, "*First, secondly, thirdly,*" etc., or, "*First, second, third,*" etc., will depend on the sense, or whether we refer to the verb or the divisions. "A hotel"—*Noah Webster;* "An hotel"— *Russell, Kinglake,* and English writers generally. "Our forces were *to have advanced* last Tuesday." Generally condemned; but it means, they did not advance. "Our forces were *to advance* last Tuesday." And perhaps they did advance; we have no news from them as yet. "I would rather be in his place." Correct. "I had rather be in his place." Good old English, and allowable colloquial modern English. See p. 36; also Cowper's Works.

5*

13. ANALYSIS OF SENTENCES.

Discourse is a general word denoting either *prose* or *poetry*.
Discourse may be divided into paragraphs.
Paragraphs are composed of sentences.
All *sentences* may be resolved into propositions.
Every *proposition* must have a subject and a predicate.
Every *subject* must be a nominative, or have a nominative.
Every *predicate* must be a finite verb, or have a finite verb.

Sentences are divided into *simple, complex,* and *compound.*
A *simple sentence* has but one predicate.
A *complex* or *compound sentence* has two or more predicates.

A *complex sentence* must have at least one proposition that is dependent, or that is used in the sense of a noun, an adjective, or an adverb.

A *compound sentence* must have at least two propositions of which neither is dependent, or used in the sense of a noun, an adjective, or an adverb.

A compound sentence may consist of complex sentences or members.

Exercises.

Tell whether the sentence is simple, complex, or compound, and why; mention the propositions or clauses, and why; mention the subjects and the predicates, and why; and whether simple or compound, and why:—

The flowers are gemmed with dew. The maple on the hill-side has lost its bright green, and its leaves have the hue of gold. As you come near, they spring up, fly a little distance, and light again.† Suspicion ever haunts the guilty mind. Hard things become easy by use; and skill is gained by little and little. The weight of years has bent him, and the winter of age rests upon his head. He touched his harp, and nations heard entranced. The union is the vital sap of the tree; if we reject the Constitution, we girdle the tree; its leaves will wither, its branches drop off, and the mouldering trunk will be torn down by the tempest. The good times, when the farmer entertained the traveler without pay; when he invited him to tarry, and join in the chase; when Christmas and Fourth of July were seasons of general festivity,—have passed away.‡ "Thy worldly hopes," said the hermit, "shall have faded, thy castles of ambition crumbled, and thy fiery passions subdued, ere thou hast reached the meridian of life." § Read this Declaration at the head of the army, —every sword will be drawn from its scabbard, and the solemn vow uttered, to maintain it, or to perish on the bed of honor. (Construe both the infinitive phrases with each of the two clauses just before them in the same member.) What

---

* A *sentence* is merely so much of discourse as makes a complete thought in the view of the person uttering it; a *proposition* is a single combination of such words as make a predication, judgment, or thought; and a *phrase* is merely two or more words rightly put together for thought, without expressing a predication. † When? ‡ What kind of times? § Said what

costs nothing, is worth nothing. That he must fail, is certain. 'Tis liberty alone that gives the flowers of fleeting life their lustre and perfume. Go, and assist him, that the work may be finished. He who is false to God, is not true to man. Though thy slumbers may be deep, yet thy spirit shall not sleep; there are shades that will not vanish, there are thoughts thou canst not banish. To dress, to visit, to gossip, and to thrum her piano, are the chief employments of the modern belle.

Every proposition is either *declarative, interrogative, imperative,* or *exclamatory.* Every sentence is the same, or a composite of these.

A *declarative* proposition expresses a declaration; an *interrogative* proposition, a question; an *imperative* proposition, a command; and an *exclamatory* proposition, an exclamation.

Ex.—"John rides that wild horse." "Does John ride that wild horse?" "John, ride that wild horse." "John rides that wild horse!" An *exclamatory* sentence is merely a declarative, an interrogative, or an imperative sentence, uttered chiefly to express the emotion of the speaker.

Exercises.

The propositions; and whether declarative, interrogative, imperative, or exclamatory, and why:—

A waving willow was bending over the fountain. Rise, and defend thyself. Shall I assist you? How beautiful is yonder sunset! If James has a hundred marbles, why does he never show us any of them? Men may, I find, be honest, though they differ. Now Twilight lets her curtain down, and pins it with a star. Green be the turf above thee, friend of my better days. What shall I say? What a piece of work is man! She is busy in the garden, among the posies. The spreading orange waves a load of gold. Hear him! hear him! There can be no study without time; and the mind must abide, and dwell upon things, or be always a stranger to the inside of them. The fly sat upon the axle-tree of the chariot-wheel, and said, "What a dust do I raise!"

Every proposition is either *independent* or *dependent.*

An *independent* proposition makes complete sense by itself.

A *dependent* proposition depends on another for complete sense.

The clause of a complex sentence on which the other clauses depend, is often called the *principal* or *leading clause;* its subject and predicate, the *principal* or *leading subject* and *predicate;* and the dependent clauses, *subordinate clauses.*

Exercises.

The propositions; and whether independent or dependent, and why:—

The morning dawns, and the clouds disperse. The dew glistens, when the sun rises. I would not enter, on my list of friends, the man who needlessly sets foot upon a worm. Stillest streams oft water fairest meadows; and the bird that flutters least, is longest on the wing. The path of sorrow leads to the land where sorrow is unknown. If the mind be curbed and humbled too much in children,—if their spirits be abased and broken much by too strict a hand over them,—they lose all their vigor and industry. Come ye in peace here, or come ye in war? In one place we saw a gang of sixty-five horses; but the buffaloes seemed absolutely to cover the ground. "Come," says Puss, "without any more ado; 'tis time to go to breakfast: cats don't live upon dialogues."

Every proposition may be divided into the *entire subject* and the *entire predicate*.

The *entire subject* must have one or more *subject-nominatives* to the same verb or verbs.

The *entire predicate* must have one or more *finite verbs* agreeing with the same subject, which may be called the *predicate-verbs*.

Hence both subjects and predicates are either *simple* or *compound*.

The subject-nominative may be a *word*, a *phrase*, or an *entire clause ;* the predicate-verb is simply a *verb*, or a principal verb with its auxiliaries.

Most grammarians call the entire subject the *logical subject ;* the entire predicate, the *logical predicate ;* the subject-nominative, the *grammatical subject ;* and the predicate-verb, the *grammatical predicate*. This mode of naming is not so simple as the one we have given.

Exercises.

The propositions ; the entire subjects, and then the subject-nominatives ; the entire predicates, and then the predicate-verbs :—

Men work. Most men work daily. The leaves rustle. The leaves rustle in the passing breeze. Leaves and flowers must perish. Flowers bloom and fade. Leaves and flowers flourish and decay. Poplars and alders ever quivering played, and nodding cypress formed a fragrant shade. In youth alone, unhappy mortals live; but, ah! the mighty gift is fugitive. The same errors run through all families in which there is wealth enough to afford that their sons may be good for nothing. Depart. In concert act, like modern friends, since one can serve the other's ends. That it is our duty to be kind and obliging, admits of no doubt. The division and quavering which please so much in music, have a resemblance to the glittering of light, as when the moonbeams play upon the water. It is often the fault of parents, guardians, and teachers, that so many persons miscarry. (Here either "It" or the clause "that so many," etc., may be considered the subject of "is," and the other term may be parsed as agreeing with the subject in case.) It is hardly practicable for the human mind to obtain a clear and familiar knowledge of an art, without illustrations and exemplifications. Ah me! the blooming pride of May, and that of beauty, are but one.

The parts into which sentences are divided in analysis, are called *elements*. Subject-nominatives and predicate-verbs are the *principal elements ;* and they may be modified by *words, phrases,* or *clauses.*

A part that *modifies* another, adds something to its meaning, or takes away something.

What modifies, is either explanatory or restrictive.

Ex.—" The town lay at the foot of a hill, *which we climbed.*" " The town lay at the foot of the hill *which we climbed.*"

Whatever modifies a substantive, is an *adjective element.*

Ex.—" *Solomon's* Temple." What temple? "David, the *king* and *psalmist.*" What David? "The land *of palms.*" What land? "A hill *crowned with majestic trees.*" What kind of hill? "A proposition *to sell the farm.*" What proposition? "The store *which is on the corner.*" What store? "A request *that you will go with us.*" What kind of request?

What modifies, may itself be modified.

A NOUN may be modified—
1. By an *article*. "*The* MAN is intelligent."
2. By an *adjective*. "A *beautiful* ROSE;" "A ROSE, *red* and *beautiful*."
3. By a *possessive*. "*John's* HORSE;" "*My* SLATE."
4. By an *appos'itive*. "JOHN *the saddler;*" "The POET *Milton*."
5. By a *participle*, with what belongs to it. "A LAW *relating to taxes*."
6. By an *infinitive*, with what belongs to it. "A PATH *to guide us*."
7. By an *adjunct*. "A MAN *of wisdom*."
8. By a *clause*. "The WILLOW *which stands by the spring;*" "A REQUEST *that you will go with us to-morrow*."

A PRONOUN may be modified in the same ways, except not by a *possessive*.
A modified word has frequently several modifications at once.

Exercises.

The nouns and pronouns, and by what they are modified:—
A dewy rose. The land of oranges. Lurking evils. Evils lurking near. Evils that lurk near. A house situated on the river. An opportunity to study. The sun's beams. Milton the poet. The deer which ran out of the field, and which I shot. A bright morning, fresh and balmy, that refreshed us all. The calumet was produced, and the two forlorn powers smoked eternal friendship between themselves, and vengeance upon their common spoilers, the Crows. The silence of the night; the calmness of the sea; the lambent radiance of the moon, trembling on the surface of the waves; and the deep azure of the sky, spangled with a thousand stars,—concurred to heighten the beauty of the scene. With loss of Eden, till one greater man restore us, and regain the blissful seat. Numerous small lakes lie inland, round which, on beaten trails, roam herds of red deer. Sweet day, so cool, so calm, so bright, the bridal of the earth and sky.

Whatever modifies a verb, an adjective, or an adverb, or may be given in answer to an interrogative adverb, or as the complement of a predicate, is an *adverbial element*.

Ex.—"The house was sold *yesterday*." When? "The house contains *much furniture*." Contains what? "The house was a *mere cabin*." Was what? "The horse fell, *crushing its inmates*." Fell how? "The house was sold *to pay the owner's debts*." Why? "The house was sold *because the owner was in debt*." Why?

A modified verb may be a finite verb, a participle, or an infinitive.

A VERB may be modified—
1. By an *objective*. "Men BUILD *houses*." "I KNEW *it* TO BE *him*."
2. By a *predicate-nominative*. "John HAS BECOME *a farmer*."
3. By an *adjective*. "TO BE *wise;*" "James IS *idle*."*
4. By an *adverb*. "The horse RAN *fast*."
5. By a *participle*+. "The stone ROLLED *thundering down the hill*."
6. By an *infinitive*+. "I HAVE CONCLUDED *to remain with you*."

---

* Owing to a slight radical difference in the modes of classifying, there is sometimes an apparent incongruity between Parsing and Analysis. Thus, in parsing, *idle* is referred to *James*, because *James* denotes the object to which the quality belongs; but, in analyzing, it is referred to *is*, because it makes with *is* the predicate.

7. By an *adjunct.* "Apples GROW *on trees.*"
8. By a *clause.* "She THINKS *he is rich;*" "He STUDIES *that he may learn.*"

Exercises.

The verbs, and by what modified :—

A light beaming brightly.   He writes with ease.   Cast not pearls before swine.   He became a partner.   She is industrious.   I intend to go.   I believe he will succeed when he makes a vigorous effort.   Among the flowering vines is one deserving of particular notice.   Each flower is composed of six leaves about three inches in length, of beautiful crimson, the inside spotted with white.   Its leaves of fine green are oval, and disposed by threes.   This plant grows upon the trees without attaching itself to them.   When it has reached the topmost branches, it descends perpendicularly, and, as it continues to grow, extends from tree to tree, until its various stalks interlace the grove like the rigging of a ship.   Nature from the storm shines out afresh.   Not even a philosopher can endure the toothache patiently.   There never yet were hearts or skies, clouds might not wander through.   Chaucer said, "If a man's soul is in his pocket, he should be punished there."

An ADJECTIVE may be modified—

1. By an *adverb.* "She is *foolishly* PROUD."
2. By an *infinitive.* "The fruit is GOOD *to eat.*"
3. By an *adjunct.* "He is CAREFUL *of his books.*"

Exercises.

The adjectives, and by what modified :—

She was uncommonly beautiful.   He is poor in money, but rich in knowledge.   Be quick to hear, but slow to speak.   The visions of my youth are past—too bright, too beautiful to last.   How dear to my heart are the scenes of my childhood!   That father, faint in death below, his voice no longer heard.   Wise in council and brave in war, he soon became the most successful leader.

An ADVERB may be modified—

1. By an *adverb.* "The horse ran *very* FAST."
2. By an *adjunct.* "He has acted INCONSISTENTLY *with his professions.*"

Exercises.

The adverbs, and by what modified :—

It is very badly done.   She studies most diligently.   You can not come too soon.   He has written agreeably to your directions.

When a dependent clause is abridged into a phrase, having a nominative absolute, the phrase retains the modifying sense of the clause.

Some grammarians call such also independent phrases, though perhaps needlessly.

Exercises.

The absolute phrases, and what they modify:—
My trunk being packed, I sent for a carriage. (Sent why or when?) The sun having set, we returned home. His father having been imprisoned, he went to rescue him. Along he sauntered, his musing fancies absorbing his whole soul.

Nominatives independent, or the phrases containing them, and interjections, are *independent elements.*

Exercises

Point out the independent words or phrases:—
O Liberty! can man resign thee, once having felt thy glorious flame! Weep on the rocks of roaring winds, O maid of Inistore! O Milan! O the golden bells which oft at eve so sweetly tolled! Alas, alas! fair Inés, she's gone into the West. The land of the heart is the land of the West; oho boys! oho boys! oho! Hist, Romeo, hist! My stars! what a fish! Ha, ha, ha! a fine gentleman, truly.

Connecting words are conjunctions, prepositions, relative pronouns, and some adverbs. Sometimes phrases.

Sometimes connectives are omitted, or the connection is sufficiently obvious by the position of the parts.

Exercises,

Point out the connectives, tell of what kind, and what they connect:—
The sun has set, and the moon and stars begin to appear. He took the horse, which was neither his nor mine. When I behold a fashionable table set out, I fancy that gouts, fevers, and lethargies, lie in ambush among the dishes. He that knows not how to suffer, has no greatness of soul. Though deep, yet clear; though gentle, yet not dull. The moment I touched it, down it fell. The deeper the water, the smoother it flows. (Connected by the correlative sense of the clauses.) To be happy is not only to be free from the pains and diseases of the body, but also from the cares and diseases of the mind.

Who steals my purse, steals trash; 'tis something, nothing;
'Twas mine, 'tis his, and has been slave to thousands:
But he who filches from me my good name,
Robs me of that which not enriches him,
And makes me poor indeed!

Propositions are sometimes *elliptical* or *inverted.*

Exercises,

Point out the elliptical parts, supply the omitted words, and restore the logical arrangement:—
And jokes went round, and careless chat. No mate, no comrade, Lucy knew. Oh, how damp, and dark, and cold! "Then, why don't you go," said I. Pride costs us more than hunger, thirst, and cold. The woman (strange circumstance!) remained obstinately silent. Out of debt, out of danger. On the cool and shady hills, coffee-shrubs and tamarinds grow. Alas for love, if thou wert all, and naught beyond, O earth! Of all the thousand stirs not one. "Sir, I can not.—What, my lord?—Make you a better answer."

Sentences, propositions, and phrases, may be analyzed according to the following

Formulas.

A *sentence*, and why; *simple, complex,* or *compound,* and why; *declarative, interrogative, imperative, exclamatory,* or a composite of, and why.

—— is a phrase;   the chief word
     an independent phrase; the independent substantive is ——, modified by ——.

—— is the entire subject;   the subject-nominative is ——, modified by ——.
                 predicate;   predicate-verb

—— is the entire subject;   the subject-nominatives are——, connected by——, and modified by——.
                 predicate;   predicate-verbs

ANALYSIS EXEMPLIFIED.
Simple Sentences Analyzed.

"Sin degrades."

This is a *sentence*, it is a thought expressed by words; *simple*, it contains but one proposition; *declarative*, it expresses a declaration.

Sin is the subject, because it denotes that of which something is affirmed; and *degrades* is the predicate, because it denotes what is affirmed of sin. *Sin* is also the subject-nominative; and *degrades*, the predicate-verb.

"My friend, were these houses and lands purchased and improved by our old senator, David Barton?"

This is a *sentence*, it is a collection of words making complete sense; *simple*, it contains but one proposition, or but one subject and one predicate; *interrogative*, it asks a question.

My friend is an independent phrase, because it has no grammatical connection with the rest of the sentence. *Friend* is the principal word, and it is modified or limited by the possessive *My.*

The phrase *these houses and lands,* is the subject, because it denotes that of which something is affirmed.

The phrase *were purchased and improved by our old senator, David Barton,* is the predicate, because it denotes what is affirmed of the subject.

Houses and *lands* are the subject-nominatives, connected by the word *and,* and modified by the adjective *these.*

Were purchased and [*were*] *improved* are the predicate-verbs, connected by *and* and modified by the phrase *by our old senator, David Barton. Our old senator* is modified by *David Barton; old senator* is modified or limited by the possessive *our;* and *senator* is modified by *old.*

Or thus: *Was* is the copula; *purchased* and *improved* are the attributes, modified by —— (as before)."

Complex Sentences Analyzed.

"A man who saves the fragments of time, will accomplish much in the course of his life."

This is a *sentence,*—it is a thought expressed by words, and comprised between two full pauses; *complex*, it contains two propositions, of which one depends on the other, or is used in the sense of an adjective; *declarative*, it expresses a declaration.

A man who saves the fragments of time, is the entire principal subject, because it denotes that of which something is affirmed; and *will accomplish much in the course of his life,* is the entire predicate, because it denotes what is affirmed of the subject. *Man* is the subject-nominative; and it is modified by the article *A*, and the clause *who saves the fragments of time: will accomplish* is the predicate-verb, and is modified by the object *much* and the adjunct *in the course of his life.*

Who saves the fragments of time, is a proposition connected to *man*, by the relative *who*, as a subordinate clause performing the office of an adjective.

Who is the entire subject and the subject-nominative: *saves the fragments of time*, is the entire predicate; *saves* is the predicate-verb, and is modified by its object *fragments*, which is itself modified by the article *the* and the adjunct *of time.*

"What pleases the palate, is not always good for the constitution."

This is a *sentence*, it is a collection of words making complete sense; *complex*, it contains two propositions, one of which is dependent on the other; *declarative*, it expresses a declaration.

What is equivalent to *that which. What*, or *that which, pleases the palate*, is the entire principal subject; and *is not always good for the constitution*, is the entire predicate. *That* is the subject-nominative, and is modified by the clause *which pleases the palate; is* is the predicate-verb, and is modified by the adjective *good*, which is itself modified by the adjunct *for the constitution* and the adverb *always*, and *always* is modified by the adverb *not.*

Which pleases the palate, is a proposition connected to *that*, by the relative *which*, as a subordinate clause performing the office of an adjective.

Which is the entire subject and the subject-nominative; *pleases the palate*, is the entire predicate; *pleases* is the predicate-verb, modified by the object *palate*, which is itself modified by *the.*

["Who were the robbers of the house, has not yet been ascertained."

This is a *complex declarative* sentence, having the incorporated clause, *Who were the robbers of the house*, as the entire subject and the subject-nominative. *Has not yet been ascertained*, is the entire predicate, etc.

Who were the robbers of the house, is a subordinate clause incorporated into the sentence as a substantive in the nominative case. *Who* is the entire subject and the subject-nominative, etc.]

"My son, if thou wouldst receive my words, and hide my commandments with thee, so that thou mayst gain wisdom; yea, if thou wouldst seek it as silver, and search for it as hidden treasure,—then live in the fear of the Lord, and find the knowledge of God."

This is a *sentence*, it is a collection of words making complete sense; *complex*, it consists of several propositions, some of which are dependent; a composite of *declarative*, or *conditional declarative*, and *imperative* clauses, or rather an *imperative* sentence, for its chief aim is to express a command or an exhortation.

"*My son*,"—

This is an independent phrase, because it has no grammatical connection with the rest of the sentence, etc. (Proceed as before.)

"*If thou wouldst receive my words, and hide my commandments with thee*,"—

· This is a proposition connected as a dependent clause, by the conjunction *if*, to the last clause of the sentence, etc. (Analyze these clauses in the same way as the clauses and sentences above were analyzed.)

" *So that thou mayst gain wisdom ;*"—
· This is a clause dependent on the clause preceding it, to which it is connected by *so that*, etc.

" *Yea, if thou wouldst seek it as silver, and search for it as hidden treasure ;*"—
This is a clause coördinate with the member preceding it, to which it is connected by the emphatic *yea;* and dependent on the last clause of the sentence, to which it is connected by *if.*

" *As silver,*"—   " *As for hidden treasure ;*"—
As silver is put for *as you would seek for silver*, and is therefore a clause connected to the preceding predicate by *as* as a subordinate clause, performing the office of an adverb of manner, etc.

" *Then live in the fear of the Lord, and find the knowledge of God.*"
This is the principal or independent clause, connected by *then* to the rest of the sentence. *Thou*, understood, is the entire subject and the subject-nominative, etc.

NOTE.—Long sentences are generally most easily analyzed, by commencing at the beginning of the sentence, and taking not more than one clause, independent word or phrase, at a time, and proceeding thus until the entire sentence is exhausted. It is generally better to defer dependent clauses, till their principal clauses are analyzed.

"There is strong reason to suspect that some able Whig politicians, who thought it dangerous to relax, at that moment, the laws against political offences, but who could not, without incurring the charge of inconsistency, declare themselves adverse to relaxation, had conceived a hope that they might, by fomenting the dispute about the court of the lord high steward, defer for at least a year the passing of a bill which they disliked, and yet could not decently oppose."—*Macaulay.*

ANALYSIS.—This is a *complex* declarative sentence. *There is strong reason to suspect*, is the principal clause, of which *strong reason to suspect*, is the entire subject; and *There is*, the entire predicate; *reason* is the subject-nominative, modified by the adjective *strong*, and by the infinitive *to suspect* performing the office of an adjective; *is* is the predicate-verb, modified by *There.*

That some able Whig politicians had conceived a hope, is the next simple declarative clause, performing the office of a noun in the objective case governed by *to suspect*, to which it is connected by *that*. *Some able Whig politicians*, is the entire subject; and *had conceived a hope*, is the entire predicate : *politicians* is the subject-nominative, modified by the adjectives *some*, *able*, and *Whig ;* and *had conceived* is the predicate-verb, modified by the object *hope*, which is itself modified by the article *a.*

Who thought it dangerous, etc., (read to *but,*) is a subordinate relative clause, connected to *politicians* by *who*, and performing the office of an adjective. *Who* is the entire subject and subject-nominative ; *thought it dangerous*, etc., is the entire predicate, of which *thought* is the predicate-verb, modified by the object *it*, which is modified by *dangerous*, and the appositive *to relax*, etc., of which *to relax* is modified by the adjunct *at that moment*, an adverbial element whose principal word is *moment*, modified by *that*, and connected to the verb by *at*; *to relax* is further modified by the object *the laws*, and *laws* is modified by the adjunct *against political offences*, performing the office of an adjective.

But who could not, without, etc. (read to *had*), is a relative clause also modifying *politicians*, and connected as a coördinate clause to the clause before it, by the adversative conjunction *but*. *Who* is the entire subject and the suoject-nominative; *could not, without incurring*, etc., is the entire predicate, of which *could declare* is the predicate-verb, modified by the negative adverb *not*, the adverbial adjunct *without incurring the charge of inconsistency*, the object *themselves*, which is modified by the adjective *adverse*, and *adverse* is modified by the adverbial adjunct *to relaxation*.

That they might, etc. (to *which*), is the next simple clause,—dependent, connected to *hope* by *that*, and performing the office of an adjective. *They* is the entire subject and the subject-nominative; *might defer*, etc., is the entire predicate, of which *might defer* is the predicate-verb, modified by the adverbial elements *by fomenting the dispute about the court of the lord high steward* (means), *for a year* (time), and the objective element *the passing of a bill*; *fomenting* is joined to *might defer* by *by* and modified by *dispute*, *dispute* is modified by *the* and *about the court*, *court* is joined to *dispute* by *about* and modified by *the* and *of the lord high steward*, *lord* is joined to *court* by *of* and modified by *the* and the appositive *high steward*; *for a year* is modified by the adverbial phrase *at least*; *passing* is modified by *the* and the adjunct *of a bill.*

Which they disliked, etc. (to the end), is a relative clause,—declarative, dependent, connected to *bill* by *which*, and performing the office of an adjective. *They* is the entire subject and the subject-nominative, *disliked* and *could oppose* are the predicate-verbs, connected by *and yet*, and modified, both, by the objective *which*, and the latter verb by the adverb *decently*, which is itself modified by the negative adverb *not*.

The sentence consists of six clauses, very finely bound together, of which the subject of the principal clause is branched out into a cluster of dependent clauses. —The student will seldom find a sentence more difficult to analyze.

Paragraphs or sentences may be briefly analyzed by simply pointing out the clauses or propositions in their logical order. Parsing, also, may be much abridged.

Ex. "Man hath his daily work of body or mind
 Appointed, which declares his dignity,
 And the regard of Heaven on all his ways;
 While other animals inactive range,
 And of their doings God takes no account."—*Milton.*

Man hath his daily work of body or mind appointed.
Which declares his dignity, and the regard of Heaven on all his ways.
While other animals range inactive.
And God takes no account of their doings.

Man is a common noun, in the nominative case to *hath*; *hath* is an irregular transitive verb agreeing with *Man*; *his* is a personal pronoun, relating to *Man* as its antecedent, and possessing *work*, etc.

☞ For exercises, use the phrases and sentences on pp. 73—87, and the poem on p. 131; and, of examples to be written on the blackboard and analyzed, the teacher will find an abundance in the Comprehensive Grammar.

THOUGHT AND ITS EXPRESSION.*

We *think*, or *have thoughts*.
We wish to express our thoughts, or to let other people know them.
We therefore put them into *words*, and *speak* or *write* them.
Every thought implies at least two things; something to think of, and something thought of it.
The former we denote by a *subject*; the latter, by a *predicate*.
We notice, in the world, *objects*, *actions*, and *qualities*, nearly all of which exist in *classes*, and some in *degrees*.
We notice the thing called *time*, and the thing called *space*, which two hold or contain all other things whatsoever.
In the operations of things, we notice *manner*, *cause*, *consequence*.
We also notice, chiefly in ourselves, *feeling*, *will*, *knowledge*, *ignorance*.
Some of these things must be found in every thought; and they are all expressed by a great variety of WORDS, PHRASES, *and* CLAUSES.
The subject or the predicate, while it refers to the same class, may often be denoted by a single word. (Simple subject or predicate.)

Ex.—" She sings;" " They sing." " Man errs;" " Men err."

When either refers to two or more classes, two or more words must be used to express it. (Compound subject or predicate.)

Ex.—" The *rose* or the *lily* | *blooms* and *fades*." " *Roses* and *lilies* | *bloom* and *fade*."

To denote what is only an occasional act or state, we must also frequently use several words to express it.

Ex.—"*That they should have endeavored to crush so great a genius*, is surprising." " The panther *gnashed his fangs in blood and foam*."

Within the same class we generally make the *same* word answer all our purposes, but we sometimes vary its form; as, Mill, *mills*; I, *we*; write, *writest*; great, *greater*. This change is called *inflection*. When we pass out of the class to a related class, we frequently still retain the word, but with a slight change; as, Mill, *miller*; write, *writer*; blue, *dark-blue*. This change is called *derivation*.

As there are many of almost every class, yet as scarcely any two have the same place, time, or qualities, we often add these, to show precisely what object, act, or state we mean. These added things are called *qualities* or *circumstances*; and the words, phrases, or clauses, denoting them, may be called *modifications*.

Hence, we may distinguish unmodified subject-nominatives and predicate-verbs from modified. Either class may be simple or compound.

Ex.—" Soldiers were marching." " The young soldiers of New York who enlisted last year, were marching, this morning, in magnificent array, to the Battery."

When some form of the verb *be* is the predicate-verb, the predicate is sometimes analyzed into copula and attribute, or into copula, attribute, and modifications.

Ex.—" The sky   *is*   *serene*." " David   *was*   *king*." " Grain, meat, and vegetables   *are*   *brought*   daily   down the river."

The proposition may vary according to the speaker's relations to what the subject denotes. These are the Persons; the first, the second, and the third.

Ex.—" I am speaking." " Thou art speaking." " He is speaking."

The proposition may vary according as we consider one or more than one of the same class. This variation lies in the Numbers.

Ex.—" I am speaking;" " We are speaking." " The squirrel climbs trees;" " Squirrels climb trees."

---

* This section is to be *studied* rather than *memorized*. It aims to give an inside view of thought and language,—to show the outbranchings of language from the germ of thought within, or the connection between the mind and the outer world with special reference to Grammar.

The proposition may vary according as one class is referred to or more than one. We thus have simple or compound subjects and predicates.

Ex.—" Wheat grows." " Wheat and barley grow and ripen."

The proposition may vary to express time. This shows itself in six forms in the Tenses; and must otherwise be expressed, like the other circumstances, by modifying words, phrases, or clauses.

Ex.—" I write; I wrote; I shall write; I have written;" etc. " I write *daily*." " I wrote *last week*." " I write *when I have the opportunity*." " I wrote *where you are sitting*."

The proposition may vary according to the relations of the subject to the act or state, the speaker's knowledge or will, or the dependence of events. These variations show themselves in Moods.

Ex.—" I wrote." " I should have written." " It may rain." " Write to him." " If it rain, we shall have good crops."

The proposition may vary according to the speaker's knowledge, doubts, will, or feelings; that is, be either *declarative*, *interrogative*, *imperative*, or *exclamatory*. See p. 71.

A proposition may itself make a sentence.

Ex.—" Glory is like a circle in the water."

A proposition may make only a part of a sentence. If it does not modify, it is called *coördinate*; if it modifies, *subordinate*.

Ex.—" The last load of grain is brought home, | and the tables are spread for the harvest feast." " The mind *that broods o'er guilty woes*, is like a scorpion girt by fire."

Two or more clauses forming a distinct part of a compound sentence, may be termed a *member*; and so may the remaining clause, or group of clauses.

To a proposition may be added an independent word or phrase denoting the person or thing addressed.

Ex.—" *Gentlemen*, your whole concern should be to do your duty, regardless of consequences.

A proposition may sometimes be abridged to a mere phrase.

Ex.—" *When the lesson had been learned*, we went to play"=*The lesson being learned*, we went to play. " I came *that I might see the show*"=I came *to see the show*.

Sometimes a phrase or an entire clause, as well as a single word, may be used in the sense of a *noun*, an *adjective*, or an *adverb*.

Ex.—" The boy *who is studious*, will learn"= The *studious* boy will learn. " He begins his work *before the sun rises*"= He begins his work *before sunrise*= He begins his work early. " It is well known *that he is incompetent*"=*That he is incompetent*, is well known = *His being incompetent* is well known = *His incompetence* is well known.

Sometimes a phrase or an entire clause may be modified or affected like a single word.

Ex.—" A great many valuable books." Here each word, beginning with " A," modifies all that comes after it. " He was so young, so generous, so *every thing that we are apt to like in a young man*." " You study grammar for your *improvement* in language."

To express the meaning with emphasis, or greater force, we sometimes omit words, or change the order of the words.

Ex.—" Tyrants no more their savage nature kept"= Tyrants kept their savage nature no more. " Far-fetched and dear-bought is for ladies"=*What is* far-fetched and dear-bought, is for ladies.

We *spell* words; *pronounce* words; *derive* words from others, *classify* them, and *prepare* them *for sentences;* *put words together* so as *to make sentences;* and *improve sentences*, chiefly by *utterance*, so as to make them most *agreeable* and *forcible*. Hence GRAMMAR may be divided into *Orthog'raphy, Pronun'ciation, Etymol'ogy, Syntax*, and *Pros'ody*.

The SYNTAX of sentences is best considered under four heads : *relation, government, agreement* (or *concord*), and *position*. The *relation* of words is their reference to one another according to the sense; *government* is the power which one word has over another in causing its case, person, number, or some other property; *agreement* is the correspondence of one word with another in case, person, number, or some other property; and *position* refers to the place which a word occupies in reference to other words.

THE SIX ELEMENTS.

All DISCOURSE may be divided into paragraphs; paragraphs into sentences; sentences into clauses or propositions; and propositions into phrases and words.

All sentences may be most conveniently analyzed, by resolving them into *six* elements; *two principal elements, two modifying elements,* a *connecting element,* and an *independent element.*

The two *principal elements* are the subject-nominatives and the predicate-verbs; both of which are easily distinguished, by their form and sense, from the other parts.

The *modifying elements* are either *adjective elements* or *adverbial elements.*

Any word, phrase, or clause, that modifies a noun, is an *adjective element.* It shows of what kind or nature the object is.

Any word, phrase, or clause, that modifies a verb, an adjective, an adverb, or an entire predicate, is an *adverbial element.* It generally shows *where, when, how, why, what, in what respect, to what extent,* or expresses negation. Its chief use is, to make with the predicate-verb the predicate. For the sake of greater precision, the *objective elements* may be distinguished, as such, from the other adverbial elements.

The *connecting elements* are the conjunctions, the prepositions, some adverbs, and the relative pronouns. Connectives may perform, additionally, some office in the parts to which they belong; they may be expressed or omitted; they may be used singly or in pairs; they may consist of one word each, or of a phrase.

The *independent element* may be a substantive denoting what is addressed, or what is the mere subject of thought; or it may be an interjection; or it may be something that represents an entire sentence, or stands as the fragment of a sentence.

A part used singly, is called a *simple element;* a pair or series of parts is called a *compound element;* and a part that is modified by another, makes with it a *complex element.*

Every proposition or clause should be separated, as soon as possible, into its *grammatical* subject and predicate; and all the dependent parts should then be referred, according to the sense, to the one or to the other.

What is inverted or elliptical, should generally be analyzed as if it stood in its logical order or fullness.

It is sometimes not easy to determine whether an adjunct, an adjective, or an adjective phrase; a participle or a participial phrase; an infinitive or an infinitive phrase,—should be referred to the subject or to the predicate. Consider carefully what constitutes the whole of that of which the affirmation is made; next consider what constitutes the whole of that which is strictly affirmed. When even this mode of judging is inadequate, it will probably be a matter of little consequence, to which part the modification is referred.

How may discourse be divided? How may sentences be analyzed? Describe each kind of elements. What else is said of analysis?

COMPLEX AND COMPOUND SENTENCES.

Note.—The ideas entertained about Analysis are so various that they have not as yet settled down into a uniform system. What we have taught on this subject from page 102, is in accordance with what is now regarded as the most approved system. Many grammarians, especially the older ones, divide all sentences into but two classes,—*simple* and *compound*; or else they regard all complex sentences as compound, but not all compound sentences as complex, using *compound* as a generic term to *complex*. The following views, however, which now prevail most in Great Britain, are more exact and philosophical, and will probably give better satisfaction to those who are in the habit of thinking closely upon the structure of language. (Both the older and the more recent mode of classifying sentences, are shown in the Comprehensive Grammar See pp. 3, 58, 68.)

There runs through discourse, more or less, a serial sense, and also a modified sense. The former gives us *compound* structure; and the latter, *complex* structure.

All sentences that have two or more distinct predicates, are either *complex* or *compound*.

A *complex sentence* contains but one principal clause, with one or more dependent clauses.

The dependent clause is combined with the principal clause, in the sense of a *NOUN*, an *ADJECTIVE*, or an *ADVERB*, or else simply depends on it for complete sense. The subordinate or dependent clauses which make with other clauses complex members or sentences, comprise the relative clauses, the adverbial clauses, the correlative clauses, and generally the conjunctive clauses that express comparison, condition, concession, exception, cause, consequence, or purpose. See p. 65.

What is grammatically dependent, may be logically principal; that is, what is dependent in construction, may be most important in sense; as, "*When the sun rises*, the birds sing." "To think *a l w a y s accurately*, is a *great* accomplishment."

A *compound sentence* contains two or more principal coordinate clauses.

Such clauses are generally connected by conjunctions of the first three classes (see p. 65), or they have no connective.

Complex and *compound*, as here used, are entirely distinct: so that a sentence may be complex without being compound, or compound without being complex.

A *complex member* consists of two or more clauses combined like those of a complex sentence, and forms only a part of a sentence.

A *compound member* consists of two or more coördinate clauses, and forms only a part of a sentence.

A phrase whose chief word is modified by another phrase, may be called *complex*.

The subject is the nucleus of the sentence, round which every thing else clusters, and which is, in fact, modified by every thing else, even by the predicate-verb itself, with all its appendages. Hence some grammarians call the entire predicate the *attribute* of the subject. If, then, we regard dependent clauses always as modifying clauses, we shall have the strange anomaly, when clauses are used as subjects, of making the subject modify the predicate. (See p. 120.) But the above definition of a complex sentence, avoids the difficulty.

The skeleton of thought which underlies the full-robed sentence, may be briefly exhibited thus:—

Which one?		Is what?	When? Where?
How many?	Subject.	Does what?	How? Why?
Of what kind?		Suffers what?	As to what?

SUMMARY OF ANALYSIS.

Literature, or discourse, may be divided into *prose* and *verse*, prose and blank-verse may often be conveniently divided into *paragraphs;* other verse, into *stanzas;* and all prose and verse, of whatever kind, may be resolved into *sentences*.

Sentences are either simple, complex, or compound; declarative, interrogative, imperative, exclamatory, or composites of these; and may be resolved into *propositions* or *clauses*.

If long, sentences may often be conveniently divided first into *members*, and then into *clauses*.

Propositions or clauses are either independent or dependent; declarative, interrogative, imperative, or exclamatory; and may be resolved into *connectives, subjects,* and *predicates*.

Subjects and **Predicates** are either simple or compound, and unmodified or modified.

For the purpose of descending still farther in analysis, all discourse may be considered as consisting of the following *six elements*, which may be again subdivided into various parts:—

Principal Elements.
Subject: Noun, pronoun, verbal noun or phrase, clause.
Predicate*: Finite verb.

The unmodified (or grammatical) subject or predicate, with all its modifications, may be called the *entire* (modified, or logical) *subject* or *predicate*.

Modifying Elements: *Modifiers,* or *Modifications.* See foot-note, p. 118.

Adjective.—A NOUN or PRONOUN may be modified—1. by an *article;* 2. by an *adjective* or an *adjective phrase;* 3. by a *possessive;* 4. by an *appositive* or an *appositive phrase* or *clause;* 5. by a *participle* or a *participial phrase;* 6. by an *infinitive* or an *infinitive phrase;* 7. by an *adjunct;* 8. or by a *clause*, sometimes abridged into a phrase.

Adverbial.—A FINITE VERB, a PARTICIPLE, or an INFINITIVE, may be modified—1. by an *object*, sometimes a phrase or clause; 2, by a *predicate nominative*, sometimes a phrase or clause; 3. by an *adjective* or an *adjective phrase;* 4. by an *adverb;* 5 by a *participle* or a *participial phrase;* 6. by an *infinitive* or an *infinitive phrase;* 7. by an *adjunct;* 8. by a *clause*, sometimes abridged into a phrase.

An ADJECTIVE may be modified by an *adverb*, an *adjunct*, an *infinitive* or an *infinitive phrase*, or a *clause*.

An ADVERB may be modified by an *adverb* or an *adjunct*.

_{A modifying element may make a part of either the entire subject or the entire predicate; and, on the other hand, the principal elements also enter into the modifying clauses.}

There are also *grades of modification;* that is, a part which modifies, may itself be modified, and this modifying part may also be modified, and so on.

Connecting Element: Conjunctions, conjunctive adverbs, relative pronouns, prepositions.

Independent Element: Interjections, nominatives independent. Sometimes a word or phrase that represents a proposition.

_{* **Predicate, Copula,** and **Attribute.**—About *predicate* there is great diversity of opinion. Some writers apply the term to the predicate-verb only; some, to all}

SYMBOLS TO SHOW THE CONSTRUCTION OF SENTENCES.

The EYE is the most powerful of the five senses. The more completely, therefore, any thing can be brought under its dominion, the more easily it is mastered. Locke, in his great work on the Human Understanding, recommends the reducing of abstractions to symbols that may be easily grasped by the eye. It is well known what wonderful power has been acquired over the abstractions of quantity, by means of the few symbols and axioms of algebra; and how completely the almost infinite world of music is subjected by means of a few representative marks.

Attempts have been frequently made, both in this country and in Europe, to present the construction of sentences to the eye, by means of diagrams or symbols. Mr. F. A. P. Barnard, many years ago, devised a system that seems to have been the germ of Mr. Clark's system. Dr. Morell, of London, and several writers in our educational journals, have tried systems in letters. All of these systems, however, are defective, and seem to be too complicated and mechanical.

What we want, is a brief, simple, and comprehensive system, by which the pupil can easily show to his teacher at a glance, what he knows of the construction of the sentences which have been assigned to him as a task. I have therefore devised the following mode of writing out *algebraically* the construction of sentences:—

First Class.

S, *s*entence.
M, *m*ember.
P, *p*roposition.
C, independent or principal *c*lause.
c, dependent *c*lause.
c',c'',c''', *degrees* of dependence below the first.
N, subject-*n*ominative, or unmodified subject.
V, predicate-*v*erb, or unmodified predicate.
N^m, abridged expression for *m*odified subject.
V^m, abridged expression for *m*odified predicate.

X, independent word or phrase.
Repeat for compound, except S.

Second Class.

+, predication.
=, equivalence.
|, ∥, ∦, separation, less or greater;
or use the punctuation marks of the sentence itself.
( ), supplied matter.
∾, placed over to show, if necessary, inversion.

Third Class.

r, a*r*ticle.
a, a*d*jective.
b, adver*b*.

d, a*d*junct.
And let *d* = p o, etc.
s, po *s* sessive.
c, appositive—*e*xplanatory or *e*mphatic.
o, *o*bject.
t, predica*t*e-nominative.
p, *p*articiple.
l, abso*l*ute phrase; *i. e.*,
nom. absol. with particíple.
And let l = n p, etc.
i, *i*nfinitive.
j, (*j*oin,) connective.
Repeat for compound.
', '', ''', *degrees* of subordination below the first or primary.

By referring to pp. 105–8, 117–29, the reader can see that these symbols exhaust the subject.

If at any time it should appear necessary, any of these symbols can be made to show the relations of others, by being placed, as superiors, over them. Thus: c^a = adjective clause; c^b, adverbial clause; c^o, objective clause; c^t, predicate-nominative clause; i^o, objective infinitive; d^b, adverbial adjunct; N^j, connecting nominative, *i. e.*, relative pronoun.

Ex.—" Large streams from little fountains flow." S = P = a N + V d. d = p a o. The stanza on page 130, an excellent specimen for illustration, would stand thus in our symbols:—

S = M; M = C c; C c = N + V^m; N ∓ V^m = N + V r a a' t c; N + V r a a t c.
p = N + V'd. d = p a a' o. c = s a N + V d j V s a o b b. d = p o.

From this example we see, that the teacher may require of his pupils *first grade* analysis only, which goes not below clauses; or *second grade*, which shows subjects and predicates and dependent clauses, and which may be abridged; or *third grade*, which shows all the minutiæ.

We have not room here to exemplify this subject at large. See pp. 118–28. The above system seems to us a good one—one that can be made really useful in schools. It can be

that is said of the subject; and some of the old logicians apply it to what follows the verb *be*, ~ to what is now generally called the *attribute*. The predicate-verb *be* is often called the

ANALYSIS OF SENTENCES.

learned in a few hours; the symbols are sufficient to exhaust the subject, or to reach all sentences whatsoever; the longest sentences can be thus analyzed in a line or two, for which diagrams or words would require pages; the analysis can be shown by descending steps, or by a regular descent from the greatest parts to the least, with all compound structure and every degree of subordination; the symbols will show of what the sentence consists, and their position will generally be sufficient to show the relation of the parts; the plus mark s readily show the predications, or ganglia, of the sentence: one large I on the right, at once shows that the sentence is *simple;* one large C, that it is *complex;* and two, *compound.* But we leave it to teachers to find out whether there is any advantage in the scheme.

EXERCISES IN ANALYSIS AND PARSING.

☞ In arranging the following examples, I have, in general, passed from *words* to *phrases* and from phrases to *clauses*, from *unmodified* to *modified*, from *simple* to *compound*, and from *regular* construction to *inverted* or *elliptical*. To make the simplest classification, it has been necessary to give sentences beyond the pupil's present ability. The latter paragraphs or the more complicated sentences should therefore be deferred for a second or third course.—Superior (¹), over the end of a sentence, shows that it is simple²; (²), compound³; and (³), complex³.

It is often a convenience to name phrases and clauses according to their leading or principal words, or according to their sense. Hence we have *sub'stantive phrases, ad'jective phrases, participial phrases, infinitive phrases, adverbial phrases, oppos'itive* or *explanatory phrases, independent phrases, ab'solute phrases, idiomat'ic phrases,* etc.; *substantive clauses, adjective clauses, adverbial clauses, relative clauses, correlative clauses, appositive* or *explanatory clauses, conjunctive clauses,* etc.

Principal Elements.
1. Simple Subjects and Predicates.
Unmodified.

I went.* N + V. Stars shine. It snows. Lights were shining. He should have been rewarded. Who sang? Could they have gone? Singing had commenced. To whisper is forbidden. Banners waved. Hark ye.

* This is a simple declarative sentence. The subject is *I*, and the predicate is *went.*

---

copula; but its chief idea is predication, rather than that of merely joining parts. (See Kerl's Comp. Gram., p. 197.) The adjective, noun, adjunct, etc., which follows the verb *be*, or any other intransitive verb, and is *descriptive* of the subject, is often called an *attribute*. (See Mill's Logic; also the Grammars of Greene, Covell, Pinneo, etc.) But it is not proper to call it an attribute, when it expresses *mere identity.*

We may say that the verb *be* is limited by an attribute of the subject; but to dispose of the attribute by referring it to the subject, as I have known some teachers to do, is wrong; for we thus convert Analysis at once into Parsing, or break up the main distinction between them, namely, that of subject and predicate.

In every language with which I am acquainted, the copula is also a verb that expresses existence; and it is therefore highly probable that existence was the fundamental idea. ' She *is rich*" = She *exists in a rich condition.* But this idea of existence appears to be now generally lost in that of predication; and hence many grammarians take the verb *be* with the attribute, as the grammatical predicate. This mode of analysis is allowable; yet it often leads to trouble, and tends to break up the distinction between the grammatical and the logical predicate. When I say, "John is idle"; *idle* certainly does not modify *is*, in the ordinary sense of *modify;* but let us extend the meaning of *modify*, or use *limit* in its place. John may be—a hundred different things. The word after the verb *be* determines what he *is*, or fixes the assertion, or limits the verb *be*. This mode of analysis has the advantage of simplicity, and it is sufficiently exact for the requirements of Grammar.

Modifiers.—The modifying elements are usually called *modifiers,* or *modifications.* Murray and Brown call them incidentally *adjuncts. Modifier* seems to be the better term; for, etymologically considered, the terms are always *modifiers,* but not always *adjuncts.* The term *adjunct* is used by nearly all grammarians in the sense which we have given to it on p. 63; yet some late writers prefer *prepositional phrase,* which, though not so *short* as *adjunct,* is a good term, and would deserve encouragement, if *adjunct* should supersede *modifier.*—*Modify* we use as the generic term, and *limit* as the specific. In analysis it will generally be found best to use *limit.*

ANALYSIS OF SENTENCES.   119

Modified by Words and Phrases.

1. These roses are very beautiful. $S = P = N^x + V^m =$ a $N + V$ b a.   2. Lies have short legs[s].   3. Too much fear is an enemy to good deliberation[s].   4. Virtuous youth brings forth accomplished and flourishing manhood[s].   5. Milton, the author of Paradise Lost, was deeply versed[10] in ancient learning.[s]

ANALYSIS.—This is a simple declarative sentence. The entire subject is *These roses*; the subject-nominative is *roses*, which is limited by the adjective *These*. The entire predicate is *are very beautiful*; the predicate-verb is *are*, which is limited by the adjective *beautiful*, or combines with it in making a descriptive assertion of the subject. *Beautiful* is modified by the adverb *very*, expressing degree. Or say, The predicate-verb is *are*, which is limited by the adjective *beautiful*, an attribute of the subject; and *beautiful* is modified by *very*, expressing degree.

Modified by Clauses.

SUBJECT.—1. They who are set to rule over others, must be just. $S = C c = N c + V a$.   2. There was one clear, shining star, that[1] used to come out into the sky before the rest, near the church[10] spire, above the graves[x].

PREDICATE.—3. Heaven has imprinted, in the mother's face, something that claims kindred with the skies[x].   4. I was assured that he would return[x].

CLAUSAL PHRASES.—5. The disputes between the majority which supported the mayor, and the minority headed by the magistrates, had repeatedly run so high that[10] bloodshed seemed inevitable[x].   6. We found, in our rambles, several pieces of flint which the Indians had once used for arrow-heads[x].

ANALYSIS.—1. This is a complex declarative sentence. The independent or principal clause is, *They must be just ;* and *who are set to rule over others*, is the dependent clause, which is joined to *They* by the relative *who*, and is used in the sense of an adjective. 2. It would be a convenience to parse *like, near,* and *worth* as prepositions; and some respectable grammarians parse them so. These words seem to have *absorbed* the governing power of the preposition. But *near*, and sometimes *like*, may be compared; and sometimes they are followed by *to*. 6. The independent or principal clause, exclusive of its longer modifications, is, *The disputes between the majority and the minority had repeatedly run so high*. (Now analyze this clause, and then the remaining parts.) The last clause modifies *so* or *so high* adverbially, by showing the *degree*.

[For beginners, it will generally be found easiest to resolve all sentences simply into their *independent* and *dependent propositions*, and to take not more for one analysis than a single predication, continually pushing aside, for subsequent analysis, the minor clauses. It may also be often best to state simply on what a dependent clause depends, or to mention with this statement the sense of the connective as shown on p. 65.   When sentences are long, it is sometimes more convenient to state first the unmodified (or grammatical) subject or predicate, and then the modifiers that make the entire (or logical) subject or predicate.]

Inverted and Elliptical Constructions.

1. In every grove warbles the voice of love and pleasure[s].   r N d $+$ V d.   2. Bursts the wild cry of terror and dismay[s].   3. How wonderfully are we made[s] !   4. To what expedient wilt thou fly[s] ?   5. Then first thy Sire, to send on earth, Virtue, his darling child, designed[s].

6. Write. 7. Sweet the pleasure. 8. Give me° the horse⁴. 9. Let nothing frighten you but sinˢ. 10. The inquisitive are generally talkative. 11. Here the wigwam blaze beamed on the tender and helplessˢ.

"Where's thy true treasure?" Gold says, "Not in me;" And, "Not in me," the Diamondᶜ. Gold is poor!

ANALYSIS & PARSING.—1. Always show first what the prose arrangement would be, and then analyze the sentence. 6. Supply *thou* or *you*. 7. Supply *is*. 9. *Let* is modified by the phrase after it as the entire object, and by *nothing* as the simple object. *Frighten* modifies *nothing*—or refers the act to it, and also depends on *Let*. "We made him *speak*;" "We made him *poor*;" "We made him a *bankrupt*;" "I feel my health *declining*;" in all these sentences, the Italic word modifies the substantive, and depends also on the verb. 10. The adjective *inquisitive* is here used elliptically for *inquisitive persons*; and, for the sake of convenience, it may be parsed as a noun. But when such an adjective is modified by an adverb, or when several such adjectives unite in describing the same persons, a substantive should be supplied. 11. Supply *ones* or *persons*.

Infinitive Phrases used as Subjects.

1. *To relieve the poor, is our dutyˢ. i r o + V s t. 2. To pay as you go, is the safest way to fortuneˣ. 3. To have advanced much farther without wagons or supplies, would have been dangerousˢ.

Inverted and Elliptical.

Unknown to them, when sensual pleasures cloy, To fill the languid pause with finer joyˣ.

* *To relieve the poor* is the entire subject ; *to relieve* is the unmodified subject.

Clauses used as Subjects.

1. That the earth is round, is now well knownˣ. c + V b b. 2. Whether we should go, was next discussedˣ. 3. How many and what enormous lies have been published in the newspapers, must have astonished every honest readerˣ. 4. "Dust thou art, to dust returnest," was not written of the soulˣ.

That the earth is round, is the entire principal subject. *That* is the connective, which is used to unite more closely into a whole the words of its clause, and to combine them in this sense with the principal predicate.

Difficult Parsing.

Give whatˢ you can spare. What¹ is that yonder? I know not what⁷ it is. What¹⁰ a simpleton he is! *What*¹ is a pronoun. What¹⁴! shall we never have any rest? Is *is* is'.

Compound Subjects and Predicates.
Compound Subjects.
Nouns and Pronouns.

1. John¹ and I¹ went. N j N + V. 2. Either James or Henry is talkingˢ. 3. Lead, iron, and coal, were foundˢ. 4. His magnificence, his taste, his classical learning, his high spirit, the grace and urbanity of his manners, were admitted even by his enemiesˢ.

—ANALYSIS.—1. This is a simple declarative sentence, with a compound subject. *John and I* is the entire subject; and *John* and *I* are the subject-nominatives, connected by *and*.

4. Where no conjunction is expressed, it is probably best to say that the parts are connected *by simple succession.*—When a predicate must be supplied with each nominative, then the sentence, not the subject, should be considered compound; as, "You or he is to be blamed." "The best books, not the cheapest, should be our object." See Comp. Gram., p. 72.

Infinitive Phrases.

1. To remain and to advance were equally dangerous. 2. *To hope and strive is the way to thrive. 3. To be wise in our own eyes, to be wise in the opinion of the world, and to be wise in the sight of our Creator, are three things that rarely coincide^x.

* *To hope and strive* is the entire subject and the subject-nominative. *To hope* is in part the subject of *is*. *Is* agrees with *to hope* and *to strive* conjointly, taken as one thing.

Clauses.

That he should take offense at such a trifle, that he should write an article about it, and that he should then publish it, surprised us all^x.

Clausal Phrases.

The wit whose vivacity condemns slower tongues to silence, the scholar whose knowledge allows no man to fancy that he instructs him, the critic who suffers no fallacy to pass undetected, and the reasoner who condemns the idle to thought and the negligent to attention, are generally praised and feared, reverenced and avoided^x. N c, N c c', N c, N c + b V j V, V j V.

Compound Predicates.

1. He rose, reigned, and fell^s. N + V V j V. 2. Read and write. 3. Slowly and sadly they climb the distant mountains, and read their doom in the setting sun^s.

4. Though the world smile on you blandly,
    Let^{11} your friends be^{12} choice^{10} and few;
    Choose your course, pursue it grandly,
    And achieve what^s you pursue.— *T. B. Read.*

5. Glass is impermeable to water, admits the light and excludes the wind, is capable of receiving and retaining the most lustrous colors, is susceptible of the finest polish, can be carved or sculptured like stone or metal, never loses a fraction of its substance by constant use, and is so insensible to the action of acids that it is employed by chemists for purposes to which no other substance could be applied^x.

S = C c c' = N + V^m, V^{m}V^m, V^m, V^{m}V^m, V^m, j V b a d c^b c'.

ANALYSIS.—1. This is a simple declarative sentence, with a compound predicate. 4. By supplying *thou* after each verb, the second member affords three simple coördinate clauses; but it is probably better to consider these three verbs as making a compound predicate.

Adjective Elements.

1. Articles.

A church stands on the adjoining hill. A statesman's character should be an honor to his country. r s N + V r t d.

Elliptical and Peculiar Constructions.

1. A man and woman were drowned. S=P=r N j (r) N + V.
2. He bought a house and lot⁸. 3. A river runs between the old and the new mansion⁸. 4. A great many adjectives are derived from nouns⁸ 5. Peter the Great is the pride of Russia⁸.

ANALYSIS & PARSING.—1. Supply *a* before *woman*. 2. *A* relates to both *house* and *lot*, for both are regarded as one thing. 4. *A* relates to all the rest of the subject; or it would perhaps be better to parse *many* as a plural collective noun, and supply *of* after it. We say, "A great many *of* them." 5. "Peter the Great" = Peter the Great Emperor; or, The Great Peter. But it is probably best to parse the whole expression as a proper noun.

2. Adjectives.

1. This little twig bore that large red apple⁸. a a' N + V a a'n'o. 2. Green fields and forests were before us⁸. 3. A swift and limpid rivulet purled over the pebbles⁸. 4. He used very forcible but courteous language⁸. 5. Two plum-trees, radiant with white blossoms on every bough, overtop the garden wall⁸. 6. The whole world swarms with life, animal and vegetable⁸.

Apple is modified by *red; red apple,* by *large;* and *large red apple,* by *that.* *Green,* in the next example, belongs to both *fields* and *forests.*

Inverted and Elliptical.

1. A bright and handsome young lady she was⁸. 2. Calm, attentive, and cheerful, he confutes more gracefully than others compliment˟. N a a j a + V b' b c. 3. Then followed a long, a strange, a glorious conflict of genius against power⁸. 4. So excellent a faculty is memory, that all other faculties borrow from it their beauty and perfection˟. 5. She was a virgin lovely as the dewy rose˟. 6. Violets meek and jonquils sweet she chose⁸.

ANALYSIS.—2. The dependent clause, *than others compliment,* limits, determines, or completes the comparison. 5. *Virgin* is modified by *lovely;* and *lovely* is modified by the adverbial clause *as the dewy rose (is lovely).*

3. Possessives.

John's horse is in our garden⁸. s N + V d. Gen. George Washington's residence was on the Potomac⁸. Soft¹⁰ blows the breeze o'er India's coral strand⁸.

Elliptical and Peculiar Constructions.

1. I will wait at Smith's⁸, the bookseller⁷. 2. I will wait at Smith' the bookseller's'. 3. Lewis' and Raymond's factory was burned⁸. 4. This is a discovery of Sir Isaac Newton's⁸. 5. That head of yours has many strange fancies in it⁸. 6. The sea is His, for He made it˟. 7. Simpson's Playfair's Euclid is the one⁷ that I studied˟. 8. The bard of Lomond's lay is done⁸.

ANALYSIS & PARSING.—1. Supply *house* or *store* after *Smith's.* 2. *Bookseller's,* rather than *Smith,* is the word in apposition. 3. *Lewis* is still in the possessive case, though used without the possessive sign. 4. Supply *discoveries.* 5. *Yours,* an idiom; equivalent to *your possession.* 6. Supply *property.* It would be a convenience to parse *His* as a possessive pronoun representing a possessive modifying word and a nominative chief word, and therefore in the nominative case, agreeing with *sea.* In a similar way, *yours,* of the preceding example. But the analogies of grammar are against this mode of parsing these words. 7. *Euclid* is limited by *Playfair's,* and the phrase *Playfair's Euclid* is limited by *Simpson's.* 8. *Bard ('s)* is governed by *lay,* and *Lomond('s)* by *of.*

4. Appositive or Explanatory Expressions.

Nouns and Pronouns.

1. Thou, thou', art the man[s]. N e + V r t. 2. I myself was present[s]. 3. The nurse, that ancient lady, preached decorum[s]. 4. The twin sisters, Poetry and Music, are my delight[s]. 5. There is but one God, the author, the creator, and the governor of the world; almighty, eternal, and incomprehensible[s]. 6. Thou sun, both eye and soul of the world. 7. John, John, John! you lazy boy! 8. A cove, or inlet', divides the island[s]. 9. The commissioners, that is, Mason and Dixon, established this line[s]. 10. She was proud of me as[15] her pupil[s]. 11. I object to his appointment as clerk[s]. 12. Messrs. William and Robert Bailey were conversing with the Misses Barnes[s]. 13. Madame de Stael calls beautiful architecture frozen music[s]. 14. I sold them for a dollar a pair[s]. 15. The saint', the father', and the husband, prays.[s]— *Burns.* 16. You are too humane and considerate; things few people can be charged with[s].—*Pope.*

ANALYSIS & PARSING.—6. Analogy seems to be in favor of making *Thou* the nominative independent, and *sun* the appositive. (See sentences beginning with *it*, next paragraph.) *Eye* and *soul* are in apposition with *sun.* 7. The first *John* is the principal word, which is modified by *John, John,* and perhaps *you* rather than *boy. You* is modified by *boy,* and *boy* by *lazy.* 9. *That is,* a conjunction. 10. *Pupil* is in apposition with *me,* and joined to it by *as.* 11. *Clerk* is in apposition with *his.* This sentence might be considered somewhat ambiguous, and it is therefore not to be commended. 12. *William (Bailey)* and *Robert Bailey* are put in apposition with *Messrs.;* but *Misses Barnes* is best parsed as but one noun. 13. *Calls* is modified by *beautiful architecture frozen music,* as the entire object, and by *architecture* as the simple object. *Music* is put in apposition with *architecture,* and is partially governed by *calls.* 14. *Pair* is in apposition with *them,* for it explains *them* distributively. 16. *Things* is probably best parsed as an *appositive absolute*—relating to the adjectives *humane* and *considerate*—and therefore in the nominative case, according to Rule II. Supply *which* as the object of *with.*

Infinitive Phrases.

1. It is foolish to lay out money in a purchase of repentance[s]. N [ie] b o d + V a. 2. It is mean to divulge the secrets of a friend[s]. 3. It is our duty to be friendly toward mankind, as much as it is our interest that mankind should be friendly toward us[x].

ANALYSIS.—1. This is a simple declarative sentence. *It,* with the explanatory infinitive phrase, *to lay out money,* etc., is the entire subject; and *It* is the subject-nominative. *It* is modified by the phrase *to lay out money,* etc., as the entire appositive or explanatory phrase; and by the infinitive *to lay,* as the simple appositive. *To lay* is modified by the adverb *out,* the object *money,* and the complex adjunct *in a purchase of repentance.*

Clauses.

1. It is through inward health, that we enjoy all outward things. N c[c] + V d. 2. It is scarcely to be imagined, how soon the mind sinks to a level with its condition[x]. 3. Study is at least valuable for this—that it makes man his own companion[x]. 4. The opinion that the soul is immortal, has always prevailed.

ANALYSIS & PARSING.—1 This is a complex declarative sentence, consisting of an independent and a dependent proposition. The unmodified independent proposition is, *It is through inward health;* the dependent proposition is, *that we enjoy all outward things,* which is used in the sense of an appositive, explanatory of *It.* 3. Supply *thing;* or say, *This is* a demonstrative pronoun representing the phrase *this thing,* and therefore in the n. g., 3d. p., s. n., and in the o. c.—being the object of the preposition *for*—according to Rule V. 4. The unmodified independent clause is, *The opinion has always prevailed;* the dependent clause is, *that the soul is immortal.*

Inverted and Elliptical.

1. Child of the Sun, refulgent Summer comes⁸. a N e d + V.
2. Thyself shalt see the act⁸. (N)e + V r o. 3. This monument is itself⁷ the orator of this occasion⁸.— *Webster.* 4. One by one the moments fly⁸. 5. They had one each⁸.

ANALYSIS & PARSING.—3. *Itself* is in apposition with *monument;* it is not a predicate-nominative. 4. *One* may be parsed as an adjective, belonging to *moment* understood; or it may be parsed as an indefinite pronoun, representing, with its adjunct, the subject distributively, and therefore in apposition with this subject. *One by one* might also be parsed as an adverbial phrase, showing the manner of flying. 5. *Each* may be parsed as a pronoun presenting distributively again the subject *they*, and therefore put in the same case with it by Rule VII. When a suitable substantive can be easily supplied after a pronominal adjective, this latter word should generally be parsed as an adjective; when a substantive can not be supplied without changing the sense, the pronominal should be parsed as a pronoun; and when a substantive can not be easily supplied, it will be generally better to parse the pronominal as a pronoun. A pronominal, when parsed as a pronoun, should be called *distributive, demonstrative, indefinite, emphatic,* etc., according to the sense in which it is used.

5. Participles.

1. Truth, crushed to earth, shall rise again⁸. N p d + V b.
2. The deer, seeing me, fled⁸. 3. The wolf, being much exasperated by the wound, sprang upon the horse⁸. 4. He had a beautiful daughter, betrothed to a chief⁸. 5. I had it done for you⁸. 6. There are twenty-six senators, distinguished for their wisdom, not elevated by popular favor, but chosen by a select body of men⁸. 7. The blast seemed to bear away the sound of the voice, permitting nothing to be heard but¹⁴ its own wild howling, mingled with the creaking and the rattling of the cordage, and the hoarse thunder of the surges, striving like savage beasts for our destruction⁸.

Inverted.

8. Close beside her, faintly moaning, fair and young, a soldier lay,
Torn with shot and pierced with lances, bleeding slow his life away⁸.

ANALYSIS & PARSING.—1. *Truth* is the subject-nominative, and it is modified by the participial phrase *crushed to earth.* 5. *Done* is here a participle rather than an *infinitive*. It is sometimes difficult to determine whether a word in this construction is a participle, or an infinitive with *to be* understood before it. Be governed by the sense. 8. This is one of the sentences in which it is hard to determine what makes the subject, and what makes the predicate. Perhaps the division is properly made thus: *A soldier, fair and young, torn with shot and pierced with lances,* | *lay close beside her, faintly moaning, and slowly bleeding away his life.* See p. 114.

6. Infinitives.

1. Contributions to relieve the sufferers, were sent in⁸. N i r o + V b. 2. The book to be adopted by us, should be compared with others of the same kind⁸. 3. Persuade Mary to let him have his books⁸. 4. Let us have some of these clams cooked for supper⁸.

ANALYSIS & PARSING.—1. *Contributions* is limited by the infinitive phrase *to relieve the sufferers.* 4 *Cooked* presents here again the difficulty of deciding between the perf. pass. participle and the pres. pass. infinitive. It is rather the infinitive.

7. Adjuncts.
Simple.

1. The roar of the lion was heard⁸. r N d + V. 2. She bought a house with its furniture⁸. 3. The promises of Hope are

sweeter than roses in the bud, and far more flattering to expectation˟. 4. The sailors did not like the idea of being treated soˢ. 5. There is a flower about to bloomˢ. 6. The question of who is to lead them, was next discussed˟.

Complex.

7. A Gothic cathedral is a blossoming in stone, subdued by the insatiable desire of harmony in manˢ. 8. The gold in a piece of quartz from the mines of California, weighed several poundsˢ.

Compound.

10. The large elm between the house and the river, seems to be the king of the forest˓. 11. Brazil is regarded as a land of mighty rivers and virgin forests, palm-trees and jaguars, anacondas and alligators, howling monkeys and screaming parrots, diamond-mines, revolutions, and earthquakesˢ.

ANALYSIS & PARSING.—1. *Roar* is modified by the adjunct *of the lion.* 5. *About* governs the infinitive after it. Compare with "*About the house*"—*nearness.* 6. *Of* governs the clause after it. 8. *Weigh* is usually parsed as intransitive; and the object after it is disposed of by a Rule corresponding to our Rule VI. But *weigh* fundamentally signifies *to lift,* as in the phrase "*to weigh* anchor;" and I therefore incline to think it should be parsed as transitive. 10. *Between the house and the river,* is an adjunct that is inseparably compound in its object.

8. Clauses.

1. The honeysuckles which bloom round our portico, are deliciously fragrant˟. $S = Cc = rNc + Vba$. 2. The man who sows his field, trusts in God˟. 3. Self-denial is the sacrifice which virtue must make˟. 4. We encamped by a limpid rivulet, that purled over the pebbles˟. 5. He paid more for the flowers and gems which he bought, than they are worth˟. 6. 'Tis the land where the orange and citron grow˟. 7. There is plain proof that⁵ he is guilty˟. 8. The man with whom love is a sentiment, ever yearns for a home of his own˟. 9. He who said nothing, had the better of it, and got what he wanted˟.

10. As one that runs in haste, and leaps over a fence, may fall into a pit, on the other side, which he did not see; so is the man who plunges suddenly into any action before he sees the consequences˟.

Inverted and Elliptical.

11. Whom ye ignorantly worship, him declare I unto you˟. 12. We have no such laws as those by which he was tried in the State from which he came˟. $C c c' c''$. 'Tis the land I love˟.

Abridged.

13. She turned,—a reddening rose' in bud,
   Its calyx half withdrawn,—
  Her cheek on fire with damasked blood
   Of girlhood's glowing dawn!—*Holmes.*

ANALYSIS & PARSING.—1. *The honeysuckles are deliciously fragrant,* is an unmodified independent proposition. *Which bloom round our portico,* is a dependent proposition, used in the sense cf an adjective describing *honeysuckles*. 5. *Than* has here a construction similar to that of the relative *as;* but it is probably best to supply *that is which.* 8. *With* shows the relation between *love* and *whom*, rather than between *is* and *whom.* Nearly equivalent to *whose love.* 10. *As* and *so* are correlatives. The principal correlatives are *such—as, such—that, so—that, so—as, as—as, as—so, the—the,* (comparative)—*than.* Clauses, joined by correlatives, sometimes modify each other; but, in most cases, only one of the clauses is strictly the modifier. "As you sow, so you shall reap." Here the reaping, not the sowing, is described. 13. *Its calyx half withdrawn,* is an absolute phrase, used here in the sense of a relative clause describing *rose. Her cheek (being) on fire,* etc., is an absolute phrase, used here for an adverbial clause of manner or cause, and modifying *turned.*

Adverbial Elements.
1. Objectives.
Nouns and Pronouns.

1. Birds build nests^s. N + V o.   2. The soil produces corn, tobacco, hemp, wheat, and grass^s.   3. Here he brought her^s the choicest food, the finest clothing, mats for her bed, and sandal-oil to perfume herself with^s.   4. The hurricane even tore down enclosures that had been lately made, trees that had stood for ages, and mansions that had been built of stone^x.

Infinitive Phrases.

1. I like to study^s. N + V i^o.   2. We preferred to remain at home, and learn our lessons^s.   3. He intended to move to the West, to purchase him a farm, and to end his days on it in peace and quiet^s.

Clauses.

1. I believe that he is honest and industrious^x. N + V c^o.
2. Who can tell where this war will end?^{x} 3. Every one must have noticed how much more amiable some children are than others^x.   4. She saw that we were tired, and needed some refreshment^x.   5. Tell us not, sir, that we are weak, unable to cope with so formidable an adversary^x.   6. They said that Halifax loved the dignity and emolument of office, that while he continued to be president it would be impossible for him to put forth his whole strength against the government, and that to dismiss him would be to set him free from all restraint^x. N+Vc, c'c, c.

ANAL"sis.—*I believe,* is the unmodified principal clause; *that he is honest,* etc., is the dependent clause, used here as the object of *believe.* See Comp. Gram., p. 79.

Inverted and Elliptical.

1. Me glory summons to the martial scene^s.   2. Him well I knew, and every truant knew^c.   3. She gave what she could not sell^x.   4. I know not what to do^s.   5. I have nothing to say^s.
6. "Life," says Seneca, "is a voyage, in the progress of which we are continually changing our scenes"^{x}.   7. O, that those lips had language^x!   8. He bade the stranger^s hail^4:   9. Teach me my own defects to scan^s.

3. To simplify the analysis, *She gave what* may be called the principal clause; *what she could not sell,* the dependent clause, whose predicate modifies or describes the object of the principal clau*se.* (But see p. 130.) 4. *To do,* object of *know ; what,* object of *to do.* 5. *Nothing (that I wish) to say.* Perhaps this idiom is best disposed of, by considering *nothing* the object of both *have* and *to do.* 7. O, *(how much I wish) that,* etc.

2. Predicate-Nominatives.
Nouns and Pronouns.

He is a soldier. N + V r t. I have become a farmer. She was appointed governess. Man is a bundle of habits and relations*. This aunt Betsy⁷ was the neatest and most efficient piece of human machinery that ever operated in forty places at once˟. Tecumseh's brother was the priest and prophet of the tribe*. A poor relation is the most irrelevant thing in nature, an odious approximation, a haunting conscience, a perpetually recurring mortification, a drawback on your rising, a stain in your blood, a drain on your purse, and a more intolerable drain on your pride*. 1. The brooks ran nectar⁷. 2. Towards the earth's centre is down⁷. 3. He is tired of being a loafer*. 4. I knew it to be him*. Where are the flowers, the fair young flowers, that lately sprang and stood, In softer airs and brighter light, a beauteous sisterhood!*

Infinitives.—To venture in was to die*. Their service was, to grind the corn and carry the baggage*. The best way to preserve health, is, to be careful about diet and exercise*.

Clauses.—5. My impression is, that you will succeed˟. The law should be, that he who can not read should not vote˟. The excuse was, that the army had not been well enough equipped, that the roads were too bad, and that the supplies were deficient˟.

Inverted and Elliptical.—6. I shall be all anxiety, till I know what⁷ his plans are˟. A joy thou art and a wealth to all*. We stand the latest, and, if we fall, the last, experiment⁷ of self-government˟.

3. Adjectives.

You are studious. N + V a. She was considered beautiful. Her countenance looked mild and gentle*. The question now before Congress, is practical as death, enduring as time, and high as human destiny˟. Envy is so base and detestable, so vile in its original, and so pernicious in its effects, that the predominance of almost any other passion is to be preferred˟. Blennerhasset is described as having been amiable and refined, and a passionate lover⁷ of music*. To bleach is to make white.—*Webster.* Correct the heart, and all will go right˟.—*Porteus.*

Inverted and Elliptical.—Lovely art thou, O Peace! Large, glossy, and black hung the beautiful fruit*. Green's the sod, and cold the clay˟.

4. Adverbs.

Verbs Modified.—He spoke eloquently. N + V b. The net was curiously woven. The bird flew rapidly away*. What he did, he did patiently, accurately, and thoroughly˟. 7. Drink deep, or taste not the Pierian spring˟.

Adjectives Modified.—The work is highly useful. r N + V b a. The well is deep enough. How various, how animated, how full of interest is the survey*! I had never seen any thing quite so beautiful before*.

ANALYSIS & PARSING.—1. To *nectar*, Rule IV is usually applied; but the sense seems to require Rule VII. The brooks *were* nectar. 2. *Toward the earth's centre*, noun. So, "For me to go, is impossible." 3. *Loafer*, nom. absol.; cut off from *He* by a governing word. 4. For want of a better name, call *him* a *predicate-substantive*, not a *predicate-nominative*. 5. *Is, that you will succeed*, is the entire predicate; *is* is the predicate-verb, limited by the explanatory clause *that you*, etc., which is used here in the sense of a predicate-nominative. 6. *All* is an adjective belonging to *I*. 7. *Deep*, remnant of an adverbial modifier; therefore an adverb. (See Comp. Gram., p. 248.) N. B. "I am *here*," adv.; "I am *near*," adj. Very little difference in analogy.

Adverbs Modified.—We marched rather slowly. You have come altogether too soon. The car runs not quite fast enough.

Clauses modifying adverbially.

The child seemed to recline on its mother's bosom, as some infant blossom on its parent stem^x. The cottage stood where the mountain shadows fell when the sun was declining^x. Remember, while you are deliberating, the season now so favorable may pass away, never to return^x. When misfortunes overtake you, when sickness assails you, and when friends forsake you, religion will be your greatest comfort^x. The farther we went, the worse we fared^x.

Inverted and Elliptical.

Up soars the lark, the lyrical poet of the sky^s. Here, all is confusion; there, all is order and beauty^c. When young, life's journey I began^x.

More and more richly the rose-heart keeps glowing,
Till from its nourishing stem it is riven^x.

5. Participles.

He walks limping. N + V p. They lay concealed^s. The oak fell shivered by lightning^s. He went on his way rejoicing. Our recruits stood shivering, and rubbing their hands, in groups on the deck of the boat^s. Now the bright morning star, day's harbinger, comes dancing from the east^s.

6. Infinitives.

Verbs Modified.—The child seemed to sleep. r N + V i. She was supposed to be rich^s. He was known to have assisted the editor^s. Here jasmines spread their silver flowers, to deck the wall or weave the bower^v. To curb him, to stand up against him, we want arms of the same kind^v.

Adjectives Modified.—She is rather young to go to school^s. It is a thing not easy to be done^s. Pope was not content to please; he desired to excel, and therefore always did his best^c.

Adverbs Modified.—It is too badly done to last^s. It was so bright as to dazzle our eyes^s. He proceeded too cautiously to fall into such a trap^s.

7. Adjuncts.

Verbs Modified.—I am in trouble. N + V d. Deliver us from evil. You are suspected of having been negligent^s. Is there not a display of infinite goodness, in the vicissitudes of the seasons?^{s} Religion dwells not in the tongue, but in the heart^s or ^{c} These two hundred drachmas will, in a little while, rise to four thousand^s. This will depend on who he is^x.

Adjectives Modified.—Let us be watchful of our liberties^s. He is indolent about every thing^s. They were invincible in arms^s.

Inverted and Elliptical.

In the same cradle was I rocked, and by the same maternal hand.^{s} or ^{c} On that plain, in rosy youth, they had fed their father's flocks^s. One hot summer's morning, a little cloud rose out of the sea, and glided lightly, like a playful child, through the blue sky, and the wide earth, which lay parched and languishing from the long drought^x. By fairy hands their knell is rung^s. Come, go with me the jungle through^c. According to some ancient philosophers, the sun quenches his flames in the ocean. (Supply *To believe*, etc.; for the sun does not set according to, etc.)

8. Clauses.

I came that I might assist you.^{x} I am afraid that he will not return^x. He was assured that every thing should be attended to^x.

This is merely a general class of modifications, including objective clauses, predicate-nominative clauses, adverbial clauses, and occasionally a clause that can not well be brought under any one of these three heads.

☞ *Connectives* and *independent elements* have been sufficiently shown elsewhere. See p. 107

Simple Sentences.

A hollow tree sheltered us from the storm.° Heaven lies about us in our infancy. Bad education and bad example increase greatly our natural depravity. All vice infatuates and corrupts the judgment. The surest way to lose power, is to abuse it. London, the capital of England, is the largest and richest city in the world. Italy is noted for its delightful climate, its beautiful scenery, and its historical recollections. He not only forgave him, but sent him home loaded with benefits. George Washington was born in Virginia, on the 22d of February, 1732. Who shall ask me for a passport at the grave of Washington? True politeness is modest, unpretending, and generous. To be without wants, is the prerogative of God only. It is too often the fate of labor, to be oppressed by capital. O blessed Health! thou art above all gold and jewels. Every day sends out, in quest of pleasure and distinction, some heir fondled in ignorance and flattered into pride. Generally speaking, large bodies move slowly.† Cats and dogs catch and eat rats and mice.‡

* This is a simple declarative sentence. The entire subject is *A hollow tree;* the entire predicate, *sheltered us from the storm*. *Tree* is the subject-nominative, modified by the adjective *hollow*, and *hollow tree* is modified by the article *A*. *Sheltered* is the predicate-verb, modified by the object *us*, and by the adjunct *from the storm*. *Storm* is modified by the article *the*, and connected to *sheltered* by the preposition *from*. † This is a simple sentence: the phrase *Generally speaking* is rather independent, though it stands as the remnant and representative of a dependent clause. ‡ This is a simple sentence; notwithstanding it has a compound subject, and a compound predicate with a compound object.

Complex Sentences.

Ah! who can tell how hard it is to climb
The steep where Fame's proud temple shines afar?°

No pleasure can be innocent from which our health suffers. When all is composed and quiet within us, the discharge of our duties is easy. A writer in physic, of the first rank, asserts that our diet is the chief cause of all our diseases. Be not discontented if you meet not with success at first. Beware lest thou sin. Show not your teeth, unless you can bite. I were to blame, were I to do so. As the flower springs and perishes, so does man. The deeper the well, the cooler the water. The value we set upon life, is seen by what we do to preserve it. Whatever is done skillfully, appears to be done well. There is not a more pleasing emotion in the heart than gratitude. I went because I was invited. To chirp is the first sound that a young bird utters. I consider a human soul, without education, like a marble in the quarry; which shows none of its inherent beauties, until the skill of the polisher fetches out the colors, makes the surface shine, and discovers every ornamental cloud, vein, and spot, that runs through it. What that principle of life is which we call soul; how it is distinguished from mere animal life; how it is connected with the body; and in what state it subsists when its bodily functions cease,—

are among those unsolvable questions with which nature everywhere abounds. For additional examples, see pp. 120-9.

* This is a complex interrogative sentence. The interjection *Ah* is independent in construction. *Who can tell* is the principal clause; *how hard it is to climb the steep*, is the primary dependent clause, which modifies the verb *can tell*, in the sense of a noun in the objective case; and *where Fame's proud temple shines afar*, is the secondary dependent clause, modifying *steep*, in the sense of an adjective.

Clauses of Complex Sentences abridged into Phrases.

Dependent clauses can frequently be abridged into *absolute phrases, participial phrases, infinitive phrases,* or *adjuncts*.

When Cæsar had crossed the Rubicon, Pompey prepared for battle^x. Cæsar having crossed the Rubicon, Pompey prepared for battle*. Since I had nothing else to do, I went^x. Having nothing else to do, I went*. When I had eaten my dinner, I returned to the store. Having eaten my dinner, I returned to the store. She did not know what she should say. She did not know what to say. It was requested that he should stay. He was requested to stay. I begged him that he would go with us. I begged him to go with us. You will suffer from cold, if you remain here. You will suffer from cold, by remaining here. As we approached the house, we saw that the enemy were retreating. On approaching the house, we saw the enemy retreating.

Compound Sentences.

What in me is dark, illumine; what is low, raise and support.*

Times change, and we change with them. Connecticut river yields the best shad, and Connecticut girls know best how to cook them. At this he laughed, and so did we: the jests of the rich are ever successful. He said nothing more, nor did I. To be content with what is sufficient, is the greatest wisdom; and he who increases his riches, increases his cares; but a contented mind is a hidden treasure which trouble can not find. The son, as well as the father, is expert in business. Strong proofs, not a loud voice, produce conviction. The slothful man is a burden to himself; he loiters about, and knows not what to do; his days pass away like the shadow of a cloud, and he leaves behind him no mark for remembrance; his body is diseased for want of exercise; his mind is darkened, and his thoughts are confused; he wishes for action without the power to move, and longs for knowledge but has no application. A rose—I know not how it came there—lay on my book.

> Man is the rugged lofty pine,
>   That frowns o'er many a wave-beat shore;
> Woman's the slender, graceful vine
> Whose clasping tendrils round it twine,
>   And deck its rough bark sweetly o'er.†

* This is a compound imperative sentence, consisting of two complex members. The subject of the first member is *thou* understood; the entire predicate is *illumine what in me is dark*, and the predicate-verb is *illumine*, modified by *what in me is dark*, as the entire object, and by *that*, comprehended in *what*, as the simple object; *that* is modified by the adjunct *in me*. *Which*, comprehended in *what*, is the subject of the dependent clause, and *is dark* is the predicate. (Thus analyze the rest.) † This is a compound declarative sentence, consisting of two complex members, of which the final clause in the latter has a compound predicate.

ELEGY

WRITTEN IN A COUNTRY CHURCHYARD.[*]

1.

THE curfew tolls the knell of parting day;
  The lowing herd wind[a] slowly o'er the lea;
The ploughman homeward plods his weary way,
  And leaves the world to darkness and to me.

2.

Now fades the glimmering landscape on the sight,
  And all the air a solemn stillness holds,
Save where the beetle wheels his droning flight,
  And drowsy tinklings lull the distant folds;

3.

Save that, from yonder ivy-mantled tower,
  The moping owl does to the moon complain
Of such, as[b] wandering near her secret bower,
  Molest her ancient, solitary reign.

4.

Beneath those rugged elms, that yew-tree's shade,
  Where heaves the turf in many a mouldering heap,
Each in his narrow cell forever laid,
  The rude forefathers of the hamlet sleep.

5.

The breezy call of incense-breathing Morn,
  The swallow twittering from the straw-built shed,
The cock's shrill clarion, or the echoing horn,
  No more shall rouse them from their lowly bed.

6.

For them no more the blazing hearth shall burn,
  Or busy housewife ply her evening care;
No children run to lisp their sire's return,
  Or climb his knees the envied kiss to share.

7.

Oft did the harvest to their sickle yield,
  Their furrow oft the stubborn glebe has broke[c];
How jocund did they drive their team afield!
  How bowed the woods beneath their sturdy stroke!

---

[*] Taken from the author's last edition, and carefully compared with the most important editions issued since.

  (a) See Kerl's Comprehensive Grammar, p. 211. (b) *As* is generally a relative pronoun, after *such, many,* or *same;* and *that* is a relative pronoun, when it has the sense of *who, whom,* or *which.* (c) See Comp. Gram., p. 334.

8.

Let not Ambition mock their useful toil,
　Their homely joys, and destiny obscure;
Nor Grandeur hear, with a disdainful smile,
　The short and simple annals of the poor.

9.

The boast of heraldry, the pomp of power,
　And all that beauty, all that wealth, e'er gave,
Await alike the inevitable hour:
　The paths of glory lead but to the grave.

10.

Nor you, ye proud, impute to these the fault,
　If Memory o'er their tomb no trophies raise,
Where through the long-drawn aisle and fretted vault
　The pealing anthem swells the note of praise.

11.

Can storied urn or animated bust
　Back to its mansion call the fleeting breath?
Can Honor's voice provoke the silent dust,
　Or Flattery soothe the dull, cold ear of death?

12.

Perhaps in this neglected spot is laid
　Some heart once pregnant with celestial fire;
Hands that the rod of empire might have swayed,
　Or waked to ecstasy the living lyre.

13.

But Knowledge to their minds her ample page,
　Rich with the spoils of time, did ne'er unroll;
Chill Penury repressed their noble rage,
　And froze the genial current of the soul.

14.

Full many a gem of purest ray serene,
　The dark, unfathomed caves of ocean bear;
Full many a flower is born to blush unseen,
　And waste its sweetness on the desert air.

15.

Some village Hampden, that, with dauntless breast,
　The little tyrant of his field withstood—
Some mute, inglorious Milton, here may rest;
　Some Cromwell, guiltless of his country's blood.

16.

The applause of listening senates to command,
　The threats of pain and ruin to despise,
To scatter plenty o'er a smiling land,
　And read their history in a nation's eyes,

17.

Their lot forbade ; nor circumscribed alone
    Their growing virtues, but their crimes confined,—
Forbade to wade through slaughter to a throne,
    And shut the gates of mercy on mankind;

18.

The struggling pangs of conscious truth to hide,
    To quench the blushes of ingenuous shame,
Or heap the shrine of luxury and pride
    With incense kindled at the Muse's flame.

19.

Far from the madding crowd's ignoble strife,
    Their sober wishes never learned to stray;
Along the cool, sequestered vale of life
    They kept the noiseless tenor of their way.

20.

Yet év'n these bones from insult to protect,
    Some frail memorial still erected nigh,
With uncouth rhymes and shapeless sculpture decked,
    Implores the passing tribute of a sigh.

21.

Their name, their years, spelt by the unlettered Muse,
    The place of fame and elegy supply;
And many a holy text around she strews,
    That teach* the rustic moralist to die.

22.

For who, to dumb Forgetfulness a prey,
    This pleasing, anxious being e'er resigned,
Left the warm precincts of the cheerful day,
    Nor cast one longing, lingering look behind?

23.

On some fond breast the parting soul relies,
    Some pious drops the closing eye requires;
Ev'n from the tomb the voice of Nature cries,
    Ev'n in our ashes live their wonted fires.

24.

For thee, who, mindful of the unhonored dead,
    Dost in these lines their artless tale relate;
If chance, by lonely Contemplation led,
    Some kindred spirit shall inquire thy fate,—

---

* See stanza 14; and Kerl's Comprehensive Grammar, p. 834.

25.

Haply some hoary-headed swain may say,
  "Oft have we seen him at the peep of dawn
Brushing with hasty steps the dews away,
  To meet the sun upon the upland lawn.

26.

"There, at the foot of yonder nodding beech,
  That wreathes its old, fantastic roots so high,
His listless length at noontide would he stretch,
  And pore upon the brook that bubbles by.

27.

"Hard by yon wood, now smiling as in scorn,
  Muttering his wayward fancies he would rove;
Now drooping, woeful wan, like one forlorn,
  Or crazed with care, or crossed in hopeless love.

28.

"One morn I missed him on the customed hill,
  Along the heath, and near his favorite tree;
Another came; nor yet beside the rill,
  Nor up the lawn, nor at the wood, was he.

29.

"The next, with dirges due, in sad array,
  Slow through the church-way path we saw him borne;—
Approach and read (for thou canst read) the lay
  Graved on the stone beneath yon aged thorn."

The Epitaph.

30.

Here rests his head, upon the lap of Earth,
  A youth to Fortune and to Fame unknown;
Fair Science frowned not on his humble birth,
  And Melancholy marked him for her own.

31.

Large was his bounty, and his soul sincere,
  Heaven did a recompense as largely send;
He gave to Misery (all he had) a tear,
  He gained from Heaven ('twas all he wished) a friend.

32.

No farther seek his merits to disclose,
  Or draw his frailties from their dread abode,
(There they alike in trembling hope repose,)
  The bosom of his father and his God.

GRAY.

14. PROSODY.

Punctuation.

Punctuation treats of the points or marks used in writing and printing.

The principal marks of punctuation are the following twelve :—

Period	(.),	Dash	(—),
Colon	(:),	Curves	(( )),
Semicolon	(;),	Brackets	([ ]),
Comma	(,),	Hyphen	(-),
Interrogation-point	(?),	Quotation-marks	(" ") or (' '),
Exclamation-point	(!),	Underscore	(_____).

The period is put at the end of the sentence; the colon, the semicolon, and the comma, are used within it. The period is the greatest pause-mark, the colon the next, the semicolon the next, and the comma the least.

Ex.—"Some books are to be tasted, others to be swallowed, and some few to be chewed and digested: that is, some books are to be read only in parts; others to be read, but not curiously; and some few to be read wholly and with diligence."—*Bacon.*

The **period** is put at the end of every phrase or sentence complete by itself, and not interrogative or exclamatory; also after abbreviations.

Ex.—" John W. Ringgold, Esq., addressed the assembly."

The **colon** is followed by something that has been formally promised; or by what adds, to an already complete sentence, an important remark, illustration, or conclusion.

Ex.—"Of cruelty to animals let the reader take the following specimen : 'Running an iron hook into the intestines of a live animal; presenting this animal to another as his food ; and then pulling up this second creature, and suspending him by the barb in his stomach.'"—*Sidney Smith.*

"Study to acquire the habit of thinking : no study is more important."

In formal letters or documents, it is now generally placed after the introductory address; but, in the familiar style, the comma, or the comma with the dash, is commonly preferred.

Ex.—" Hon. Edward Everett.
   " *Dear Sir:*
    - " I thank you for your, etc.
           " Joseph Story."

" Dear Sir,
  " The latest news from Boston, giving information of, etc.
           " James Madison."

" George W. Taylor, Esq.
   " *Dear Sir,*
    " As you write me to give," etc.

" George W. Taylor, Esq.—*Dear Sir:* As you write me to give my opinion,", etc.—*The Printer.*

The **semicolon** separates parts of a sentence that are too closely related for the colon, and too loose in sense for the comma, or that have the comma within them; and sometimes it separates clauses or phrases similarly construed, and accumulated into one sentence.

Ex.—" That the world is overrun with vice, can not be denied ; but vice, however predominant, has not yet gained unlimited dominion."—*Johnson.* " He is, indeed, a horse; and all other jades you may call beasts.—*Shakespeare*. "Every thing has its time to flourish; every thing grows old; every thing passes away." "Though deep, yet clear; though gentle, yet not dull."—*Denham*.

The **comma** is used where a slight pause is needed.

1. Three or more serial terms, or two terms without their connective, are separated by the comma.

Ex.—"*Hedges, groves, orchards*, and *gardens*, were in bloom." "Far above us towered an iron-bound coast, *dark, desolate, barren*, and *precipitous*, against which the *long, rolling* swell of the Pacific broke with a *dull and disheartening* roar." So, where the verb is understood; as, "Indolence produces poverty; and *poverty, misery*."

Two long predicate phrases, even when the conjunction is expressed, are also generally separated; as, "The prairies of Iowa are covered with a rich coat of grass, and not unfrequently interspersed with hazel thickets."

2. Two parts, when contrasted or emphatically distinguished, or when a part of one might be improperly referred also to the other, are separated by the comma.

Ex.—"*To soften, not to wound*, the heart." "It is used so, but erroneously." "*He holds, and ever has held*, the legal title." "Othello, and Prince Hamlet." "He retreated, and loaded his gun."

3. A word, phrase, or clause, that is parenthetic, or that breaks the connection of parts closely related, is set off by the comma.

Ex.—"Moral culture, *especially in youth*, is of the greatest importance." "They set out early, and, *before the dawn of day*, arrived at the destined place." "Adjectives, *when something depends on them*, should, *with their adjuncts*, be set off by the comma."

4. A phrase used as an adverbial or adjective element and adding a distinct idea, is set off by the comma when it is not in close connection with what it modifies, and especially when removed from it by inversion.

Ex.—"*In a central region,* | *midway on the continent,* | *though somewhat nearer the Pacific than the Atlantic Ocean,* | *at an elevation of nearly 7,500 feet,* | lies the remarkable valley of Mexico, *encircled by a colossal rampart of the hardest rocks,* | *and forming a circumference of about 67 leagues,* | *with a sky of the deepest blue, a serene atmosphere, and a magnificent landscape.* Apply, also, rules 3d, 2d, and 1st.

But when such a phrase is merely restrictive, and stands in close connection with what it modifies, it is not usually set off; as, "Gladly would I pour *into thy bosom* | *the balm of consolation*." What is *restrictive*, merely *modifies* an idea; what is not restrictive, *adds* an idea, or is *explanatory*.

5. Independent or absolute words, and words in apposition, are generally, with what belongs to them, set off by the comma. See pp. 68, 69, 72.

Ex.—"And so, *Don Gomez*, you will accompany us." "*Shame being lost*, all virtue is lost." "*O, yes, sir*, I do." "Paul, *the apostle of the Gentiles*."

6. A merely explanatory noun after *or*, or a part relating to each of two or more separated parts, is set off by the comma.

Ex.—"The marmot, *or ground-hog*, resembles the raccoon." "This is the first, though perhaps not the best, *of my books*."

7. The comma is used to separate the clauses of a compound sentence, when they are too closely related for the semicolon.

Ex.—"Columbus, who discovered America, was a Genoese." "There mountains rise, and circling oceans flow."

But when a clause or phrase is *restrictive*, that is, depends closely on something else, in the sense of a noun, an adjective, or an adverb, it is not set off.

Ex.—"He was a man | whom nothing could turn aside from the path | which duty pointed out." (Restrictive relative clauses.) "I will sell you *whatever you wish to buy.*" "It is probable *that you are very nearly right.*" "Go *when it suits you.*"

8. When the entire subject is a clause, or a long participial or infinitive phrase; when it has a clause, a long adjunct or other similar phrase, or p rts requiring the comma; when it ends with a verb, or with a noun that might improperly be read as the nominative; or when a word precedes the verb, that would otherwise be of doubtful character or reference,—it seems best to separate the subject from its predicate.

Ex.—" That one bad example spoils many good precepts, is well known." "He that has much nose, thinks every one speaks of it." "Whatever improves him, delights him." "To be totally indifferent to praise or censure, is a real defect in character." "For me to furnish him so large and expensive an outfit, is utterly impossible." "His having been seen in the neighborhood, was the ground of suspicion." "Honor, wealth, and pleasure, seduce the heart." "Necessity, that great excuse for human frailty, breaks through all law." There is a strong tendency to omit the comma from before the predicate of such sentences as the first seven of the foregoing.

9. When the predicate-nominative is a long clause or infinitive phrase, and immediately follows the verb *be*, it is usually set off by the comma, especially when it has the air of importance, and might be made the subject.

Ex.—" One of the greatest secrets in composition is, to know when to be simple." "The consequence is, that most animals have acquired a fear of man." "The question that is to be discussed to-night, is, 'Would the Extension of our Territory endanger the Perpetuity of our Government?'"

The **interrogation-point** is placed after every direct question.

Ex.—" What books do you like best?" But, "He asked me what books I like best."

The **exclamation-point** is placed after what expresses some sudden or strong feeling; as, surprise, wonder, joy, grief, anger, or horror.

Ex.—" Left his *bed* and *board!* He never had any!"

It is also placed after unusually earnest or solemn addresses, and generally after interjections.

Ex.—" Spare me, O merciful God!" "Ah! few shall part where many meet."

The **dash** generally denotes emphasis or unusual structure.

1. It is placed after what is left unfinished, generally from interruption.

Ex.—" 'HERE LIES THE GREAT'—False marble! where?"—*Young.*

2. It is generally used in sentences that are fragmentary and emotional.

Ex.—" The pulse fluttered—stopped—went on—throbbed—stopped again—moved—stopped.—Shall I go on?—No."—*Sterne.*

3. It is used to show an unexpected turn in the sentence; and, in dialogue without names or breaks, it marks the transition from one speaker to another. See last example.

Ex.—" If thou art he, so much respected once—but, oh! how fallen! how degraded!"—*Milton.*

4. It is now generally used to set off a parenthesis, especially when emphatic, or when there are other points within it.

Ex.—" He was dressed—and, indeed, so were they nearly all—in coarse homespun."

5. It is often used before echoes, or where *that is* or *namely* is understood; and also after a loose series of particulars, leading to an important conclusion.

Ex.—" Angry thoughts canker the mind to the worst temper in the world,—that of fixed malice and revenge." See 8th rule, under comma.

6. It is placed after side-heads, and generally before authorities when in the same line with the end of the paragraph.

Ex.—"THE ABUSE OF THE IMAGINATION.—He who can not command his thoughts, must not hope to control his actions."—*Jane Taylor.*

The **curves** enclose something thrown in hastily or incidentally, and so little related to the chief matter that it may be omitted.

Ex.—"Pride, in some disguise or other (often a secret to the proud man himself), is the most ordinary spring of action among men."—*John Wilson.*

The **brackets** [the writer means the *hooks* used in printing] enclose what is inserted by another person; but authors sometimes enclose with them their own explanations, especially when these stand detached, or by themselves. [*Brachium*, in Latin, denotes an arm.]

The **hy'phen** is placed at the end of a syllable of a word so long that a part of it must be put into the next line. It is also used to separate the parts of compound words that do not coalesce, in pronunciation, like mere syllables of the same word; as, *tender-hearted, electro-magnetism.*

The **quotation-marks** enclose what is formally presented as the language of another person. "Single quotation-marks enclose a 'quotation within a quotation'."

The **underscore** is a line used only in writing. It is drawn under words once, to denote *slanting* or *Italic letters;* twice, to denote SMALL CAPITALS; three times, to denote CAPITALS; and four times, to denote *ITALIC CAPITALS.* Words are thus printed for the sake of emphasis or distinction.

Capital Letters.

[This subject does not properly belong to either Punctuation or Prosody. It is inserted here, merely because this seems the best place for it.]

A *capital letter* should begin—
1. The first word of every distinct sentence or phrase.
2. The first word of every direct quotation or saying. See p. 103.
3. The first word of every line of poetry. See p. 131.
4. Every name of the Deity; as, the Almighty, the Supreme Being.
   Also personal pronouns when applied to the Deity, except when used in connection with their antecedents; as, "I turn to Thee." "God provides for all *his* creatures."
5. Every proper name, and the titles that may be used with it; each chief word of a phrase used like a proper name; and most words derived from proper names.
6. Titles of office, honor, or distinction; also any very important word, especially when it denotes the principal subject of discourse.
7. The name of an object personified, when it is used like a proper noun; as, "O Grave! where is thy victory?"
8. The words *I* and *O* should always be capitals.

Figures.

A **met'aphor** is the name of one object given to another, on account of some *resemblance* between the objects.

Ex.—"The *ear* of a pot" looks like an ear on a head; but the "*key* of an arithmetic" does not look like a key, yet it serves to unlock the mysteries of the arithmetic. "Life is an *isthmus* between two eternities."

A **meton'ymy** is the name of one object given to another, on account of some *relation* between the objects. The chief of these relations are those of *cause* and *effect*, *container* and *thing contained*, *sign* and *thing signified*.

Ex.—" I have read *Shakespeare ;*" *i. e.*, his works. " We drank but one *bottle ;*" *i. e.*, what was in one bottle. " My son, give me thy *heart;*" *i. e.*, thy affections.
" Here the *sword* and *sceptre* rust ;
Earth to earth, and dust to dust !"—*Croly.*

Synec'doche is the figure by which we give the name of a part to the whole, or that of the whole to a part.

Ex.—" We bought a hundred *head* of sheep." " Give us, this day, our daily *bread ;*" *i. e.*, our food. "They paid my price in paltry *gold ;*" *i. e.*, in money.

Nearly one half of all the meanings of words are but *faded* figures,— faded metaphors, faded metonymies, faded synecdoches.

Versification.

Versification is the act or the art of making verse.

Verse is beautiful language keeping time like music.

Verse consists of measured lines, each having seldom less than two syllables or more than twenty-two.

Each measure consists of two or three syllables, has a stress, or accent, on the first or the last syllable, and is called a *foot.*

The principal feet are *four ;* the *iambus*, the *anapest*, the *trochee*, and the *dactyl.*

Iambic verse is divisible into little portions of two syllables each, accented on the second syllable ; *anapestic verse*, of three syllables each, accented on the last syllable ; *trochaic verse*, of two syllables each, accented on the first syllable ; and *dactylic verse*, of three syllables each, accented on the first syllable.

Iambic Verse.—1. Afár. 2. The stárs shone bríght. 3. Thou moón that rúl'st the níght. 4. The woóds are húshed, the wáters rést. 5. How swéet, at éve, the víllage múrmur róse ! 6. The déw was fálling fást, the stárs begán to blínk. 7. The flámes that lit the báttle's wréck, shone roúnd him ó'er the déad.

Anapestic Verse.—1. From afár. 2. Like a róse pearled in déw. 3. I am mónarch of all I survéy. 4. At the clóse of the dáy when the hámlet is still.

Trochaic Verse.—1. Túrning. 2. Géntly flówing. 3. Gó where glóry wáits thée. 4. Dó not sáy that lífe is fléeting. 5. Cóme, O, cóme with mé ; the moón is béaming. 6. On' a moúntain strétched benéath a hóary wíllow. 7. Lét us séek the grássy bánk by lófty máples sháded. 8. Béams of noón, like búrning lánces, thróugh the trée-tops flásh and glísten.

Dactylic Verse.—1. Féarfully. 2. Bird of the wílderness. 3. Pléasures in éndless varíety. 4. Cóuld he but háve a glimpse ínto futúrity.

To each of the foregoing species of lines, we sometimes find a part of another foot added.

Ex.—" Réstless mórtals tóil for *naúght.*"
" Far adówn the long aísle sácred músic is stréam-*ing.*"

Most verse is still further divided into agreeable portions, by making some of the feet, or parts of feet, answer to each other by similarity of sound. These corresponding sounds are called *rhymes*, and they occur usually at the ends of the lines. Verse that has no rhyme, is called *blank verse.*

What can you say of Punctuation? The points in general? The period? The colon? The semicolon? The comma? The interrogation-point? The exclamation-point? The dash? The curves? The brackets? The hyphen? The underscore? Capital letters? Metaphor? Metonymy? Synecdoche? The meanings of words? Versification? Verse? Feet? Iambic verse? Anapestic? Trochaic? Dactylic? Examples. Of syllables that overrun the line? Rhyme? Blank verse?

☞ The subject of capital letters and that of punctuation, when taught merely by rules, and a few examples to illustrate them, are not sufficiently tangible to be comprehended by pupils; I have therefore annexed a series of exercises, that, I trust, will teach the pupil more about these things than is generally learned from grammars.

Capital Letters.—Exercises.

Copy the following examples, and apply the rules given on p. 138 for the use of capital letters; also correct the examples which are incorrect, or the paragraphs which follow the stars:—

1. No, my son; a life of independence is generally a life of virtue. It is that which fits the soul for every generous flight of humanity, freedom, and friendship. Do not serenity, health, and plenty attend the desire of rising by labor? Lovely, far more lovely, is the sturdy gloom of laborious poverty than the fawning smile of flattery; and the man who can thank himself alone for the happiness he enjoys, is truly blest.

* this terrible chasm must be filled up. but how? here is a list of proprietors. choose from the wealthiest, in order that the smallest number of citizens may be sacrificed.

"The gunpowder overboard! Out with the boat. Here."

* for Rent or Sale. total, $25. balance, $9.25.

Exercises.

2. Solomon said, "Pride goeth before destruction." They shouted, "Victory!" He answered, No. Christianity does not spread a feast before us, and then come with a "Touch not, taste not, handle not." One truth is clear: Whatever is, is right.

Resolved, That we endorse the course pursued by our delegates, etc.

* Remember this ancient maxim: "know thyself." And, "this to me!" he said. Every tongue shall exclaim with heart-felt joy, welcome, welcome! La Fayette. The question, then, will naturally arise, how is the desired improvement to be effected? Ah! that maternal smile, it answers—yes.

Be it enacted, that, after the 1st of August, 1862, a tax, etc.

Exercises.

3. Now bright the sunbeam on St. Lawrence smiles,
Her million lilies, and her thousand isles.

* Believe not each aspersing tongue,
as most weak people do;
but still conclude that story wrong
which ought not to be true.

Exercises.

4. The Most High; the Infinite One; Providence; the All-wise; the Son of God; our Lord Jesus Christ; the Father, the Son, and the Holy Ghost; God and his angels. To Him be the honor and the glory. Oh, give relief, and Heaven will bless your store. The Son of man shall come in the glory of his Father.

* The holy spirit; the eternal; the omnipotent; the king of kings, and lord of lords; the judge of the world; our creator; our savior; great parent of good. O thou all-seeing searcher of our hearts! To him who is the friend of the widow and the orphan.

When the words *heaven* and *hell* are used in their most ordinary sense, they begin with small letters; but when used in a specific sense, or when *Heaven* denotes God, they begin with capitals. The Indian always says, "Great Spirit," or uses both words to denote God; but when Pope wrote, "Thou great First

Cause," he used *great* in its ordinary descriptive sense. The *King of kings* shows preëminently God's relation to worldly kings; but the *Angel of Death* does not show the relation of any angel to death. The *Devil* denotes *Satan;* but a *devil* may be simply a bad person or spirit. When the words *god, goddess, deity, divinity*, etc., are applied to the heathen deities, they do not begin with capitals. When *Muses, Graces, Naiads*, etc., are regarded in the splendor of ancient imagination, they are generally favored with capitals; but our own *fairies, sylphs, ghosts, hobgoblins*, etc., are rather too puny and undignified in idea to be thus distinguished.

Exercises.

5. Thomas, Susan, Dr. Jno. B. Johnson, Mrs. Elizabeth B. Browning, Monday, Tuesday, January, February, New York, Pennsylvania, United States, Sandwich Islands, Isle of Man, Long Island, American, Americanism, Roman, Italics, Christian, Jesuits. This out-Herods Herod himself. A Southern man is from the South.

* george, mary, sunday, friday, kentucky, tennessee, august, sept. 10th, rev. henry L gaylor, mr. jones, north America, cape fear, christmas, frenchified, irishman, columbia, maj. holt; jas. m. marlow, esq.

When words derived from proper names have assumed ordinary meanings of the language, and lost their reference to the proper names, they are not usually capitalized; as, *turkey, guinea, damask, colossal, daguerreotype, galvanize, champagne, china-ware.*

Proper names consist chiefly of the names of persons, places, and time. They are therefore very numerous, amounting to millions. And since it is not always easy to make a new and acceptable proper name, a common word or phrase of the language, whose meaning is supposed to suit, is often taken and made a sort of proper name.

A new proper name is often made from an old one, by the addition of some common word; and the common word then generally begins with a capital letter.

Orleans, *New Orleans;* Cambridge, *East Cambridge;* Clinton, *Governor Clinton;* Jefferson, *Jefferson City;* Madison, *Madison Square;* Astor, *Astor House;* Vernon, *Mount Vernon;* Pike, *Pike's Peak;* Mexico, the *Gulf of Mexico;* Magellan, the *Strait of Magellan;* Britain, the *British Channel.*

* Rhode island, Miller's landing, lower California, new Hampshire, Japan sea, Harper's ferry, mount Mitchel, Apollo garden, Lafayette place, Hudson's bay, the bay of Honduras, William and Mary's college, the Indian ocean, lake Ontario, point Barrow, Cook's inlet, Behring's strait, Queen Charlotte's sound.

When a common word or phrase of the language is raised to the dignity of a proper name for a particular object, the word or chief words begin with capital letters.

The Park, Salt River, Great Bear Lake, Lake Superior, the Black Sea, Big Sandy, Land's End, the Cape of Good Hope, the United States, the Western States, the Mountains of the Moon, the Old South Church, the City Hall, a book called—The Temple of Truth.

* The laurel hills, the dead sea, white river, sandy hook, a hill called cedar crest, the lake of the woods, point lookout, the five points, pea ridge, the white sulphur springs, the rocky mountains, union square, central park; on fifth avenue, near spruce street.

The two principles just given, express what seems to be the best usage according to analogy and custom; many writers, however, use not more capital letters than seem absolutely necessary to distinguish the designated objects from others of the same kind.

When objects are very common and comparatively insignificant, we often find that only the specific words, and not the general words—especially when the latter are plural—begin with capital letters; as, "in Cass and Butler counties." The words *county, township, hill, creek, river,* when used in connection with specific words, are not generally commenced with capital letters. *Street* we find written—*Fifth Street, Fifth* and *Madison Streets ; Fifth-street, Walnut-street, Fifth* and *Walnut streets* (the hyphen being omitted from the plural phrase, to show the common reference of *streets* to the two words before it); and, lastly, *Fifth street.* The first two modes are best authorized. The same remark applies occasionally to such words as *place, square, house, church,* etc. But, in all cases, *when the specific word is also a common word of the language, the tendency is, to begin the general word with a capital letter too.*

Callaway county is usually called *Callaway ;* but *Kansas City* is not called *Kansas.* The *Ohio river* is as well denoted by *the Ohio,* which is a sufficient name to call it by, and which implies the word *river ;* but the *Red River* is not called the *Red,* nor is the *Blue Ridge* ever called the *Blue,* for it takes both words to make the name. The *city of New York,* or *New-York city,* is generally called *New York ;* but *Jersey City* needs both words to make the name. *Van Dieman's Land* is not the *land* belonging to Van Diemen. The *lake of Nicaragua* is the *lake* belonging to Nicaragua; but the *Lake of Nicaragua* is merely a name; so, the *Grecian Archipelago. Crabbe's Prairie* was once *Crabbe's prairie.* *Sutter's Mill* is now a little town, and the *mill* is washed away. The *London Times* is a newspaper, and *London times* are something else. The *Planter's House* is simply a hotel, and not the *house* of a *planter.* The *Missouri railroad* is a railroad in Missouri; but the *Missouri Railroad* could be located anywhere. We can see *white mountains* in almost any mountainous country; but the *White Mountains* are in New Hampshire. The *South Pass* denotes not only a *pass,* but also a locality. *Niagara Falls* means not merely a *fall* of water. The *Erie Canal* is wholly a name; but the *Erie and Ohio canal* is understood as being simply the canal between Lake Erie and the Ohio river. The phrases *Elegy in a Country Churchyard, Battle of Hohenlinden, The Task,* are as much the names of particular poems, as *John, James,* and *Henry,* are the names of particular boys. *Lord's Day* is equivalent to *Sunday ;* and *New-Year's Day,* the *Fourth, Good Friday,* or any other holiday, is as much a particular day as *Sunday, Monday,* or any other day of the week.

Exercises.

6. The President, the Vice-President, the Senate, and the House of Representatives; Daniel Webster, Secretary of State; the City Council; the Board of Directors for the Southern Bank; the Vigilance Committee; the Democracy of New Orleans; the Catholics and Protestants; a Methodist; the Supreme Court: the Navy Department; the Auditor of Public Accounts; the Tax Bill; The guests were entertained by Mayor Rice, at his residence, No. 34, Union Place. The flag bore this motto: The Union, the Constitution, and the enforcement of the Laws. "You are old, Father William," the young man replied. Begin your letter thus: Dear Sir, Dear Brother, *or,* My dear Aunt, etc.

* Alexander the great; Charles the second; To Jos. Aikin, esq.; To the secretary of the interior department; gen. Scott and col. Richardson; the southern states; the fourth *number* of the *new monthly ;* John Bull to brother Jonathan.

When I speak of the *Company* or the *Convention,* I mean to guard you against thinking of the wrong one, or to make you think of a particular one. The *Insurrection* was printed with a capital, only while the excitement lasted; but the *Revolution* and the *Reformation* are still matters of interest, and retain their capitals. Our *Constitution* does not refer to our health, nor does our *State* refer to our condition. Missouri is a part of the *South,* though it lies *west.* If the *North, East, South,* and *West,* make the *United States,* then one of these states is a *State.* The *Lunatic Asylum* is a particular and distinguished institution in our State, though there are *lunatic asylums* in most parts of the world.

* I went with him to visit the Lakes;" that is, a celebrated group of lakes. Macaulay calls *Satan*, the *Tempter*, the *Evil Principle*; and he also writes, "the mercenary warriors of the Peninsula," applying the word in a specific sense, or to Spain and Portugal. If I should use the phrase *Old Dominion* as a specific substitute for the proper name *Virginia*, I would use capital letters; but if I should merely call Goldsmith's *Deserted Village* Goldsmith's *great poem*, I would not begin the latter words with capitals. We must often judge whether the specific or titular sense, or the ordinary meaning of the words, is uppermost in the mind, and use capitals or small letters accordingly. *Webster's Speeches* refers to a book, or to their title; while *Webster's speeches* refers simply to the speeches. A chapter in your *history* refers to your life; but a chapter in your *History* refers to a book so named. When I speak of the *principal* of a school, I refer to his duties; but when I speak of the *Principal* of a school, I refer to his title. "Part I, Remark, Observations, Rules of Spelling," refer to certain divisions or headings of a book. Our Club, President, Treasurer, and Secretary, are such in title as well as in fact. The *London Times* says, "Her Majesty, the Prince Consort, the Bride, the Prince of Wales, and other members of the Royal Family, were present." Common folks would not have been thus honored with capitals. An astronomer writes, "The Sun is the centre of the System," because these capitalized words denote subjects of which he treats. And merchants, in their accounts, generally begin with capital letters the names of those things in which they deal.

When entire phrases or sentences are made headings, or otherwise made prominent, only the nouns, the descriptive adjectives, and other important words, are begun with capitals.

ADVERTISEMENT.—"Just published. A Collection of Songs, Duets, Trios, and Choruses. Together with a New and Complete Course of Elementary Instruction, and Lessons in Singing, for the School-room and Social Circle.' Price 62½ cents." In Advertisements and Notices, the liberty of capitalizing is carried to a great and almost indefinite extent.

Exercises.

7. The Wind and the Sun loved the Rose,
But the Rose loved but one ;
For who rocks the wind where it blows,
Or loves not the sun ?—*Bulwer*.

* I hate when vice can bolt her arguments,
And virtue has no tongue to check her pride.

Pride, poverty, and fashion, once undertook to keep house together.

Exercises.

8. O, I understand you now.
* He knew i was there. Such, o music! is thy heavenly power.

The pupil may have noticed, that the names of the *days* of the week and *months* of the year; the chief words in the *titles of books*; the names of *sects, parties*, and *associations*; and, generally, the names of *public bodies*—as, Senate the General Assembly,—are capitalized.

He may also observe, that rules 1st and 2d, are fundamentally one, applying to distinct phrases or sentences; rules 3d and 8th, implying distinction; and rules 4th, 5th, 6th, and 7th, since the words merely designate, or designate honorably, rather than describe by their ordinary meaning.

Capital letters should not be used, where small letters will express the sense as well or better

Punctuation.—Exercises.
Period.

Copy the following examples, and apply the rules; also correct what is incorrect, or the paragraphs after the stars:—

As yet, the forests stand clothed in their dress of undecayed magnificence. The winds, that rustle through their tops, scarcely disturb the silence of the shades below. The mountains and the valleys glow in sunlit verdure.

* give, then, generously and freely recollect, that, in so doing, you are exercising one of the most godlike qualities in your nature go home, and look at your families, smiling in rosy health, and then think of the pale, famine-pinched cheeks of the poor children of Ireland—*S S Prentiss*

For Sale. Opinions of the Press. Dr. Chas. F. Persinger, Chairman. St. Louis, Aug. 1st, 1857. To the Hon. Jas. Fenton.

* Preface Contents Apollo Garden From the *Gentleman's Magazine* "H. Clay Select Speeches of 8vo Price $1.00."

Albany, N. Y., Sept., 1860. Henry Holmes, Esq., addressed the assembly. Sir David Brewster, K. H., LL.D., F. R. S., L. & E. I have two good reasons: 1. I can not give my attention to it; 2. I have no money to invest in it. 15.3 yds. of cloth, for $9.45. (The period is also used to separate decimals from whole numbers, and after enumerative figures or letters.)

* T S Glover, Esq, was called to the chair To Mr and Mrs Lindsay Dr Wm R Rector, Sup't of Com Schools On the 4th inst, he disappeared 3 cwt 2 qrs 5 lbs Let us consider—1 Its soil; 2 Its climate 40 chickens, @ 12c each, cost $4.80

Colon.—Exercises.

Make a proper use of time: the loss of it can never be regained. Make a proper use of time; for the loss of it can never be regained.

* Avoid affectation it is a contemptible weakness.
Honor and shame from no condition rise
Act well your part; there all the honor lies.

The grant was absolute and conclusive: it conceded the land and the islands; the rivers and the harbors; the mines and the fisheries. (Here the sense is, How so? Why so? Explain more fully what you mean.) There are two questions which grow out of this subject: 1st, How far is any sort of classical education useful? 2dly, How far is that particular classical education adopted in this country useful?

* The procession was as follows The President, the Vice-President, the Speaker of the House, etc. All our conduct toward others should be influenced by this important principle Do unto others as you would have them do unto you.

This is the state of man to-day he puts forth
The tender leaves of hope; to-morrow blossoms,
And bears his blushing honors thick upon him;
The third day comes a frost, a killing frost.

Semicolon.—Exercises.

Without dividing, he destroyed party; without corrupting, he made a venal age unanimous.

* The miser grows rich by seeming poor but the extravagant man grows poor by seeming rich.

A salad should be, as to its contents, multifarious; as to its proportions, an artistic harmony; as to its flavor, of a certain pungent taste.

* False in institutions, for he retrograded false in policy, for he debased false in morals, for he corrupted. Listen to the advice of your parents treasure up their precepts respect their riper judgment and endeavor to merit the approbation of the wise and good.

This lovely land, this glorious liberty, these benign institutions, are ours; ours to enjoy, ours to preserve, ours to transmit. Mercer was upright, intelligent, and brave; esteemed as a soldier and beloved as a man, and by none more than by Washington. He is my major-domo; that is, my steward over household affairs.

* Among the oaks I observed many of the most diminutive size some not above a foot in height, yet bearing bunches of acorns. Charles the Twelfth, of Sweden born, 1682 killed by a cannon-ball, 1718. Rio, 9 cents Maracaibo, 12 cents Java, 15 cents.

"I have always," says Ledyard, "remarked that women in all countries are civil and obliging; that they are ever inclined to be gay and cheerful, timorous and modest; and that they do not hesitate, like men, to perform a generous action."

* If thou art a child, and hast ever added a sorrow to the soul or a furrow to the silvered brow of an affectionate parent if thou art a husband, and hast ever caused the fond bosom that ventured its whole happiness in thy arms, to doubt one moment of thy kindness or truth if thou art a friend, and hast ever wronged in thought, or word, or deed, the spirit that generously confided in thee, —then be sure that every unkind look, every ungracious word, every ungentle action, will come thronging back upon thy memory, and knocking dolefully at thy soul then be sure that thou wilt lie down sorrowing and repentant on the grave, and utter the unheard groan, and pour the unavailing tear, more deep, more bitter, because unavailing.

"The pride of wealth is contemptible; the pride of learning is pitiable; the pride of dignity is ridiculous; but the pride of bigotry is insupportable." Here the *dash* would have been too sentimental; the *comma* would have slurred the matter over too lightly; the *colon* would have indicated a different connection in thought; the *period* would have been too deliberate; but the *semicolon* gives due distinction to the parts, and the greatest energy to the whole.

Comma.—Rule I.—Exercises.

Days, months, years, and ages, shall circle away,
And still the vast waters above thee shall roll.

The little, round buds unfolded into broad white leaves. From law arises security; and from security, industry.

* This part of Arabia is populous and fertile; yielding oranges lemons almonds dates figs raisins honey and an abundance of corn cattle sheep and the finest of horses. The little ragged untaught child made me think of the little lonely blossom that is born to wintry days. Hamilton was more declamatory imaginative and poetical; Burr clear pointed concise and compact.

The white-washed wall the nicely sanded floor
The varnished clock that clicked behind the door.

"John, James and William are going to town," implies that I am telling John what the other two boys are doing; and should therefore be, "John, James, and William, are going to town."

Rule II.—Exercises.

Liberal, not lavish, is kind Nature's hand. We often commend, as well as censure, imprudently. Was it you, or the wind, that shut the door? He should, and shall, relinquish his claim. The gleam of the ocean, and vast prairies of verdure, were before me.

* Though grave yet trifling; though submissive vain. John and also his sister went into the country. Is he sick or well? They not only attacked but also captured the army and city. Here all is order; there all is discord. 'Twas certain he could write and cipher too. He went and addressed the crowd. The troops landed and killed a hundred Indians.

Rule III.—Exercises.

No society, of which moral men are not the stamina, can exist long. There, lightly swung, in bowery glades, the honeysuckles twine. They knew their powers not, or, as they learned to know, perverted them to evil.

* Burns however to be justly judged must be estimated by the times in which he lived. She is to be sure a very amiable woman. A virgin of eighteen tall and straight bright and blooming seems to our old age a very delightful object.

Common parenthetic expressions are such as *on the contrary, by no means, without doubt, in general, now and then, in short, for the most part, beyond question, generally speaking,* etc.

Rule IV.—Exercises.

Tired of his toilsome flight, and parched with heat,
He spied, at length, a cavern's cool retreat.

The work is probably not worth the labor and care spent upon it.

* From the hills in his jurisdiction he could behold across the clear waters of a placid sea the magnificent vegetation of Porto Rico which distance rendered still more admirable as it was seen through the transparent atmosphere of the tropics.

The ship Ann Alexander a stanch vessel Captain S. Deblow sailed from New Bedford the 1st of June 1850 for a cruise in the South Pacific in search of whales.

Rule V.—Exercises.

Friend John, what is wanted? And now, sir, what is your conclusion? No, no, Gerald; there are too many of them already. Nocturnal silence reigning, a nightingale began. To be a merchant, the art consists more in getting paid than in making sales.

Wept o'er his wounds, or, tales of sorrow done,
Shouldered his crutch, and showed how fields were won.

* To you Osman I consign half the city; and to you Mustapha the remainder The terms being settled he produced the cash. Front to front their horns locked every muscle strained they were fighting as bulls only can fight. Well to be sure how much I have fagged through!

Rule VI.—Exercises.

The skull, or cranium, protects the brain. Again, we conceive that natural religion, though not a demonstrative, is yet a progressive, science.

* The English dove or cushat is noted for its cooing or murmuring. This street is an important if not the principal highway in the city.

Rule VII.—Exercises.

How wretched, were I mortal, were my state! The rain fell in sheets, the thunder rolled, the lightning flashed fierce and lurid, and the wind swept in gusts over the thicket as if it would uproot it altogether. 'I his small group of our wounded, who were left behind, were captured by a party which lay in ambush.

* Since life is short let us not be too solicitous about the future. The farmer who had never been in a city before and who was therefore most easily duped at once bid on the watch. The variety of wild fruits and flowering shrubs is so great and such the profusion of blossoms with which they are bowed down that the eye is regaled almost to satiety.

Rule VIII.—Exercises.

What pleases, soon becomes popular. He who is much in love with himself, will have few rivals. To be always attentively observing what is passing around them, is one of the means by which men improve their circumstances.

* To maintain a steady course amid all the adversities of life marks a great mind. Family feuds violated friendships and litigation among neighbors are the banes of society. Divide and conquer is a golden principle equally applicable in science and in policy.

Rule IX.—Exercises.

But the question is, are the examples correct in syntax? All that a man gets by lying, is, that he is not believed when he tells the truth. That it is so, can not be denied.

* The great mystery about the theft was that the door was still found locked as before. Our intention is to start early in the morning.

Finally, the comma is put after a word repeated; as, "Home, home! sweet, sweet home!" after a surname followed by the given name; as, "Tyler, George W.": used to separate numbers into periods; as, Population of the United States, 31,443,790 : used to separate words in pairs, that are construed in pairs; as, "Old and young, rich and poor, high and low, attended the meeting:" sometimes used, or not used, according as a word has a conjunctive or an adverbial sense; as, "On these facts, *then*, I *then* rested my argument:" omitted from expressions of close apposition; as, " Allen the bookseller," "the poet Milton," "ye mountains."

Interrogation-point.—Exercises.

Well, James, what have you got there ? "They say, if the bill is rejected, Government must stop. What must stop ? The laws ? The judicial tribunals ? The legislative bodies ? The institutions of the country ? No, no, sir! all these will remain, and go on." He asked me why I wept. He asked me, "Why do you weep ?" Let us consider, first, of what use will it be ? and, secondly, what will it cost ? Let us consider, first, of what use it will be; and, secondly, what it will cost.

* "Is this reason Is it law Is it humanity" "Will you go" said he, "or will you stay" Is the law constitutional is the question for discussion Whether the law is constitutional is the question for discussion Dr. Johnson wrote, "When Diogenes was asked what wine he liked best? he answered, That which is drunk at the expense of others." Is this sentence correctly punctuated

Exclamation-point.—Exercises.

Lo! Newton, priest of Nature, shines afar,
Scans the wide world, and numbers every star!

O home! magical, all-powerful home! how strong must have been thy influence, when thy faintest memory could cause these bronzed heroes of a thousand battles to weep like children! What, ho! Endymion, sleepest thou so soundly? Macbeth, Macbeth, Macbeth! beware McDuff! "Banished from Rome!" What's banished but set free from daily contact of the things I loathe?

* O Absalom, Absalom my son, my son Charge, Chester, charge On, Stanley, on Yoho yoho through lanes, groves, and villages. Gentlemen, what does this mean? "Chops and tomato sauce. Yours, Pickwick." Chops Gracious heavens And tomato sauce Is the happiness of a sensitive and confiding female to be trifled away by such shallow artifices as these? Sweet child lovely child thy parents are no more

     The knell, the shroud, the coffin, and the grave,
     The deep damp vault, the darkness, and the worm

<small>The exclamation-point is sometimes repeated, for greater effect; as, "Selling off below cost!! great sacrifices!!!" The interrogation and exclamation points are sometimes used sneeringly to express the unbelief of the speaker; as, "The measures which he introduced to Congress, and which ought to have been carried by overwhelming majorities (?), proved him to have been in every sense a great statesman (!).</small>

Dash.—Rule I.—Exercises.

Gil Blas. Your Grace's sermons never fail to be admired; but— *Archbishop.* It lacked the strength—the—Do you not agree with me, sir?

I take—eh! oh!—as much exercise—eh!—as I can, Madam Gout!

  Oh! when the growling winds contend, and all
  The sounding forest fluctuates in the storm,
  To sink in warm repose, and hear the din
  Howl o'er the steady battlements——

* She was

  "A great fool," said a trooper.

It was to inquire by what title General but catching himself Mr. Washington chose to be addressed.

Rule II.—Exercises.

But you are hungry—want a breakfast—turn into a restaurant—call for ham, eggs, and coffee—then your bill—six dollars!—*Travels in California.*

* Another wave lifts the schooner another fearful crash she rolls over her decks are rent asunder her crew are struggling in the water all is over!

Rule III.—Exercises.

These are—ah, no!—these *were* the gazetteers! Approaching the head of the bed, where my poor young companion, with throat uncovered, was lying with one hand the monster grasped his knife, and with the other—ah, cousin! —with the other—he seized a ham, which hung from the ceiling.

"I am told he is a man of excellent understanding."—"Is he?"—"Very virtuous and generous."—"I believe I shall like him."—"And very handsome."— "My dear papa, say no more; he's mine—I'll have him."

  * Whatever is, is right. This world, 'tis true,
  Was made for Cæsar but for Titus too.

In combustibility it agrees with cannel coal It does Have you examined its fracture I have

Rule IV.—Exercises.

Their female companion—faded, though still young—possessed nevertheless a face whose expression often drew my gaze. If I should buy the farm,— though, I must say, it is very uncertain as yet,—I would build a new house upon it.

* Setting aside a rare virtue in this clime her aristocratic pretensions, she set up as a baker for the public. All seemed very well; but for there was one of those dreadful *buts* in the case but he had a very small amount of money to begin with.

When the parts separated by a parenthesis would require separation by a point even if the parenthesis were omitted, the point is placed before each dash; but many writers use, for the sake of simplicity, only the dash.

Rule V.—Exercises.

No, sir; I always thought Robertson would be crushed by his own weight—would be buried under his own ornaments. I gave him all I had,—my blessing. (See last sentence under semicolon, p. 145.)

* On this was he willing to stake all he had character and life. Which is more five square feet, or five feet square? The crisp snow and the woolly clouds, the delightful rustle of the summer forest and the waving of the autumn corn, the glory of the sunset and the wonder of the rainbow the world would have wanted these, had not the winds been taught to do their Master's bidding.

Rule VI.—Exercises.

HONOR AND MONEY.—A French officer said to a Swiss officer, "Why is it that you Swiss are always *hiring* yourselves out to fight?" "And what do *you* fight for?" replied the Swiss. "For *honor*, of course," said the other. "Then," resumed the Swiss, "I suppose each of us fights for what he stands most in need of."—*Percy's Anecdotes*.

Finally, the dash is sometimes added to the common points to lengthen the pause a little, show emphasis, or mark transition; it is generally used in composite headings; (see newspapers;) it is often used where a line is broken off, and the subject is resumed in the next line; (see p. 106;) it is used to show omission of letters or figures; (as, pp. 71—3 — pp. 71, 72, and 73;) and it is often used at the left of newspaper extracts, to show they are such, or as a more modest request to notice than the ☞.

Curves.—Exercises.

The next day the landlord inquires (and all landlords are inquisitive), and after inquiry talks (and all landlords are talkative), concerning the private business of his new guest.   Gladiator (Lat. *gladius*, a sword); a sword-player, a prize-fighter.   I gave (and who would not have given?) my last dollar to the poor beggar.

* The Hon. Mr. Spendthrift to borrow a name from John Bunyan wishes to represent the county of ———.

Thou idol of thy parents—Hang the boy!
There goes my ink.
With pure heart newly stamped from Nature's mint—
Where did he learn that squint?

The parts enclosing a parenthesis are punctuated as if they had it not; but, if a point is required after the first part, it is generally placed after the entire parenthesis, or before each curve; and when the parenthesis itself is interrogative, exclamatory, or stands detached, the proper point precedes the latter curve.

Brackets.—Exercises.

"He [Mr. Clay] never wrote such a letter." (Explanation)   "Do you know if [whether] he is at home?" (Correction.)   "Abbotsford, May 12th," [1820.] (Omission.)

* LESSON LV.—LLEWELLEN AND HIS DOG.

A true story, showing the lamentable effects of hasty wrath.

The spearman heard the bugle sound, and cheerily smiled the morn,
And many a brach and many a hound attend Llewellen's horn, etc.
Here the writer was interrupted by a visitor.

Hyphen.—Exercises.

Compounded.—*One idea rather than two; a different meaning from the separated words:* Horse-fly, orang-outang, gooseberry, to-night; * to morrow, straw berry, twenty five, touch me not (a flower). *A phrase made an adjective:* The tree-and-cloud-shadowed river; * a life and death struggle. *A familiar term for a particular object:* Apple-orchard, boarding-house, white-oak; * black berry, humming bird, rain bow. *Imitative words made of rhyming or otherwise musical elements:* Picnic, sing-song, helter-skelter; * hodge podge, wishy washy. *Foreign phrases not yet altogether anglicized:* Piano-forte, camera-obscura; * concavo convex, electro magnetism. *Change in the part of speech:* The end-all and the be-all, a setting-forth of; * a run away, many flowered. *A word qualifying the word next to it, yet liable to be referred to the word beyond:* A light-armed soldier, battle-hymns and dirges; * the deep tangled wild wood, some four footed animals, New York Directory.

Uncompounded.—*A mere or temporary adjective, or noun so used—especially when equivalent to the adjunct beginning with* OF: A gold ring — a ring of gold, Malaga wine; * common-sense, a brick-wall. *Capitalized phrases made proper names:* Long Island, Hudson's Bay, St. John's College; * New-York, Prince-Edward's-Island. *Idiomatic phrases, and phrases whose meaning is kept clear by their syntax:* By and by, a carefully selected assortment; * tit-for-tat, ill requited love, love ill-requited. *An element making compounds with two or more others before it, to show its common reference—or else it must be compounded with each:* Riding and dancing schools, *or,* riding-schools and dancing-schools; his son and daughter in law, *or,* his son-in-law and daughter-in-law; the clock and watch repairing business; * Seed and Feed-Store; with fresh water and land-shells.

Hyphened.—*Prefixes before capital letters:* Anti-American, Neo-Platonic; ° pre Adamite. *Prefixes not uniting fluently in sound with what they are joined to, or liable to have their meaning lost:* Vice-president, semi-cylindrical, re-collect (to collect again); * counterrevolution, reformation (a new formation), cooperate (or else, coöperate). *Elements coming in contact with letters liable to be confounded:* Ant-hill, one-eyed, chain-shot; * pineapple, snowshoe.

Consolidated.—*Generally, prefixes with what they are joined to:* Reconstruct, undergraduate ; * pre-possession, under-rate. *Most compound words used as adverbs, prepositions, or conjunctions:* Everywhere, upon, notwithstanding; * any-where, here-by. *Frequently, compounds when again compounded:* Quartermaster, quartermaster-general. *Elements yielding their accents to a new and chief accent:* Black'berry, *from* black *and* ber'ry; * book-seller, run-away. *Compounds newly formed or but little used, generally require the hyphen; but by long and general use they tend to drop it:* "Steamboats and railroads have driven all the romance out of travel."—*Irving.*

A crow is a *black bird,* but not a *blackbird.* A *dog's-ear* is the corner of a leaf turned over; but a *dog's ear* is the ear of a dog. A *sugar tree* is made of sugar; but a *sugar-tree* is a maple that yields sugar. A *glass house* is made of glass; but a *glass-house* is a house in which glass is manufactured. *Many colored* birds are not necessarily *many-colored* birds; nor is a *negro merchant* necessarily a *negro-merchant;* nor a *live oak,* a *live-oak.* A *dancing master* is simply a master that dances; but a *dancing-master* teaches dancing.

Quotation-marks.—Exercises.

He is, indeed, "*a bright particular star,*" and will some day make his mark in the world. Some of us have killed "brown-backs" and "yellow-legs" [birds; as much as to say—So the people call them] in the marshes.

* I rise for information, said a member of Congress. I am very glad to hear it, cried another, sitting by; for no one needs it more.

Underscore.—Exercises.

We *must* FIGHT; I repeat it, sir, we MUST *fight*. We have petitioned, we have *supplicated*, we have REMONSTRATED, we have PROSTRATED ourselves at the foot of the throne.

The names of boats, ships, newspapers, magazines, and other periodical literature, are generally printed in Italics; also words used as the names of themselves, and foreign words introduced into English.

The *White Cloud* arrived yesterday. The poem first appeared in the *Louisville Journal*. *Woven* is the perfect participle of *weave*. They remained in *statu quo*.
* Here I reign king, and, to enrage thee more, thy king and lord. He was appointed secretary, pro tem. The Neptune and the Great Eastern sailed yesterday. A story in the New-York Ledger.

Apostrophe.—Exercises.

The apostrophe shows possession or omission, and sometimes assists in expressing the plural number.

Possession.—John's book; Mary's bonnet; boys' sports; King James's Bible; the men's knapsacks; the Duke of Wellington's achievements.
* Josephs pony; my brothers estate; the girls lessons; Watts works.

Contractions.—Th' or t' for *the*; 'm for *am*; 'rt, *art*; 're, *are*; they're, *they are*; 's, *is*, *us*, *has*; let's, *let us*; 'd, *had* or *would*; 'll, *will*; he'll, *he will*; * I ll, *I will*; * I d, *I would*; n't, *not*; don't, *do not*; * wont, *will not*; * cant, *can not*; 'tis or it's, *it is*; e'en, ev'n, *even*; e'er, *ever*; * ne er, *never*; o'er, *over*; 'gan, *began*; * gainst, *against*; * neath, *beneath*; o'clock, *of the clock*.
* The rank is but the guineas stamp, the mans the gold for a that.

Plurals.—"Cross your *t's* and dot your *i's*," is not the same as "Cross your. *ts* and dot your *is*."
* There are no *is* in English "*eyes*;" but *es* there are in "*ease*." *A* does want *ye* to make it "*aye*;" theres but one *p* in "*peas*."

The *double dash* (———), or *stars* (* * *), or *periods* (. . . .), are often used to show the intentional omission of something.

The *caret* (∧), used only in writing, shows where to insert letters or words that have been accidentally omitted.

The *macron* (‾) marks a long sound, as in *live*.

The *breve* (˘) marks a short sound, as in *live*.

The *acute accent* (′) shows stress of voice, as in *op-po'-nent*.

The *di-er'-e-sis* (¨) shows that the vowel under it, is not connected with the vowel before it; as in *preëminent*.

The *brace* (}) unites parts, or refers them in common to something else.

The *section* (§) and the *paragraph* (¶) mark the divisions of a book, or show where something new begins.

The *hand* (☞) directs special attention to something.

The *star* (*), the *dagger* (†), the *double dagger* (‡), and the *parallels* (‖), refer to notes in the margin. Letters or figures are often used for the same purpose.

☞ The Comprehensive Grammar contains a great variety of examples to illustrate the rules of Punctuation and of Capital Letters. It will be well for the teacher to select the most instructive illustrations given in that book, and use them as a sort of "Dictation Exercises."

MATTERS OF REFERENCE.

Words belonging to Two or More Parts of Speech.

All is used—
    As an *adjective*. "*All* flowers must fade."
    As a *noun*. "Not *all* that glitters, is gold."
    As an *adverb*. "*All* [*altogether*] listless roamed a shepherd swain."

As is used— ["*As* cold as ice"—*degree*.
    As an *adverb*. "Skate *as* I skate"—*manner*. "It fell *as* I entered"—*time*.
    As a *conjunction*. "*As* [*since*] we all must die, why not be charitable?"
    As a *pronoun*. "Let such *as* hear, take heed."

Before is used—
    As an *adverb*. "I came *before* it rained."
    As a *preposition*. "He stood *before* me."
So are also used *above, after, below, ere*, etc.

Both is used
    As an *adjective*. "*Both* trees are in blossom."
    As a *corresponding conjunction*. "She is *both* handsome and intelligent."
So are also used *either, neither*, etc.

But is used—
    As a *conjunction*. "Sin may gratify, *but* repentance stings."
    As a *preposition*. "Whence all *but* [*except*] him had fled."
    As an *adverb*. "Words are *but* [*only*] leaves."

For is used—
    As a *preposition*. "He works *for* me."
    As a *conjunction*. "Improve each day, *for* [*because*] life is short."
So is also used *notwithstanding*.

Much is used—
    As an *adjective*. "*Much* money is often an evil."
    As an *adverb*. "He is *much* better than he was."
    As a *noun*. "Where *much* is given, *much* will be required."
So are also used *more, little, less*, etc.

Since is used—
    As a *preposition*. "*Since* last year."
    As an *adverb*. "It happened long *since*."
    As a *conjunction*. "*Since* no one claims it, I will keep it." (Cause.)

That is used— [years."
    As an *adjective*. "*That* book belongs to me."
    As a *conjunction*. "Few people know *that* some crows live a hundred
    As a *relative pronoun*. "The same flag *that* [*which*] we saw before."
    As a *demonstrative pronoun*. "The court of England or *that* [*the court*] of

What is used— [France."
    As an *interrogative pronoun*. "*What* ails you?"
    As a *relative pronoun* with one case. "I know *what* ails you."
    As a *relative pronoun* with two cases. "Take *what* I offer."
    As an *adjective*. "*What* news from Genoa?"
    As an *interjection*. "*What!* take my money, and my life too?"

Rules for Spelling.

Spelling is the art of expressing words by their right letters, properly arranged. This art must be learned chiefly from spelling-books, dictionaries, and observation in reading.

Rule I.—Doubling.

Words of one syllable, ending in a single consonant preceded by a single vowel; and words of more syllables, ending in the same way, with the accent fixed on the last syllable,—double the consonant before a vowel in the derivative word.

Ex.—Sad, *sadder, saddest;* rebel', *rebelled, rebellion;* rob, *robber;* win, *winning,* fop, *foppish;* drum, *drummer;* up, *upper;* admit, *admittance;* quiz, *quizzed.*

In other cases, no doubling takes place.

Ex.—Seal, *sealed;* gild, *gilded;* hard, *harder;* infer', (infer'red,) *in'fer ence;* bigot, *bigoted;* tax, *taxed.* *X* final—two consonants, *ks* or *gz;* therefore never doubled.

There is a difference between *robed* and *robbed, planing* and *planning, hater* and *hatter.*

Good writers sometimes double *l,* contrary to the Rule above.

Ex.—"Traveller"—*Prescott, Bryant;* "marvellous," "carolled"—*Irving.*

Rule II.—Final Y.

Y final, preceded by a consonant and followed by any letter except *i,* is changed into *i* in the derivative word.

Ex.—Fly, *flies;* glory, *glories, glorify, glorified, glorifying, glorification;* try, *trial;* pretty, *prettier, prettiest;* merry, *merrily, merriment;* pity, *pitiable;* ivy, *ivied.*

Exceptions: The derivatives of *sly, dry,* and *shy;* as *slyly, dryly, shyness.*

Y final, preceded by a vowel, or followed by *i,* remains unchanged in the derivative word.

Ex.—Chimney, *chimneys;* gay, *gayer, gayest, gayety;* cry, *cried, crying, crier;* buoy, *buoyant;* destroy, *destroyer;* annoy, *annoyance;* joy, *joyful.*

Exceptions: Pay, *paid;* said, *laid, daily;* staid (remained), *stayed* (checked.)

Rule III.—Final E.

E final, when silent, is *rejected* before a *vowel* in the derivative word. But it is *retained* when needed to keep *c* or *g* soft, or to preserve the identity of the word.

Ex.—Bite, *biting;* force, *forced, forcible;* sale, *salable;* rogue, *roguish.* Agree, *agreeable;* peace, *peaceable;* tinge, *tingeing;* glue, *gluey.*

There is a difference between *dying* and *dyeing, singing* and *singeing.*

Words ending with *ie* change *i* into *y,* before *i,* to prevent the doubling of *i;* as, Die, *dying;* vie, *vying;* tie, *tying;* lie, *lying.*

E final is *retained* before a *consonant* in the derivative word. Sometimes it is *rejected,* when not needed.

Ex.—Base, *baseless;* rue, *rueful;* definite, *definitely;* eye, *eyelet;* whole, *wholesome,* (but *wholly.*) Due, *duly;* true, *truly;* awe, *awful;* judge, *judgment.*

Monosyllables that end with *f, l,* or *s,* preceded by a single vowel, generally have this consonant double, as *cliff, mill, pass;* words that end with any other consonant in the same way, generally have it single, as *man, cat, map.* The final consonant of a primitive word may generally remain double, but not be trebled, in the derivative word, as in *blissful, skillful, fully.* One *l* is often dropped from *ll*, especially when the accent is on some other syllable; as in *shall, always, welcome; fulfill', use'ful*. Derived verbs generally prefer the ending *ize* to *ise*, as *legal, legalize. Ei* after *c*, as in *ceiling, deceive;* generally *ie* after any other letter, as in *siege, lien, sieve. Seize, inveigle,* and some other words, are exceptious.

Compound words generally retain the spelling of the words from which they are formed; as, *Housewife, juryman, illness, wherein*. Where, *wherever;* whoso, *whosever;* sheep, *shepherd;* feet, *fetlock;* pass, *pastime;* well, *welfare;* holy, *holiday*,—are some of the exceptions.

Formation of Words.*

Frequently, words are formed from other words.

Words formed from others, are either derivative or compound; and hence all words may be divided into *primitive* (or *radical*), *derivative,* and *compound*.

The elements of words, in regard to meaning, are *roots, prefixes,* and *suffixes*.

A **root** is the chief simplest part of a word, or that part which receives the prefix or suffix.

A **prefix** is a letter or letters joined to the beginning of a word, to modify its meaning.

A **suffix** is a letter or letters joined to the end of a word, to modify its meaning.

Derivative words are formed from primitives, by means of prefixes or suffixes; and compound words are formed by uniting primitives or derivatives.

Ex.—Plant, *re*-plant, *trans*-plant, *im*-plant.   Act, act-*or*, act-*ive*, act-*ivity;* great, great-*est;* form, *re*-form-*ation. Blacksmith, blameworthy, spelling-book.*

Roots are either native or foreign, and sometimes much disguised.

Frequently, the same root may be combined with several different prefixes or suffixes, or have more than one at the same time, or be combined with some other root.

Ex.—*Struct* (build), in-*struct*, con-*struct*, re-con-*struct; thermos* (heat), *metron* (measure), *thermometer*.

Prefixes usually modify the sense, without changing the part of speech.

Suffixes usually modify the part of speech, without materially affecting the sense in other respects.

Ex.—*De* (from, separation), *de*-stroy, *de*-stroy-*er*, *de*-struct-*ive, de*-struct-*ive-ly, de*-struct-*ive-ness, de*-struct-*ion, in-de*-struct-*ible, in-de*-struct-*ibil-ity*.

There are different prefixes capable of expressing the same sense, and there are also different suffixes capable of expressing

---

* This section is one of the richest in the book; at least, great care has been taken to make it such. It will require some skill to teach it as it should be taught; but if it is rightly taught, it will be found very entertaining and instructive to pupils, and will enable them to dispense with the special book which is usually devoted to this subject.

MATTERS OF REFERENCE. 155

the same sense; because the choice is to be determined not merely by the meaning of what is added, but also by euphony, analogy, and the character of the root.

Ex.—Generous, *un*-generous; accurate, *in*-accurate; throne, *de*-throne, *un*-throne; confess, confess-*ion*; acknowledge, acknowledg-*ment*.

The meaning of a prefix is sometimes very obvious, sometimes obscure, and sometimes it has faded altogether.

Ex.—*Trans*-plant, *in*-correct; *trans*-act, *under*-stand; *com*-plete, *be*-take.

Sometimes a prefix or a suffix is added to a word, simply to lengthen or to strengthen it a little; as *be-loved* for *loved*, and *dear-y* for *dear*. Such a prefix may be disposed of, by saying that it is simply *prosthĕt'ic*; and such a suffix, by saying that it is simply *paragōg'ic*.

In making a combined form, some of the parts frequently undergo a change for the sake of euphony or analogy. This consists in the *change, omission,* or *insertion* of some letter or letters. The initial consonant of the root often requires the final letter of the prefix to be like it.

Ex.—Con-lect, *col-lect*; dis-fer, *dif-fer*; in-moderate, *im-moderate*; con-operate, *co-operate*; dis-vulge, *di-vulge*; a-archy, *an-archy*; mucilage-ous, *mucilag-inous*.

Prefixes.

The prefixes in Roman letters are Latin; in Italic, Greek; in black, Saxon or native.

A ; *on, in, at, to.* In a few words it is merely intensive.
Form, spell, and define:—
Bed, ground, shore, cross, sleep, pace, slant, field, side; wake, rise.
Thus: *Abed;* a—b-e-d—abed; on or in bed.—See dictionary, when you can not determine the meaning otherwise.

A, AB, ABS; *from, separation.*
Vert (turn); solve (loosen), rupt (broken); tract (draw), tain (hold).
AD, A, AC, AF, AG, AL, AN, AP, AR, AS, AT; *to, at.*
Join, judge; mount, scend (climb); cord, cuse (cause, charge); fix, fusion (pouring); gress (step), gravate (heavy); lot, luvial (washing); nex (join), nihilate (nothing); portion, preciate (price); rogate (lay claim); sure, sail (leap); sist (stand); tract, tribute (give).
A, AN; *without, privation.* [ernment).
Theist (God), pathy (feeling), tom (cut); onymous (name), archy (gov-
AMPHI; *two, double.* Theatre, bious (living).
ANA; *up, throughout, parallel, back, again.* [tist.
Tomy (cutting), lysis (separation), logy (discourse), gram (letter), bap-
ANTE; *fore, before.* Chamber, date, meridian (noon), cedent (going).
ANTI, ANT; *against, opposition.*
Bilious, febrile, pathy (feeling), dote (given); arctic, agonist (contend).
APO, AP; *from, off.* [(sun).
Gee (earth), strophe (turning), logy, stle (from *stello*, send); helion
Be ; *action directed to an object; intensity; by, near, about.*
Daub, dew, moan, lie, set, siege, cloud, spatter; side, fore, cause.
BENE; *good, well.* Fit (deed), volent (wishing), factor (doer), diction (say-
BIS, BI ; *twice, two.* [ing).
Cuit (baked); angular, valve, gamy (marriage), sect (cut), ped (foot).

CATA, CAT; *down, against, throughout.* (The opposite of ANA.)
Ract (flowing), strophe, pult (throw); hedral (seat), holic (whole).
CIRCUM, CIRCU; *round, about.*
Navigate, jacent (lying), spect (looking), stance (standing), scribe, (mark, write), ference (bearing); late (borne), itous (going).
CIS; *on this side.*   Alpine, Atlantic.
CON, CO, COG, COL, COM, COR; *with, together, jointly.*
Join, tract, fuse (pour), vene (come), ceive (take), tain, flict (strike), flagration (burning); extent, heir, operate; nate (born); league, lect (gather), loquy (speaking): press, mingle, pose, (place); respond, relative.
CONTRA, CONTRO, COUNTER; *against, in opposition, answering to.*
Dict (say), distinguish; vert; part, pressure, feit (make), act, plot.
DE; *from, down, destruction.*
Tract, press, ject (throw), throne, scend, pend (hang), tect (cover), tach (tie), sist, cline (lean), spise (look), moralize.
DIA, DI; *through, across.*   Meter, lect or logue (speech), gonal (angle).
DIS, DI, DIF; *away, apart, undoing, negation.*
Join, organize, appear, miss (send), ease, sect, tract, cover, perse (scatter), please, inter, arm, order, similar; verge (incline), stance, gress; fer (bear), fuse.
E, EX, EC, EF; *out, out of, from.*
Ject (throw), lect (pick), vade (go), mit (send); pectorant (breast), press, pand (spread), port (carry), pose, ceed (go), clude (shut), tort (twist), pire (breathe); centric (centre), stasy (standing); fuse, fect (done), fulgence (shining).
EN (Greek or French), *EM;* *in, into, upon.*
Tangle, shrine, rage, gulf, large, grave (scrape), tomb; broider, blazon, bark, bitter, brace (arm).
EPI, EP; *upon, over, after.*
Taph (tomb), demic (people), thet (placed), logue; hemeral (day), ode.
EXTRA; *beyond.*   Ordinary, vagant (going), mural (wall).
For, fore; *from, against, the contrary.* Bid, get, sake (seek), give, swear; go.
Fore, for; *before.*
Tell, run, see, know, taste, man, father, noon, arm, mast, head; ward.
HYPER; *beyond, over, excess.* Borean (north), critical, meter (measure).
HYPO; *under.*   Thesis placing, sulphuric, crite (thoughts).
IN, IG, IM, IL, IR; *not, privation, the contrary.*
Human, discreet, elastic, consistent; noble; modest, mortal, patient; legal, liberal; reverent, regular, resolute.
IN, IM, IL, IR; *in, into, upon, over.*
Flame, struct, lay, here (stick), cline, vade, sist, flect (bend), cision (cutting), scribe, wrought; plant, pearl, print, press, port, pend, pose; luminate or lustrate (throw light); radiate (throw rays).
INTER; *between.*   Weave, line, cede, regnum (reign), mix, marriage.
INTRO; *inwards, within.*   Duce (lead), mission (sending).
META, METH; *over, beyond, with, change.*
Thesis, morphose (form), physics, phor (convey); od (way).
Mis; *wrong, ill.*   Apply, call, deed, place, use, spell, take, fortune.
NON; *negation.*   Conductor, conformity, sense, resident, payment.

MATTERS OF REFERENCE. 157

OB, OC, OF, OP; *in the way, to, against.*
Trude (thrust), ject (throw), stacle (standing); cur, casion (falling); fer, pose, press.

Out; *beyond, not within.*
Bid, grow, last, live, let, side, law, cast.

Over; *above, beyond, excess.*
Balance, hang, top, leap, spread, do, flow, look, load, shoot, value, wise.

PARA, PAR; *beside, against, from.*
Dox (opinion), graph (writing), phrase, site (food); helion, ody (song).

PER, PEL; *through, by.*
Use, form, ennial (year), ccive, sist (stand), fect, forate (bore), chance, cent (hundred); lucid (shining).

PERI; *around, about, near.*
Patetic (walking), helion, od, phery (bearing), cranium, style (pillar).

POST; *after.* Script (writing), humous (ground), pono (place), mortem
PRE; *before.* [(death), meridian.
Judge, mature, engage, dispose, sentiment, fer, sume (take), vent (come), scribe, side (sit), text (weaving), cision.

PRETER; *past, beyond.* Natural, imperfect, mission.

PRO, PROF; *for, forth, forwards, before.*
Noun, cced (go), gress, tect, pel (drive), spect (look), duce (lead, bring), ject, fusion, logue; fer.

RE; *again, back.*
Build, call, enter, new, view, pel, lapse (fall), sonant (sounding), strain (draw), bound, place, sist, cline, tain.

RETRO; *backwards.* Cede, vert, spect, grade (walk).

SE; *aside, apart.* Cede, clude (shut), cant (cutting), duce (lead), lect.

SEMI, DEMI, HEMI; *half.*
Annual, circle, colon, diameter, vowel; god, cannon; sphere.

SINE; *without.* Cure (care).

SUB, SUC, SUF, SUG, SUP, SUR, SUS,—SUBTER; *under, after, inferior.*
Soil, divide, scribe, ject, marine; cor (run), cumb (lie down), cced; fer, fuse, fix; gest (bring); plant, press; rogate (ask); tain; fuge (fly).

SUPER, SUPRA, SUR; *above, over and above.*
Structure, fine, cargo, fluous, natural; mundane; pass, charge, mount.

SYN, SYL, SYM, SY; *with, together.*
Thesis, tax (placing), opsis (view), agogue (lead); lable (taking), logism (counting); phony (sound), pathy; stem (to make stand, set).

TRANS, TRAN, TRA; *through, across, over, on the other side of.*
Act, plant, gress, Atlantic, pose, port, fer or late (carry), migrate, form, it (going); scribe (write), scend; dition (giving).

TRI; *three.* Colored, angular, meter, foliate (leaf), ennial.

Un; *not, negation, privation, undoing.*
Able, happy, wise, truth, aided, bar, chain, ship, do, twist, horse.

Under; *beneath, inferior.*
Agent, brush, current, ground, rate, sell, hand, go, mine, sign.

UNI; *one.* Corn (horn), form, florous (flowering), valve (shell).

Up; *motion upwards, above, subversion.*
Turn, raise, rise, hold, land, hill, right, start, set, root.

With; *against, from, back.* Hold, draw, stand.

Suffixes, or Affixes.

The derivatives of this class consist almost entirely of *nouns, adjectives, verbs,* and *adverbs.*

The same suffix is not usually confined to one meaning, but ranges with the principles given under the head of Figures. (See p. 138.) The following are the chief suffixes, with their ordinary meanings:—

Able; *can be.* Conquer-*able;* can be conquered.
    can or *should be.* Piti-*able;* can or should be pitied.
    having, giving. Comfort-*able;* having or giving comfort.
Ac; *belonging to, like.* Elegi-*ac;* belonging to or like elegy.
Aceous; *having the qualities of, consisting of, resembling.* "Herb-*aceous* plants." "Crust-*aceous* animals;" like crabs or lobsters.
Ade; *thing.* Lemon-*ade;* drink made of lemons. [ade.
    group of things or acts. Arc-*ade,* continuation of arches. Cannon-
Age; *state.* Bond-*age;* state of being in bonds, slavery.
    act or *thing.* Carri-*age;* act of carrying, or that which carries.
    allowance. Mile-*age;* what is paid per mile.
    collection. Cord-*age;* collection of cords, a ship's tackle.
Al; *having, consisting of.* Crim-in-*al;* having crime. Ornament-*al.*
    belonging to, suitable to. Parent-*al;* belonging or suitable to a parent.
    act. Remov-*al;* act of removing.
An; *belonging to, resembling.* Hercu'le-*an;* large or strong as Hercules.
    person. Afric*an;* a person from Africa. Guard-i-*an.*
Ance, ancy; *act* or *thing.* Resist-*ance;* act of resisting, thing resisting.
    state. Constan*cy;* state of being constant. See Cy.
Ant; *doing.* Pleas-*ant;* applied to something that pleases.
    person. Serv-*ant;* one that serves.
Ar; *belonging to.* Po-*lar;* belonging to the poles.
    like, consisting of. Glob-u-*lar;* like a globe. Titu*lar.*
    person. Beg-*gar;* one that begs.
Ard; *person.* Drunk-*ard;* one that is habitually drunk.
    resembling. Hag-*gard;* resembling a hag in appearance, withered.
Ary; *belonging to, consisting of.* Custom-*ary;* belonging to custom.
    person. Ad'vers-*ary;* one that is adverse or hostile.
    thing or *place.* Infirm'-*ary;* a house or place for the infirm.
Ate; *to make, to do.* Perpetu-*ate;* to make perpetual. Offici*ate.*
    belonging to. Collegi-*ate;* belonging to a college.
    office, government. Caliph-*ate;* office or dominion of a caliph.
Atic, etic. See Ic. Emblem-*atic.* Sympath*etic.*
Cy; *act.* Pira-*cy;* act or crime of pirating.
    state. Secre-*cy;* the state of being secret.
    office, district. Cura-*cy;* the office or district of a curate.
Dom; *state* or *thing.* Free-*dom;* state of being free. Wis-*dom.*
    country or *district, government.* King-*dom;* country ruled by a king.
Ee; *person, person to whom.* Absent-*ee;* one that is absent. Trust*ee.*
Ed; *did* or *received.* Past tense or perfect participle. See p. 47.
    furnished with, having. Hilt-*ed;* furnished with a hilt. Beard-*ed.*
En; *to make.* Black-*en;* to make black.
    made of, resembling. Gold-*en;* made of gold, resembling gold, precious as gold. [Dependen*t.*
Ence, ency, ent. See Ance, Ancy, Ant. Reverence. Solvency.

MATTERS OF REFERENCE. 159

Er, eer, ier, or; *person.* Driver; one that drives. Engineer. Financ*ier.*
    thing. Revolv-*er;* something that revolves, a pistol.
Er, *more;* **Est,** *most.* Comparison of adjectives or adverbs. See pp. 25, 60.
Escent; *growing, becoming.* Putrescent; becoming putrid.
Ess; *female.* Host-*ess;* a female host.
Ferous; *bearing, producing.* Coni*f-erous;* producing cones, like the pine.
Ful ; *full of, having of.* Care-*ful;* full of care, cautious.
Fy ; *to make.* Puri-*fy ;* to make pure.
Hood ; *state* or *thing.* False-*hood;* state of being false, what is false.
    state or *qualities.* Man-*hood ;* state of being a man, noble qual-
    group. Sister-*hood;* a group of sisters. [ities.
Ible. See **Able.** Corrupt-*ible.* Contempt-*ible.* Sens-*ible.*
Ic, ical ; *consisting of, resembling.* Metal'-*lic;* consisting of metal.
    Spher-*ical.* [a hero.
    belonging to, suitable to. Hero-*ic;* belonging to or becoming
    having, inclined to. Dropsi*cal;* having dropsy. Whimsi*cal.*
Ice; *act, state,* or *thing.* Serv-*ice ;* act of serving, state of serving, thing
Ics; *science* or *art.* Mechan-*ics ;* the science of machinery. [done.
    things collectively. Statist-*ics ;* facts showing the condition of a nation.
Ile ; *belonging to, resembling.* Serv-*ile;* belonging to or like a servant,
Ine; *belonging to.* Alpine; belonging to the Alps. [mean.
    consisting of, resembling. Alkaline; consisting of or like alkali.
Ing; *doing.* Ending of the present participle. See p. 57.
    act or *thing.* Shav-*ing ;* act of shaving, what is shaved off.
    group, material in mass. Bed-d*ing ;* materials of a bed.
    occupation, science, or *art.* Hunt-*ing.* Engineer-*ing.* Farm-*ing.*
Ion; *act* or *result.* Un*ion;* act of uniting, things united.
    act or *state.* Commun*ion;* act or state of communing.
    The endings *tion* and *sion,* which occur so often, belong to this head.
Ish ; *somewhat.* Green-*ish ;* somewhat green.
    like. Boy-*ish;* like a boy.
    inclined to. Thiev-*ish;* inclined to thieve or steal. Snapp*ish.*
    to make, to do. Publ*ish;* to make public. Van*ish* (vain), pass away.
Ism; *act* or *mode.* Bapt*ism;* act or mode of baptizing.
    doctrine or *peculiarity.* Jesuit-*ism.* American-*ism.*
    Idiom. Latin-*ism ;* a Latin mode of speech.
Ist ; *person* or *doer.* Art-*ist;* one that practises art.
Ite ; *person,* usually of a race, clan, or party. Israel-*ite.*
Ive ; *doing.* Abus*ive;* abusing.
    person or *other object.* Relat*ive;* one related. Capt*ive.*
Ize, ise ; *to act the part of.* Tyrann*ize;* to act the tyrant.
    to make, to give. Legal-*ize;* to make legal. Author-*ize.*
Less; *without, wanting.* Care-*less;* without care, heedless.
Ling; *an object.* Year-*ling;* something a year old. World-*ling.*
    a small one. Gos-*ling ;* a small or young goose. So, -KIN, -OCK,
    -CLF, -EL, -ULE, -ET.
Ly ; *like.* Mother-*ly ;* like a mother, kind.
Ment; *act* or *result.* Abridg-*ment ;* act of abridging, thing abridged.
    state. Content-*ment ;* state of being contented.
    something that does. Amuse-*ment ;* something that amuses.
Ness ; *state* or *quality.* Happi-*ness;* state of being happy. Hard-*ness.*

MATTERS OF REFERENCE.

Ory; *doing.* Declarat*ory;* declaring.
    place. Deposit*ory;* place of deposit.   [joke.
Ose; *consisting of, inclined to.* Jocose; consisting of jokes, inclined to
Ous; *consisting of, having.* Fibr*ous;* consisting of fiber. Ambiti*ous.*
    doing, inclined to. Studi-*ous;* studying, inclined to study. Malici*ous.*
Ric (akin to *rich, right, realm*); *district, government, dominion.* Bishop-*ric.*
Ship; *state or thing.* Hard-*ship;* hard condition, what causes it.
    act or thing. Wor-*ship.* Court-*ship.*
    office, dignity. Clerk-*ship,* office of a clerk. Lord-*ship.*
Some; *tending to, somewhat.* Weari-*some;* tending to weary. Glad-*some*
    inclined to. Quarrel-*some;* inclined to quarrel.
Ster; *person or other object.* Song-*ster;* one that sings. See Er.
Ude; *state or thing.* Infinit*ude.* Multit*ude.*
Ure; *act or state.* Expos*ure;* act of exposing, state of being exposed.
    thing or result. Enclos*ure.* Temperat*ure.*
    science, art, or result. Architect-*ure.*
Y, ry, ty; *having.* Ston*y;* having stones. Dirt*y.* Gloom*y.*
    consisting of, resembling. Wir*y;* consisting of or resembling wire.
    worthy of. Trust*y;* worthy of being trusted.
    state or quality. *Honest*y;* state or quality of being honest. Safe-*ty.*
    objects collectively. Soldier*y;* soldiers collectively. Revel-*ry.* Nav*y*
    (navis, *ship*).
    place. Grocer*y;* place in which groceries are kept and sold.
    art, science, or result. Mason-*ry.*

Nouns.

Person or Instrument: Ard, ary, ee, ess, ine, ist, ite, ive, ix, n, nt, r.

Thing, Act, or State: Ade, age, al, dom, hood, ice, ics, ion, ism, ment, ness, nce, ry, ship, t, th, ude, ure, y.

Most derivative nouns are formed from *verbs, adjectives,* and *nouns.* A derivative noun may denote either a *person,* a *thing,* an *act,* or a *state.*

The *person* denoted by a derivative noun, when it denotes a person, must be the doer of an act, the receiver of an act, or simply one in some way related to that from which the name is formed. See pp. 158-60.

From the *thing,* the mind naturally passes to whatever is obviously related to it.

From the *act,* the mind readily passes to what caused it,—whether a person or an object, or some faculty, skill, or principles,—to the result, or to the manner.

From the *state,* the mind readily passes to what caused it, to what follows from it, to what sustains it, or to what necessarily accompanies it.

Hence affixes are perplexingly variable in their meanings; indeed, so much so, that the pupil will often find it safer to learn, from a dictionary, the meaning of the entire word, than to determine this meaning from his knowledge of the affix.

Form and spell, making the requisite euphonic changes; and define:—
    Ard.—Drunk,* dote, slug, dull, cow (verb), Spain, Savoy.

    * Throughout the following exercises, the student should spell and define, from his dictionary if necessary, each word given; and then the derivative word in like manner. Thus:

Ary.—Adverse, statue, note, mission.
Ee. (Generally passive; the person to whom.)—Indorse, pay, patent, assign, consign, trust, commit, legate, mortgage, lease, *less;* absent, refuge.
Ess, ine, ix; female.—Lion, heir; hero, Joseph; administrator.
Ist.—Copy, tour, journal, natural, novel, algebra, drug, duel, art, violin, pian-o; drama, *-tist;* enthusiasm, *-ast,* encomium.
Ite.—Favor, Israel, Moab, Jacob.
Ive.—Capture, operate.
N.—America, Africa, Virginia, Kentucky, college, music.
Nt.—Claim, *-ant,* account, inhabit, combat, dispute, confide, protest, assist, assail, appeal; study, *-ent,* preside; oppose, *-ponent;* act, *-gent;* receive, *-cipient.*
R.—Oversee; lie, *-ar,* beg, school; farm, *-er,* hunt, ride, drive, make, teach, preach, write, speak, wait, plaster, settle, pipe, widow, hat, foreign; visit, *-or,* edit, profess, survive, speculate, create, govern, conquer, direct, conduct, protect,; conspire, *-ator;* compete, *-itor;* auction, *-eer,* mountain, engine, gazette, pamphlet, chariot; cash, *-ier,* cannon, finance, cloth, glaze; save, *-ior;* law, *-yer,* saw; team, *-ster,* web; poke, *-er* (thing), revolve, shut, boil, read, speak, fend, steam, knock, wrap.

Diminutives. (These often imply endearment or contempt.)—Man, *-ikin;* lamb, *-kin;* ring, *-let,* stream, leaf, plant, cover; lock, *-et,* mall; duck, *-ling,* lord, hire, suckle. Globe, glob*ule;* grain, gran*ule;* ball, bull*et;* cat, *kitten;* island, *isle;* isle, *islet.*

Ade.—Gascon, stock, lemon, baluster; stamp, *-ede.*
Age.—Use, marry, mile, post, equip, till, folium (leaf), herb, bag, bond, pupil, parson, hermit, anchor.
Al.—Peruse, remove, recite, requite, deny, propose, refuse, dismiss.
Dom.—Free, wise, martyr, thrall, king, duke, earl.
Hood.—Child, brother, man, woman, boy, sister, priest, hardy, lively.
Ice.—Serve, just, lath, *lat-tice.*
Ics.—Poet, harmony, mechanic, statist (state), phys (nature).
Ion.—Commune, precise, act, reflect, possess, expand; and many other words, in which the ending shows itself in the form of *tion* or *sion.*
Ism.—Fanatic, despot, critic, hero, baptize, heathen.
Ment.—Move, pave, content, case, punish, acquire, agree, battle, settle, complete, refresh, conceal, excite, refine, retire, manage, abridge, amend, nourish, arm, *-ament.*
Nce, ncy.—Acquaint, *-ance,* concord, resist, observ-e, convey, elegant; innocent, *-ence,* resident, differ, precede; pliant, *-ancy,* constant; despond, *-ency,* ascend.
Ness.—Good, bad, white, bold, sweet, holy, busy, comprehensive.
Ship.—Partner, clerk, scholar, professor, town, workman, horseman, apprentice, hard, friend, lord, court. See Hood.
T, th.—Constrain, join, restrain; warm, wide, true, long, strong.
Ude.—Disquiet, serve, solitary, right, *rect-.*
Ure.—Please, depart, moist, seize, legislate, sign-*ature,* nourish, *nurt-.*

D-r-u-n-k-drunk, *intoxicated with liquor;* d-r-u-n-k-drunk-a-r-d-ard-drunkard, *one that is habitually drunk, a sot.* A-d-ad-v-e-r-s-e-verse-adverse, *opposing, contrary;* a-d-ad-v-e-r-ver-adver-s-a-sa-adversa-r-y-ry-adversary, *one that opposes, an enemy.* So comprehensive is the collection of words here presented, that the defining of the words in the manner indicated, will amply repay the labor of using the dictionary.

Y.—Honest, modest, discover, master, armor, glutton, injure; lunatic, *-acy*, private, secret, *-cy;* hypocrite, *-sy;* pedant, *-ry*, gallant, revel, bigot, bake, scene; brew, *-ery*, cook, witch, mock, fish, crock; loyal, *-ty*, novel; null, *-ity*, dense, fertile, hostile, captive, divine, pure, infirm, opportune, secure, sincere, elastic.

Words ending in *y* or *ry*, are often collective in sense, denoting groups of objects or acts; as, Orange-*ry*, shrub-*bery*, soldier-*y*, sorcer-*y*, trigonome*try*. So is the ending *ing* not unfrequently collective in sense; as, Bed, *bedding;* shop, *shopping; bagging, carpeting, hedging, gunning* (elements of science, or science as drawn from a multitude of acts or experiments).

Adjectives.

Al, an, ar, ate, ble, en, ern, ful, ic, (ific,) ile, ine, ish, ive, less, nt, ous, some, ward, y, (ly, ary, ory).

Most derivative adjectives are formed from *nouns* and *verbs;* and these adjectives generally signify—

Having of or having the nature of, more or less; or that the object described, in some ways belongs or is related to that from whose name the adjective is formed.

The same word may frequently be used either as an adjective or as a noun.

Form and spell, making the requisite euphonic changes; and define:—

Al.—Nature, nation, origin, music, autumn, tropic; senator, *-ial*, manor, matter, part, commerce; spirit, *-ual*, sense, habit; consequence, *-tial*, influence, essence; benefit, *-cial;* nose, *nas-*, pope, *pap-*, feast, *fest-*.

An.—Europe, epicure, Africa, America, Italy, suburbs.

Ar.—Column, consul; globe, *-ular*, circle, muscle, title, particle.

Ate.—Rose, globe, affection, consider, compassion.

Ble. (Passive, if from a transitive verb.)—Detest, *-able*, cure, eat, change, honor, tolerate, utter, value, fashion; corrupt, *-ible*, resist, sense, destroy, *destruct-*, accede, *access-*, perceive, *percept-*, divide, *divis-*.

En. (Of what substance made.)—Beech, wood, wool, earth, brass,

Ern.—North, south, east, west. [*braz-.*

Ful. (Opposed to Less.)—Art, mind, thought, peace, hope, brim, care, fret, waste, cheer, fear, youth, tune, play, sin, shame, wake, law, mourn, truth, mercy, duty.

Ic.—Angel, hero, poet, sphere, lyre; vertex, *-ical*, dropsy; sympathy, *-etic*, pathos, theory; barometer, *-etric*, diameter; emblem, *-atic*, problem, system, drama; color, *-ific*, dolor; science, *-tific;* romance, *-tic;* pharisee, *-saic;* tragedy, *-gic;* Plato, *-nic.*

Ile.—Infant, serve, merchant, *mercant-*, puer (boy). [tracted).

Ine.—Serpent, adamant, amaranth, crystal, *-line*, leather, *-n* (con-

Ish.—Salt, black, yellow, sweet, fop, fool, knave, scare, *skit-;* Spain.

Ive. (Generally active.)—Create, abuse, attract, invent, prevent, progress, retain, *retent-*, attend; perceive, *-ceptive;* presume, *-sumptive;* produce, *product-*, destroy; disjoin, *disjunct-;* adhere, *-hesive*, corrode, intrude, decide; impel, *-pulsive*, repel.

Less.—Art, blame, faith, fear, care, help, hope, name, fruit, worth, ground, guilt, thought, mercy.

Nt. (Generally active.)—Tolerate, *-ant*, please, buoy, triumph, attend, expect, luxury; solve, *-ent*, consist, abhor; compose, *-ponent.*

Ous.—Bulb, pore, pomp, fame, clamor, joy, grieve, ruin, peril, danger, murder, mountain, solicit, covet; bile, *-ious*, perfidy, vary, malice, caprice, pity, *-eous*, beauty, duty; tempest, *-uous*, contempt, tumult; enormity, *-mous*; merit, *-orious*; mucilage, *-inous*; bulb, *-iferous*.

Some.—Toil, tire, dark, glad, quarrel, lone, weary. See Isn.

Y.—Grass, rock, sand, flint, hill, shade, swamp, meal, flower, curl, mud, cloud, wealth, grease, flesh, sponge, sleep; heart, pearl, oil, mire, wire; fire, *fiery*; clay, *-ey*; friend, *-ly*, beast, brother, father, mother, heaven, man, time, state, home; residue, *-ary*, imagine, element; subsidy, *-iary*; contradict, *-ory*, conciliate, declare, satisfy, explain.

Up*ward*, out*ward*, arm*igerous*, spher*oid*, Arabe*sque*, statue*sque*, grote*sque*.

Verbs.
Ate, en, fy, ish, ize, ise.

Most derivative verbs are formed from *nouns* and *adjectives;* and these verbs generally signify—

To make or become; to impart the thing or quality to, or to exercise it; to make the ordinary use of; an act or state consisting of some common or permanent relation between the subject of the verb and the thing.

Form and spell, making the requisite euphonic changes; and define:—

Ate.—Alien, origin, germ, populous, luxury, fabric, facility, spoil, *spoli-*, grain, *granu-*, stimulous, office, vacant, circular.

En.—Black, white, sharp, red, soft, moist, less, sweet, bright, strength, haste, glad, sad, ripe, quick, thick, fright.

Fy.—Beauty, pure, just, simple, glory, class, sign, clear, *clari-*, right, *recti-*, peace, *paci-*, special, *speci-*, example, *exempli-*, fruit, *fructi-*; prophet.

Ish.—Brand, bland, public, famine, languid. [*-esy*.

Ize, ise. (These generally signify *to make, to apply, to act the part of.*)—Legal, theory, modern, moral, organ, botany; tyrant, melody, familiar, character, apology; critic.

Sharp ending to flat or rough.—Cloth, breath, wreath, bath, price, advice, grass, excuse, abuse, grief, half, thief.

Accent changed.—Abstract, conflict, absent, frequent, rebel.

Word unchanged. (To make that use of which mankind generally make; some customary or habitual act or state; some active relation to.)—Hoe, shoe, shovel, plane, chisel, hammer, smoke, garden, farm, weed, plant, coop, soap, shear, gem, fire, lance, and the names of instrumental things generally.

Adverbs.
Ly, ward or wards, wise or ways.

Most derivative adverbs are formed from *adjectives*.

Form, spell, and define:—

Ly; *like, manner, quality.*—Bitter, strange, bright, plain, faint, fierce, swift, playful, studious, mere, scarce, in, one, *on-*, spiral, fearless, infallible.

Ward, wards; *direction.*—Back, in, out, up, down, home, heaven, east, lee, wind.

Wise, ways; *manner, way.*—Length, cross, other, side, edge; straight.

A *compound word* generally consists of a principal word and its modifier, abridged both into one word. (See pp. 105, 150.) The first part of a compound word is usually the descriptive part; and the most numerous compounds are those in which a noun is combined with a noun.

Additional Words Explained.

Pages
67-87. (Correct) Syntax.—*Rule;* something fit to be obeyed, something of great importance because often true, or true of much: *rules* are great truths according to which words are rightly put together to make sentences, or which we must mind in order to understand sentences or make them. *Governing word,* a word that causes the form of some other word; a preposition or a transitive verb. *Term,* from the Latin *term'inus,* a boundary; what *bounds* or *circumscribes* a meaning; a word or an expression.

Apposition, from *ad,* changed to *ap,* and *position;* placing near or beside, for the explanatory term is placed beside the other one. *Absolutely* (Note 10th) without a noun or pronoun to which the adjective belongs. *Construction,* arrangement and sense with other words. *Absolutely or independently* (Note 12th), without a noun or pronoun to which the participle or infinitive belongs.

Independently (Note 13th), without modifying any word in the sentence. *Same construction* (Rule 15th),—two or more nouns are in the same construction, when they are nominatives to the same verb, or are governed by the same word; two or more verbs are in the same construction, when they have the same nominative; two or more adjectives are in the same construction, when they qualify the same noun or pronoun, etc. *No grammatical connection,* no such connection as a grammar can treat of; independent of, free from.

Parsing, from the Latin *pars,* part; literally, *parts-ing* or *piercing,* to get at the sense: separating into the *parts* or simple ideas which make up a thing or complex idea. *Form'ula,* something to show how a thing should be done.

88-101. False Syntax; the wrong words put together, or the right words improperly put together, to make sentences. *Politeness;* kindness that shows good breeding on our part, and a delicate regard for the feelings or happiness of others. *Ambig'uous,* having two meanings. *Ac'cent;* a greater stress of voice on some syllable of a word than on the remaining syllables, made for the sake of distinction or for euphony and easy pronunciation. *Vol'untary,* coming from a person's free will, of one's own accord. *Contin'gent,* happening to. *Compul'sory,* compelled, forced. *Anal'ogy,* resemblance in the relation of things,—thus, scales on a fish are anal'ogous to shingles on a house; some similarity belonging to a number of words. *Consistent,* not improper, making good sense with. *Promis'cuous,* mixed. *Connection,* tie, arrangement, construction. *Inel'egant;* not so polite, refined, or good as it should be. *Appro'priate,* suitable, fit.

102-29. Analysis, from the Greek *ana,* up, and *lysis,* loosening; literally, a loosening up. (Compare with our phrase *to cut up a thing.*) The *analysis of sentences* is a kind of higher parsing, being in some respects to parsing as algebra is to arithmetic. *Discourse',* in its original meaning, refers to the flow of thought; and thence it has been applied to whatever is said or written. *Paragraph,* from the Greek *para,* near, beside, and *graphē* writing; written beside, what is written apart or separate. *Declar'ative,* saying boldly. *Exclam'atory,* crying out. *Independent,* having nothing to do with others. *Dependent,* relying on others. *Log'ical,* belonging to Logic; and *grammatical,* belonging to Grammar; because, formerly, the parts so named, belonged peculiarly to these sciences.

Element, one of the simple things that makes a part of a larger. *Ellip'sis,* the omission of such words as can be easily supplied by the mind. *Ellip'tical,* having words omitted. *Inverted;* so arranged that what ordinarily follows, precedes. *Correlative,* mutually dependent. *Logical order and fullness;* according to Logic, in the reasoning manner, or as a cool and deliberate mind would state a thing. An *idiom* is a peculiar form of expression, through which the sense generally runs like the grain through a knot of wood.

135-151. Punctuation, from *punctum,* a point; the art of using points. *Period* means, literally, a circuit of words; *colon,* a member; *semicolon,* half a member; *comma,* a part cut off; and thence the words were applied to the points showing these parts. *Abbreviation,* a word shortened by omitting some of its letters. *Par-en-thet'-ic;* what brings out the full sense, but can be omitted without destroying the sense. The *curves* are often called *marks of parenthesis,* or *parenthesis;* but *parenthesis* properly denotes what is enclosed by them, by dashes so used, or by brackets. *Capital,* from the Latin word *caput,* head; chief, large.

Figure, shape, form; a form or mode of speech. *Met'aphor,* transfer. *Meton'ymy,* change of name. *Syn-ec'-do-che,* understanding one thing with another. *Verse;* a turning, that is, a turning back at the end of the line to make another line. *Iam'bic,* attacking; being first used in satire. *Trochee,* tripping, running. *Dactyl,* finger; because it has three parts, like a finger. *An'apest;* reversed, i. e., reversed dactyl. *Im-ag-in-a'-tion;* that faculty or power of the mind which calls up the shapes of things that are absent, or which pictures forth things that do not exist.

www.ingramcontent.com/pod-product-compliance
Lightning Source LLC
Chambersburg PA
CBHW020309170426
43202CB00008B/552